# Little Victories

**Autism Through a Father's Eyes**

# TITAN COMICS

Managing Editor MARTIN EDEN
Editor JAKE DEVINE
Art Director OZ BROWNE
Production Controller PETER JAMES
Senior Production Controller JACKIE FLOOK
Sales & Circulation Manager STEVE TOTHILL
Publicist IMOGEN HARRIS
Ad & Marketing Assistant BELLA HOY
Marketing Assistant GEORGE WICKENDEN
Commercial Manager MICHELLE FAIRLAMB
Head of Rights JENNY BOYCE
Publishing Director DARRYL TOTHILL
Operations Director LEIGH BAULCH
Executive Director VIVIAN CHEUNG
Publisher NICK LANDAU

# LITTLE VICTORIES

ISBN: 9781787732308

Published by Titan Comics

A division of Titan Publishing Group Ltd.

144 Southwark St.

London SE1 0UP

Originally published in French as: Les Petites Victoires by Rue de Sevres © Yvon Roy 2017. All rights reserved.

First edition: July 2020

10 9 8 7 6 5 4 3 2 1

Printed in China.

www.titan-comics.com
Follow us on Twitter @ComicsTitan
Visit us at facebook.com/comicstitan

Yu[redacted]

# Li[redacted]
# Victo[redacted]

## Autism Through a Father's Eyes

TITAN COMICS

# [redacted] time...

[redacted] making this book. The idea was [redacted] educator who had worked [redacted] what we had accomplished together [redacted] through our experience, other parents [redacted], if not a little hope.

[redacted] up my mind because I knew that plunging [redacted] be painful; but so many people around me advised [redacted] our story… They would not leave me alone!

Here is the story in comic book form. This is not a book about autism – I leave that to the specialists – even if this condition is at the heart of my story. It was important for me to make a book for all parents, as everyone, with no exception, will have challenges with their kid; the greatest of them being to love unconditionally, without ever faltering the child who is given to us.

Yvon ROY

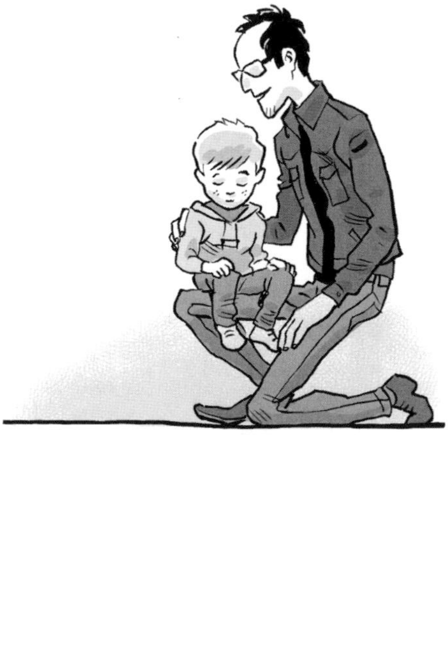

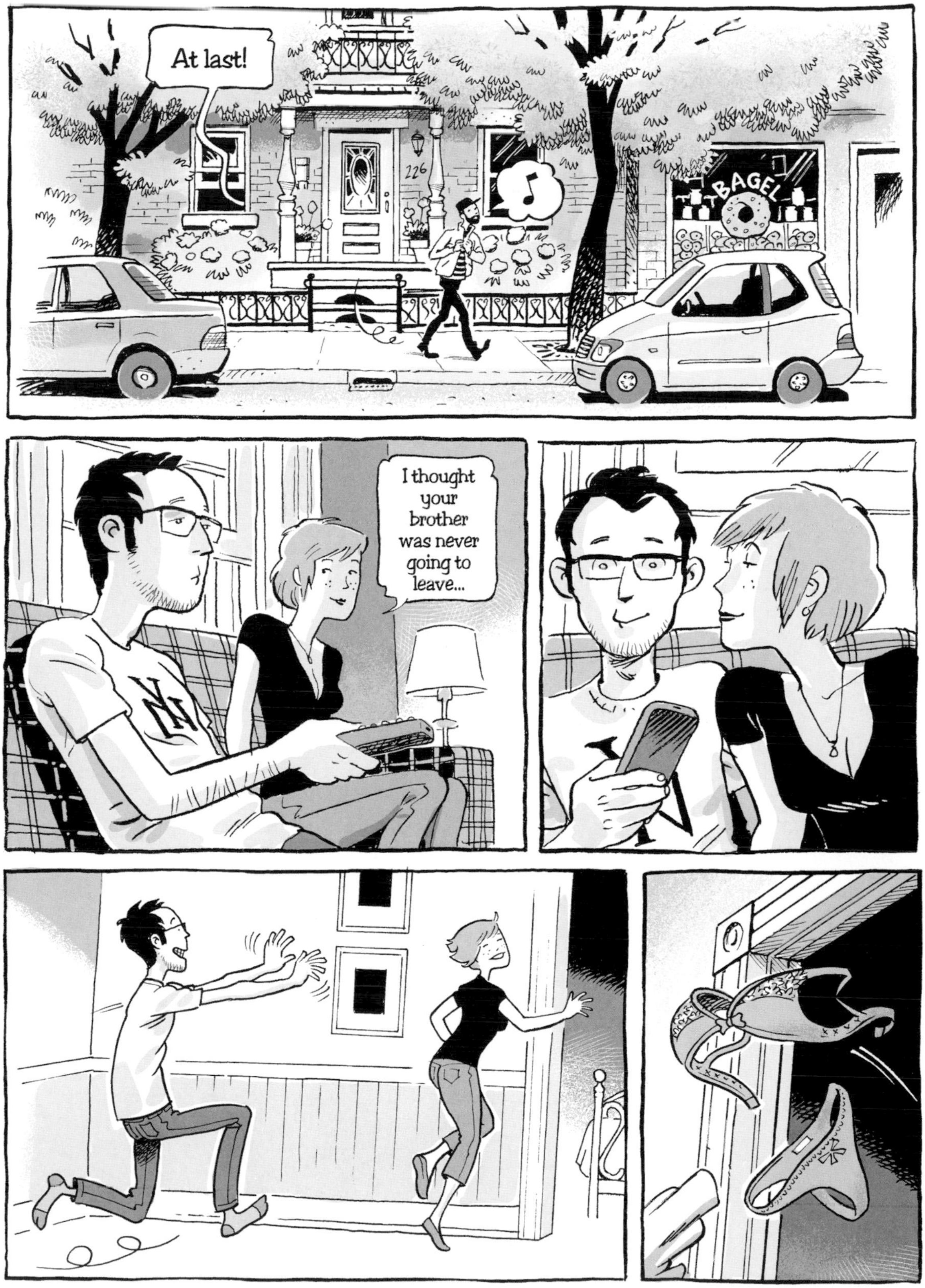
At last!
BAGEL
226
I thought your brother was never going to leave...

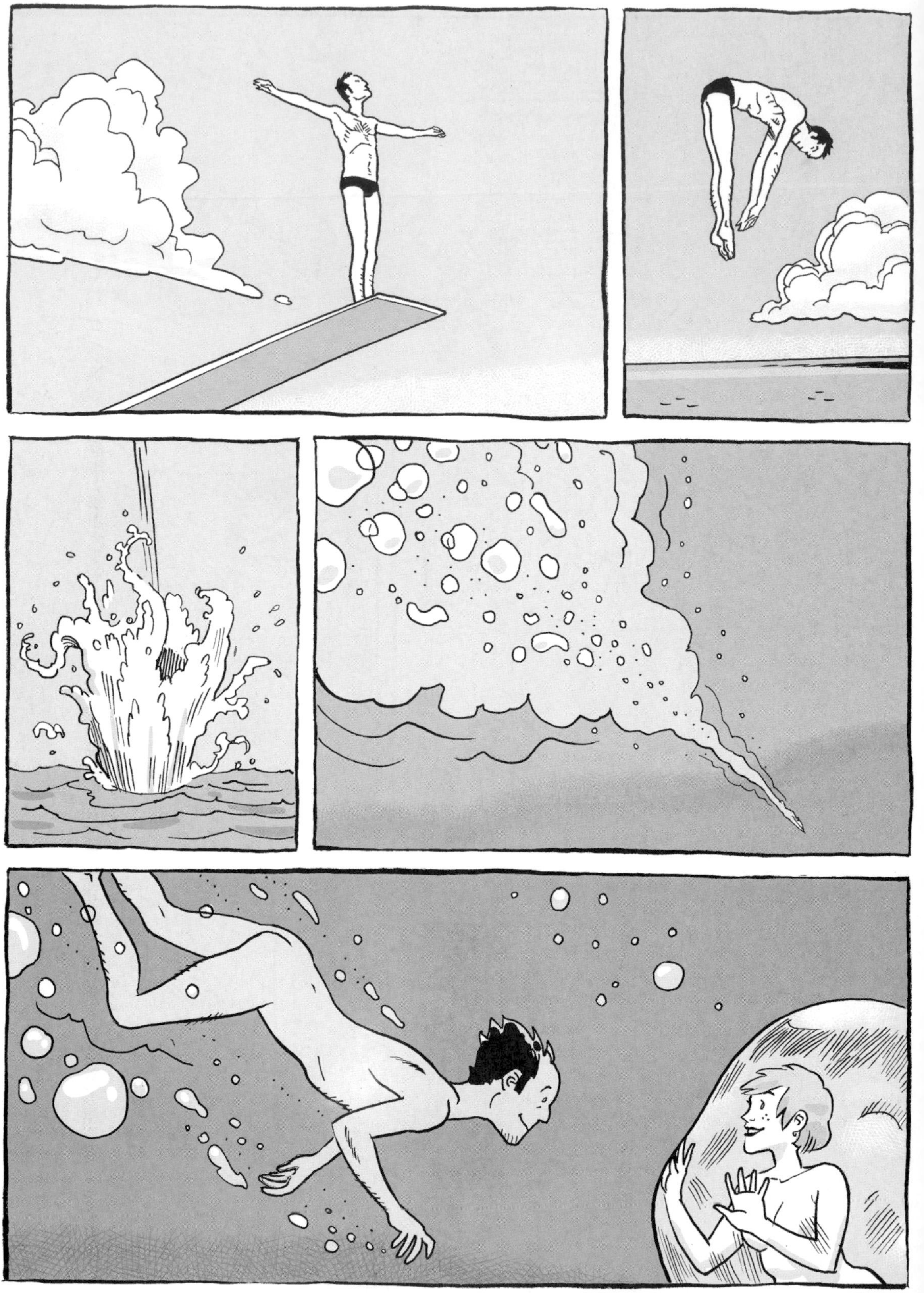

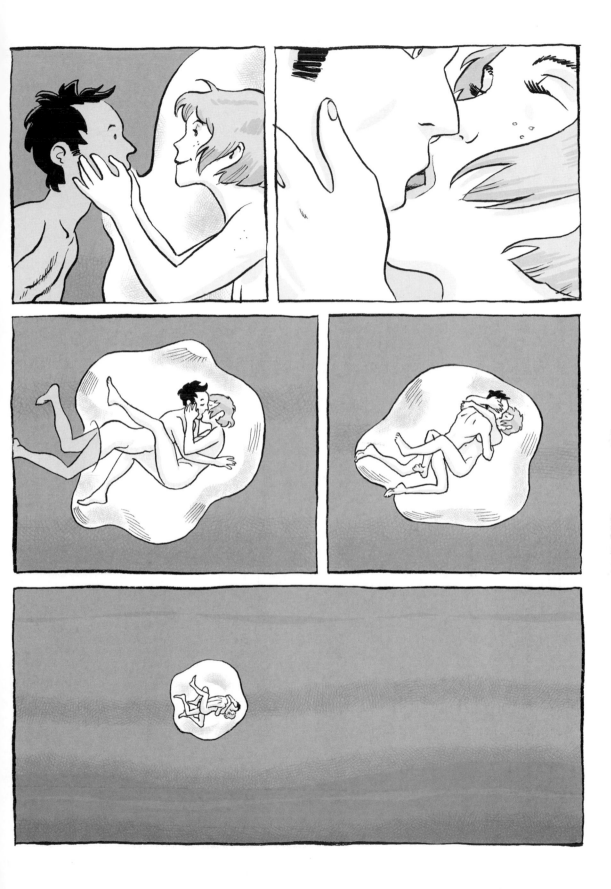

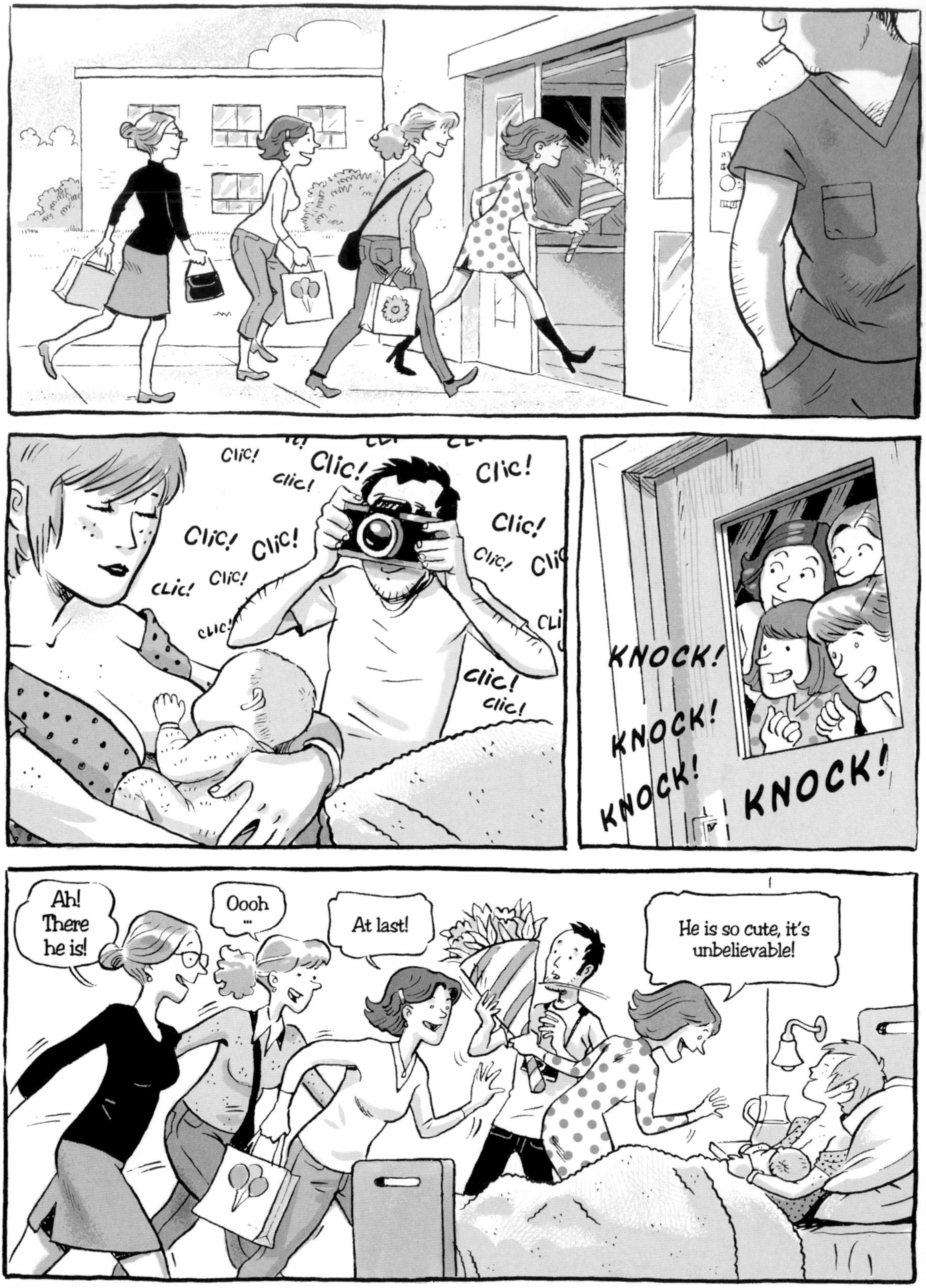
Clic!
Clic!
Clic!
Clic!
Clic!
Clic!
Clic!
Clic!
Clic!
Clic!
Clic!
Clic!
KNOCK!
KNOCK!
KNOCK!
KNOCK!
Ah! There he is!
Oooh ...
At last!
He is so cute, it's unbelievable!

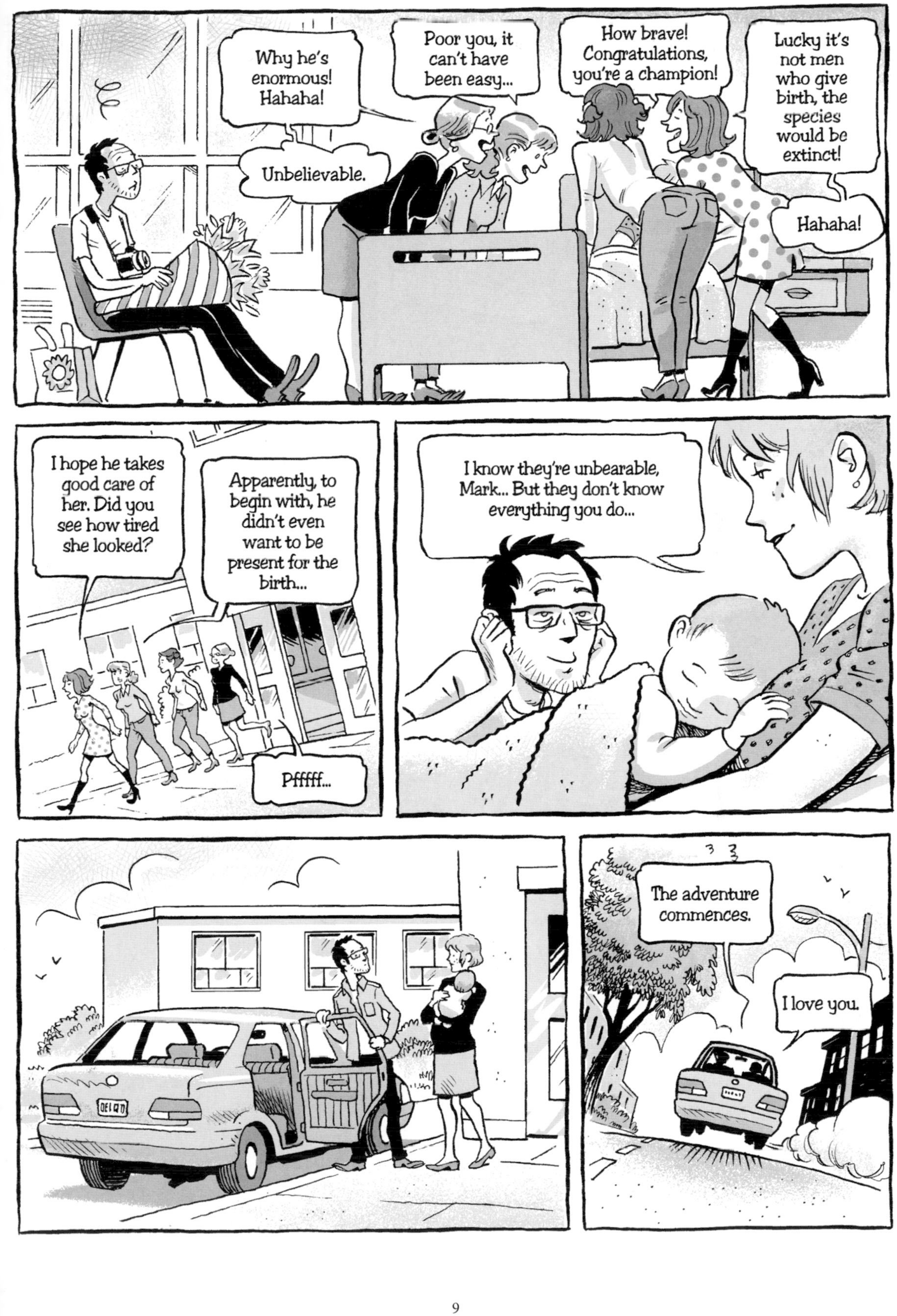
Why he's enormous! Hahaha!
Unbelievable.
Poor you, it can't have been easy...
How brave! Congratulations, you're a champion!
Lucky it's not men who give birth, the species would be extinct!
Hahaha!
I hope he takes good care of her. Did you see how tired she looked?
Apparently, to begin with, he didn't even want to be present for the birth...
Pfffff...
I know they're unbearable, Mark... But they don't know everything you do...
The adventure commences.
I love you.

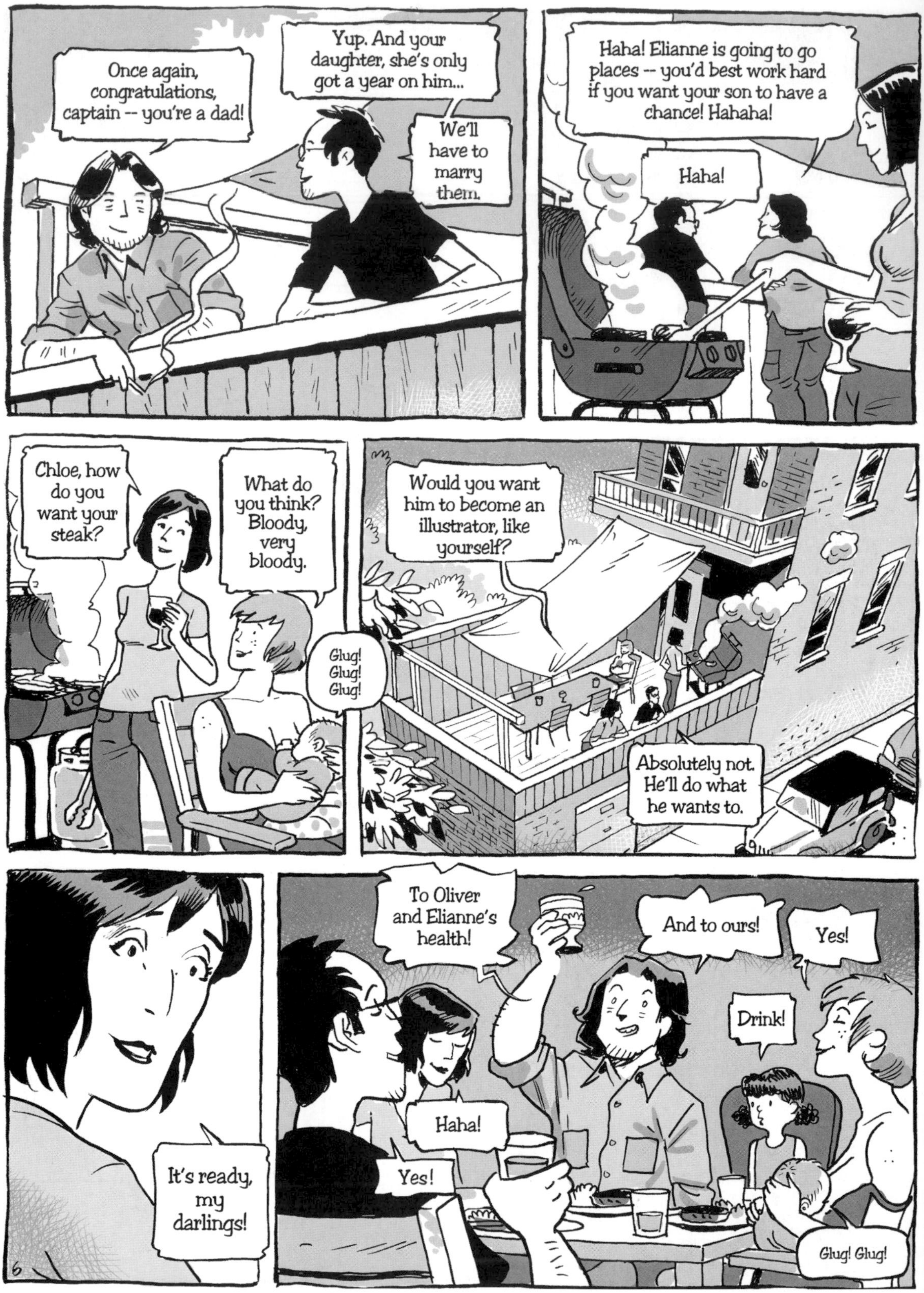

Once again, congratulations, captain -- you're a dad!
Yup. And your daughter, she's only got a year on him...
We'll have to marry them.
Haha! Elianne is going to go places -- you'd best work hard if you want your son to have a chance! Hahaha!
Haha!
Chloe, how do you want your steak?
What do you think? Bloody, very bloody.
Glug! Glug! Glug!
Would you want him to become an illustrator, like yourself?
Absolutely not. He'll do what he wants to.
It's ready, my darlings!
To Oliver and Elianne's health!
And to ours!
Yes!
Drink!
Haha!
Yes!
Glug! Glug!

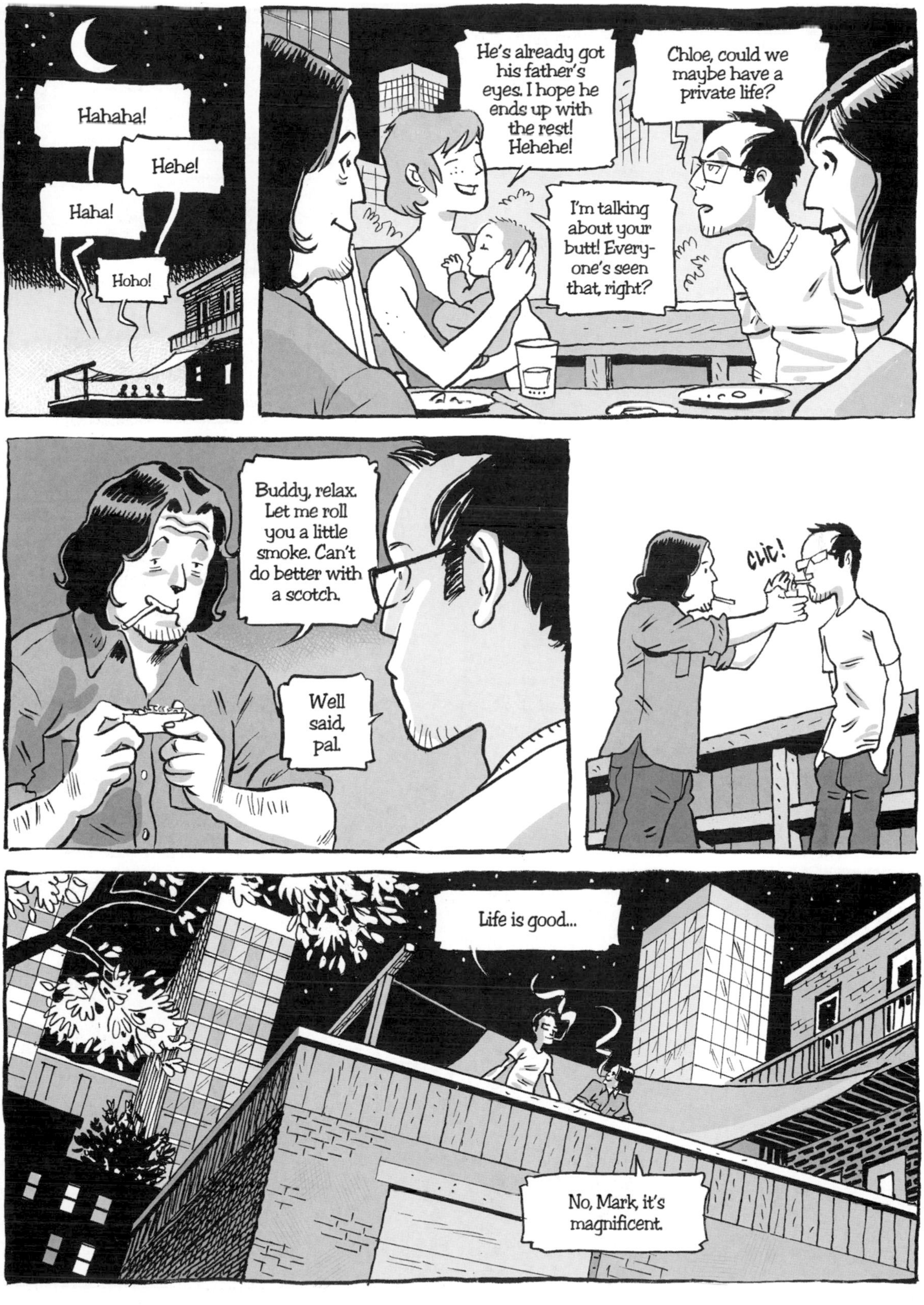
Hahaha!
Hehe!
Haha!
Hoho!
He's already got his father's eyes. I hope he ends up with the rest! Hehehe!
Chloe, could we maybe have a private life?
I'm talking about your butt! Everyone's seen that, right?
Buddy, relax. Let me roll you a little smoke. Can't do better with a scotch.
Well said, pal.
CLIC!
Life is good...
No, Mark, it's magnificent.

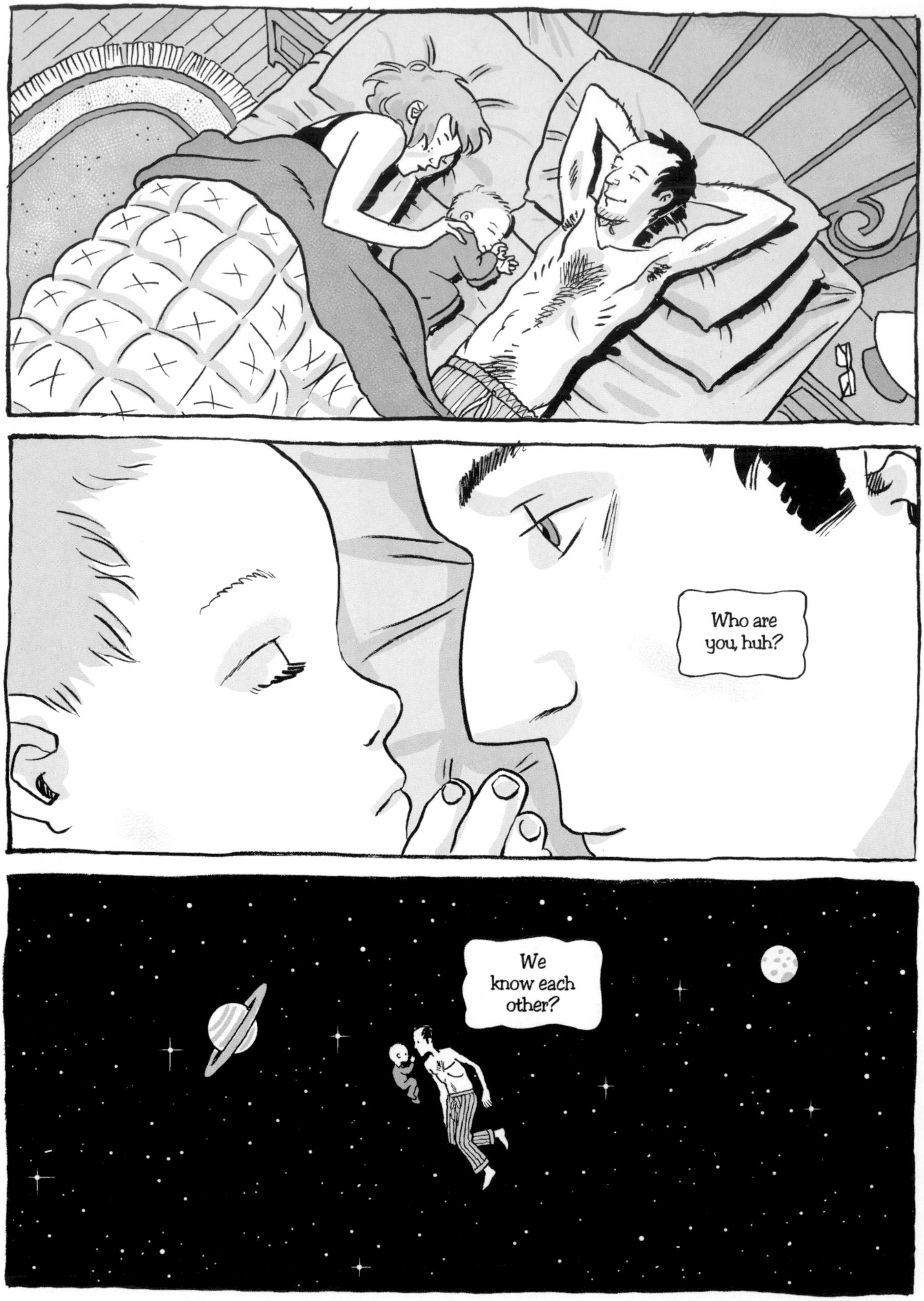
Who are you, huh?
We know each other?

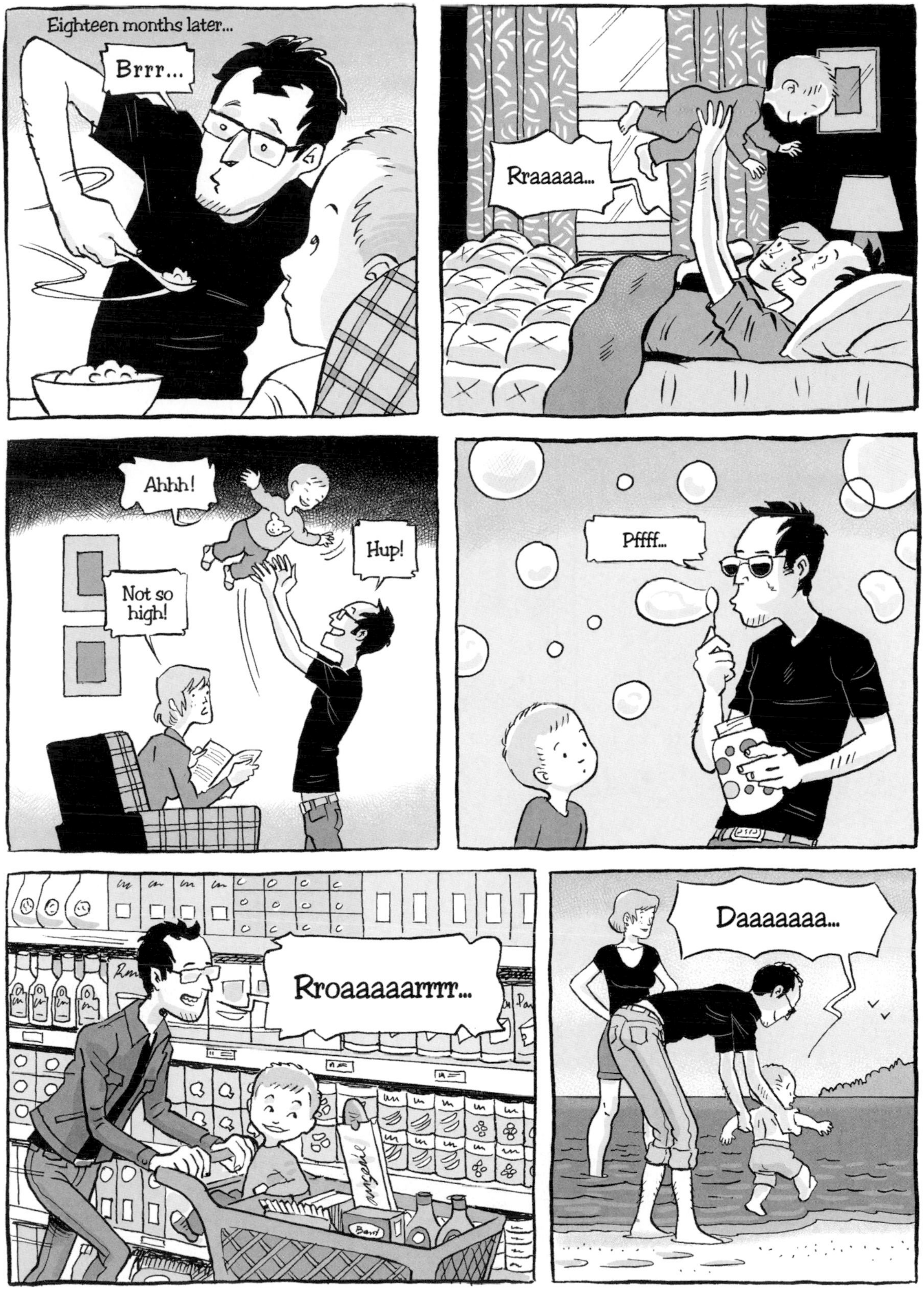
Eighteen months later...
Brrr...
Rraaaaa...
Ahhh!
Hup!
Not so high!
Pffff...
Rroaaaaarrrr...
Daaaaaaa...

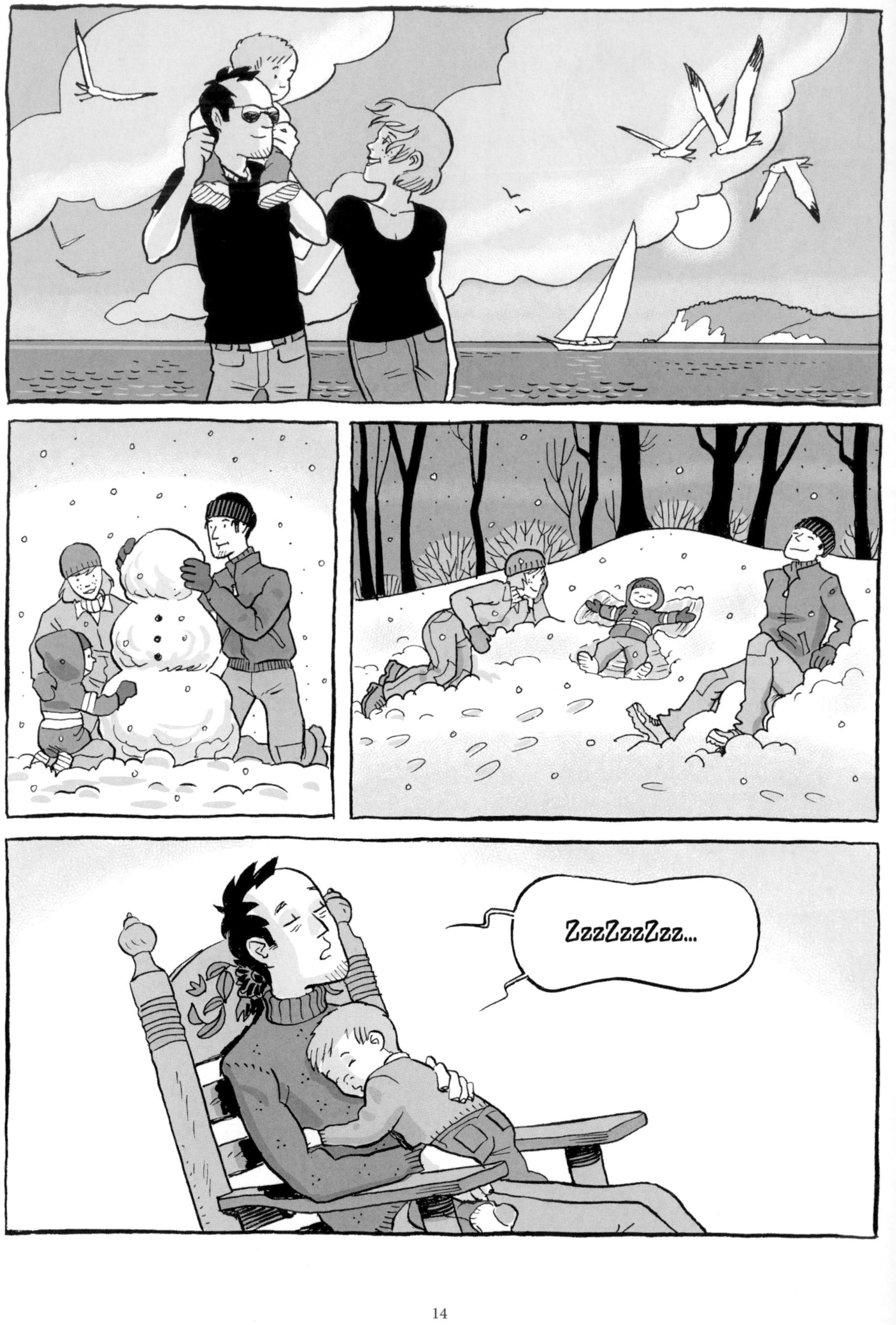
ZzzZzzZzz...

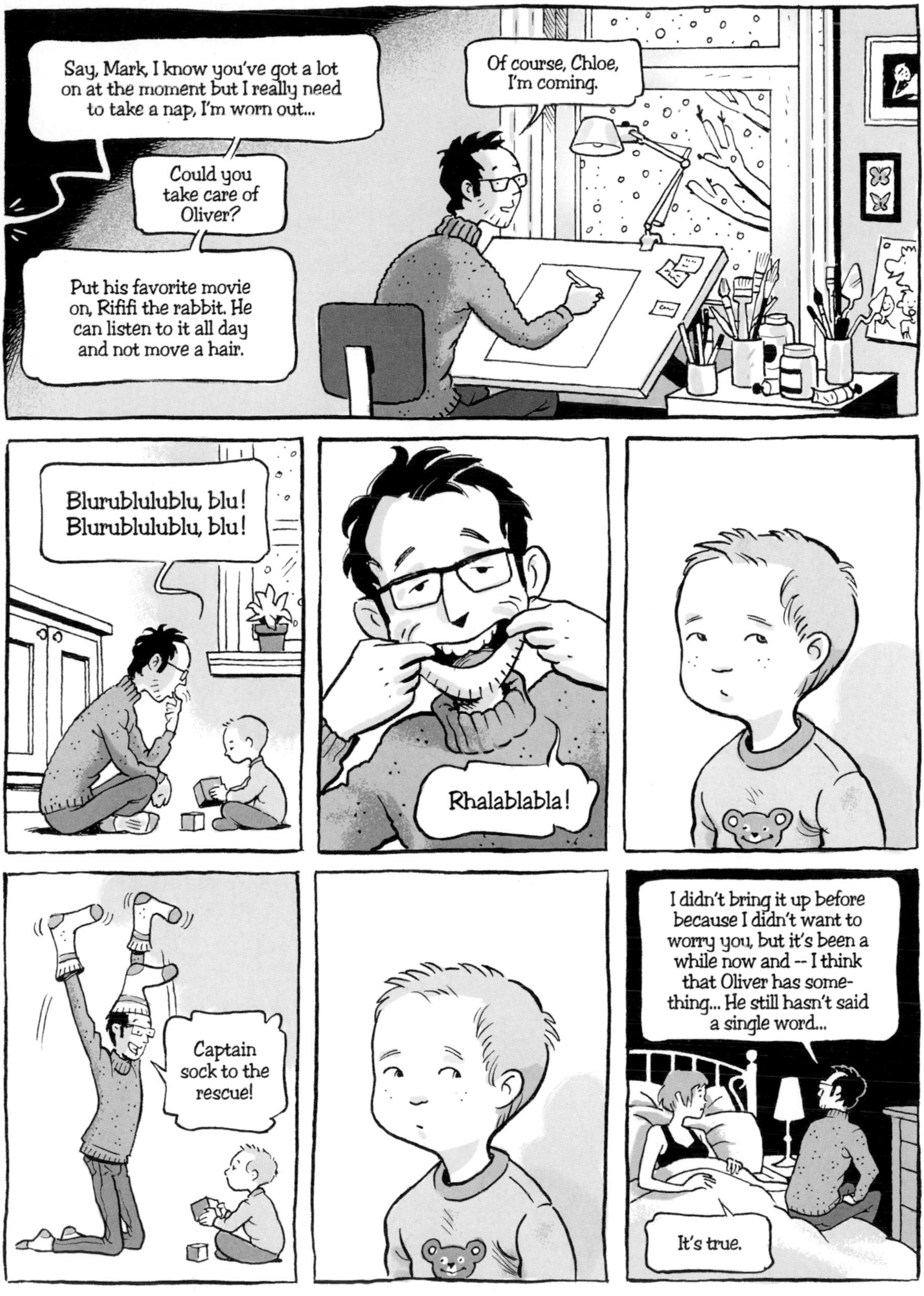
Say, Mark, I know you've got a lot on at the moment but I really need to take a nap, I'm worn out...
Of course, Chloe, I'm coming.
Could you take care of Oliver?
Put his favorite movie on, Rififi the rabbit. He can listen to it all day and not move a hair.
Blurublulublu, blu! Blurublulublu, blu!
Rhalablabla!
Captain sock to the rescue!
I didn't bring it up before because I didn't want to worry you, but it's been a while now and -- I think that Oliver has some-thing... He still hasn't said a single word...
It's true.

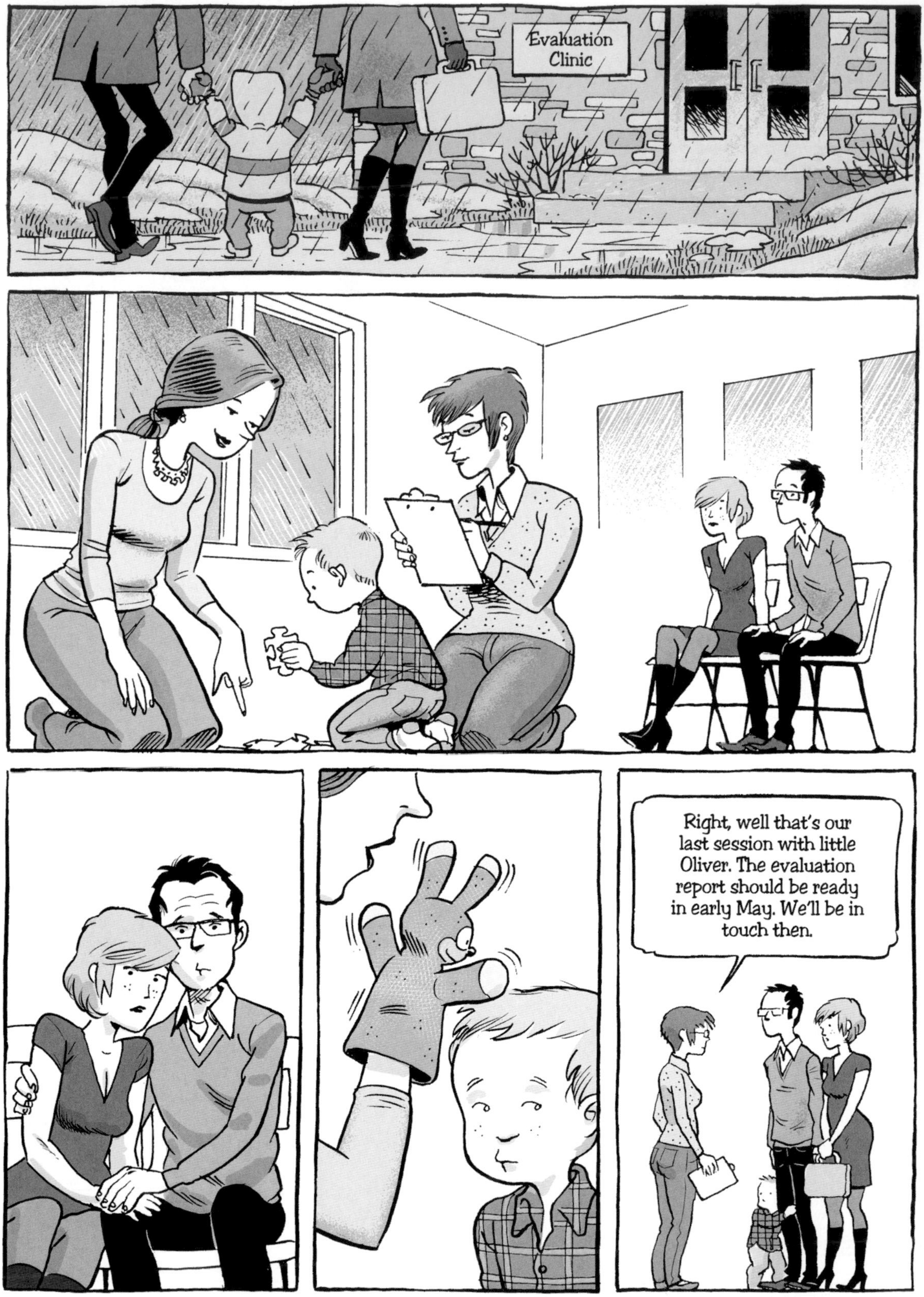
Evaluation Clinic
Right, well that's our last session with little Oliver. The evaluation report should be ready in early May. We'll be in touch then.

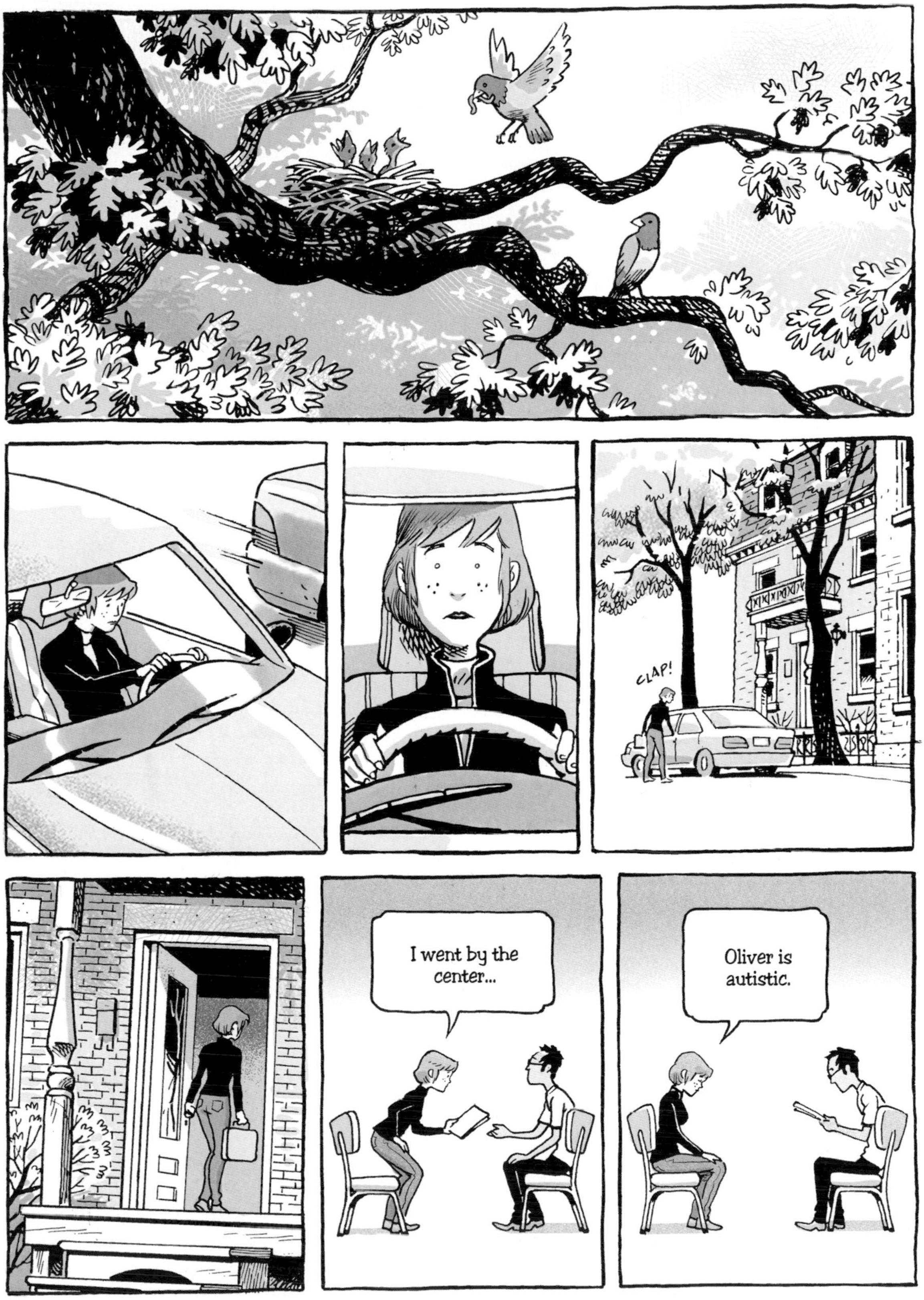
CLAP!
I went by the center...
Oliver is autistic.

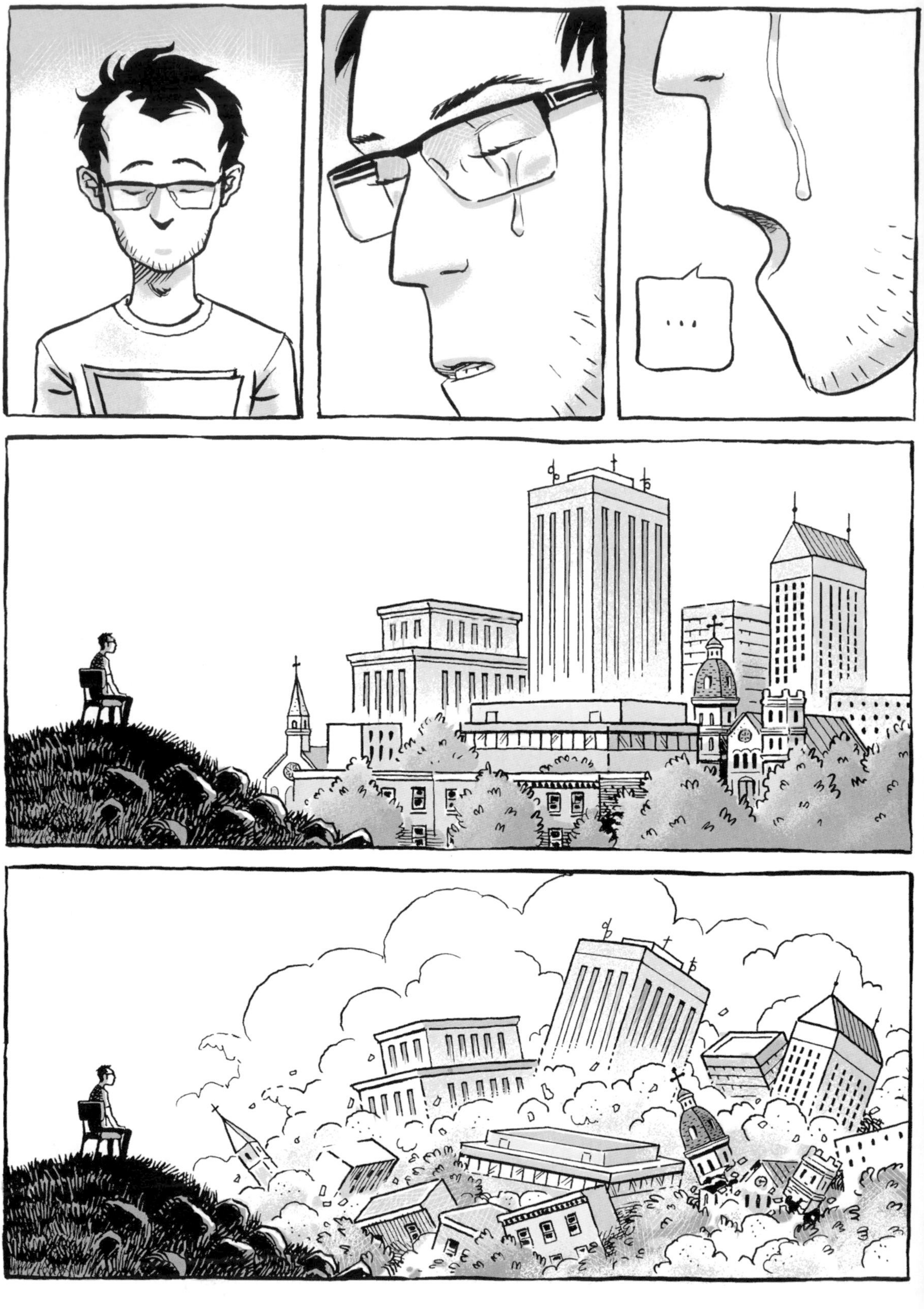
...

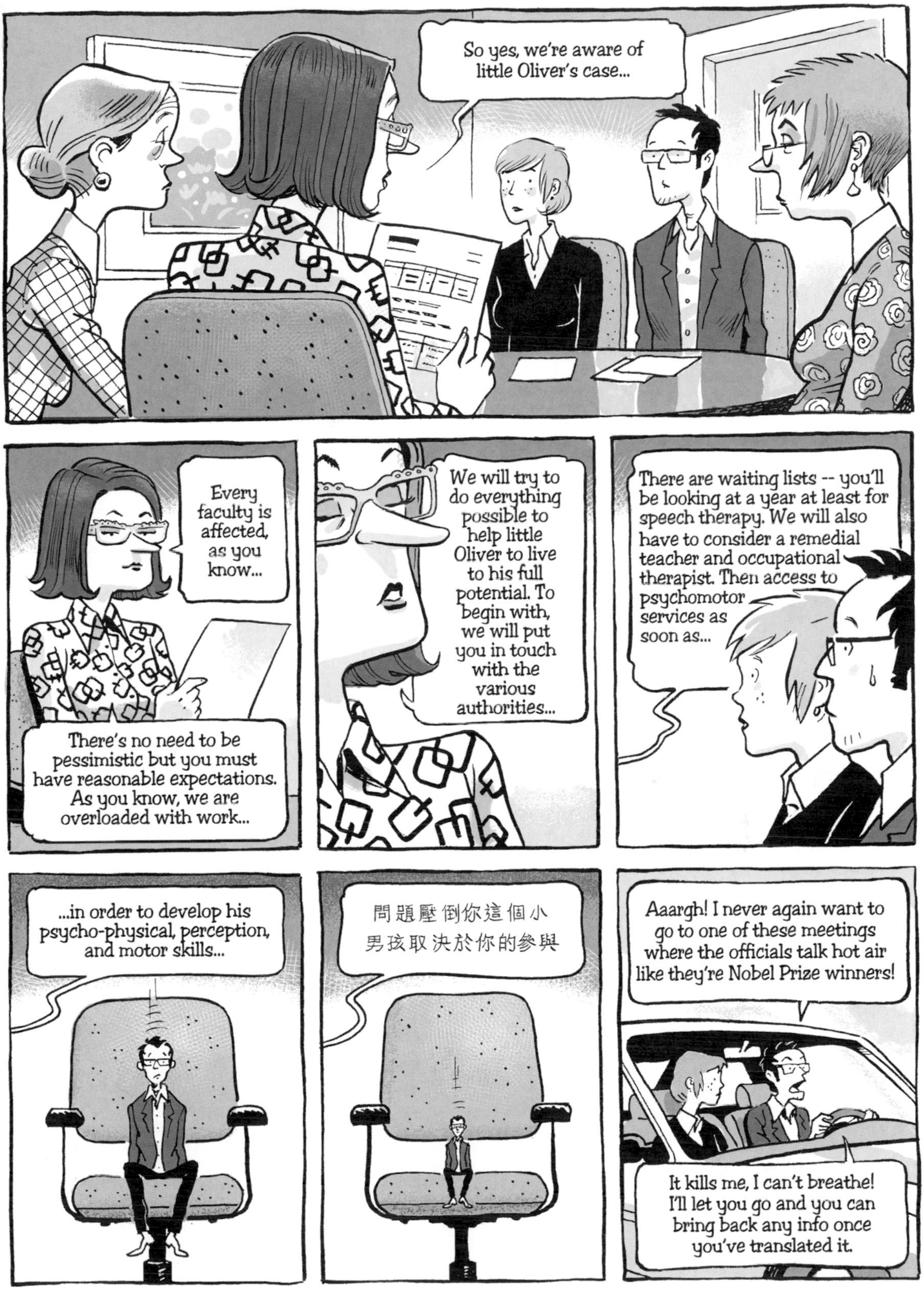
So yes, we're aware of little Oliver's case...
Every faculty is affected, as you know...
There's no need to be pessimistic but you must have reasonable expectations. As you know, we are overloaded with work...
We will try to do everything possible to help little Oliver to live to his full potential. To begin with, we will put you in touch with the various authorities...
There are waiting lists -- you'll be looking at a year at least for speech therapy. We will also have to consider a remedial teacher and occupational therapist. Then access to psychomotor services as soon as...
...in order to develop his psycho-physical, perception, and motor skills...
問題壓倒你這個小男孩取決於你的參與
Aaargh! I never again want to go to one of these meetings where the officials talk hot air like they're Nobel Prize winners!
It kills me, I can't breathe! I'll let you go and you can bring back any info once you've translated it.

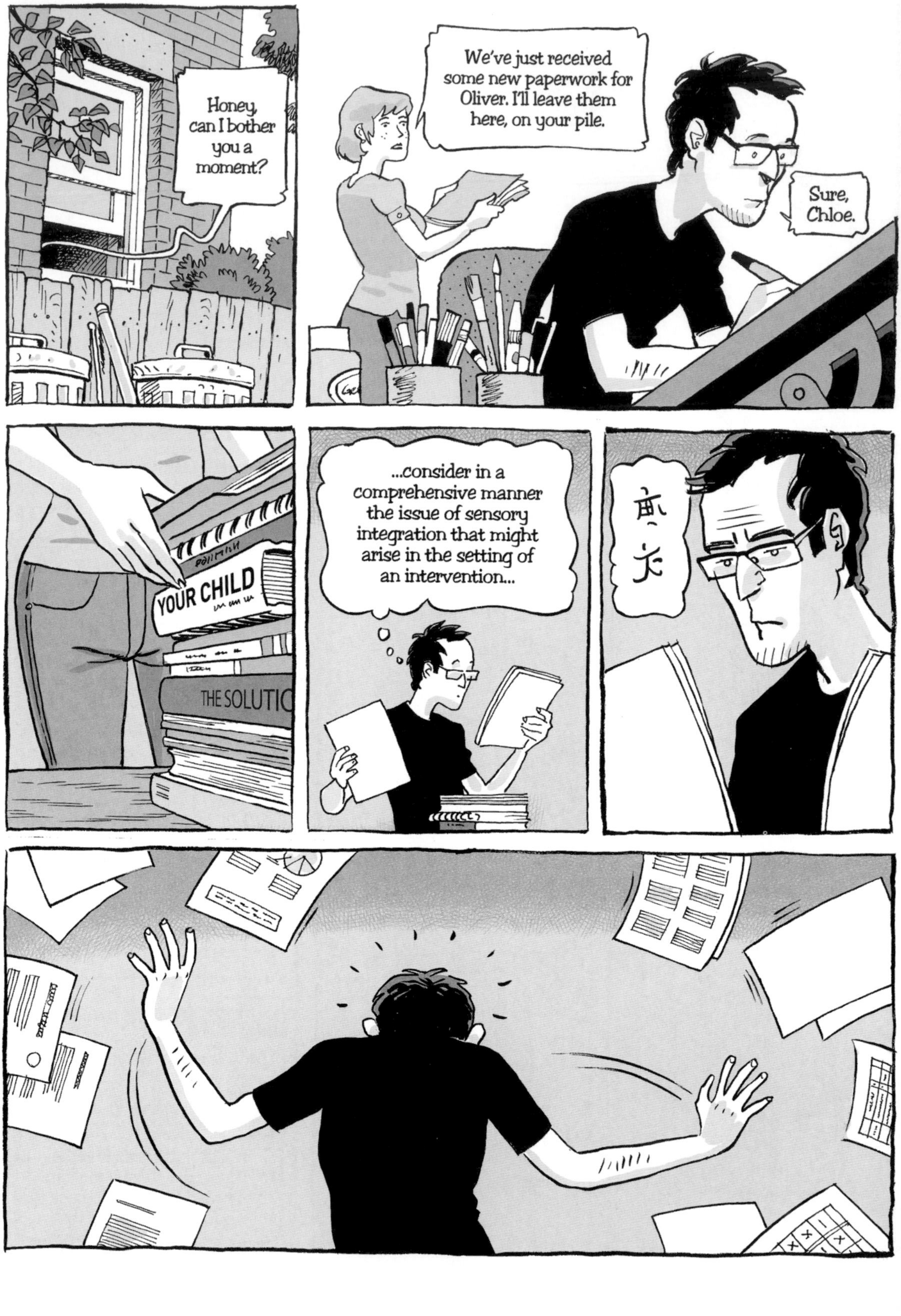
Honey, can I bother you a moment?
We've just received some new paperwork for Oliver. I'll leave them here, on your pile.
Sure, Chloe.
YOUR CHILD
THE SOLUTIO
...consider in a comprehensive manner the issue of sensory integration that might arise in the setting of an intervention...

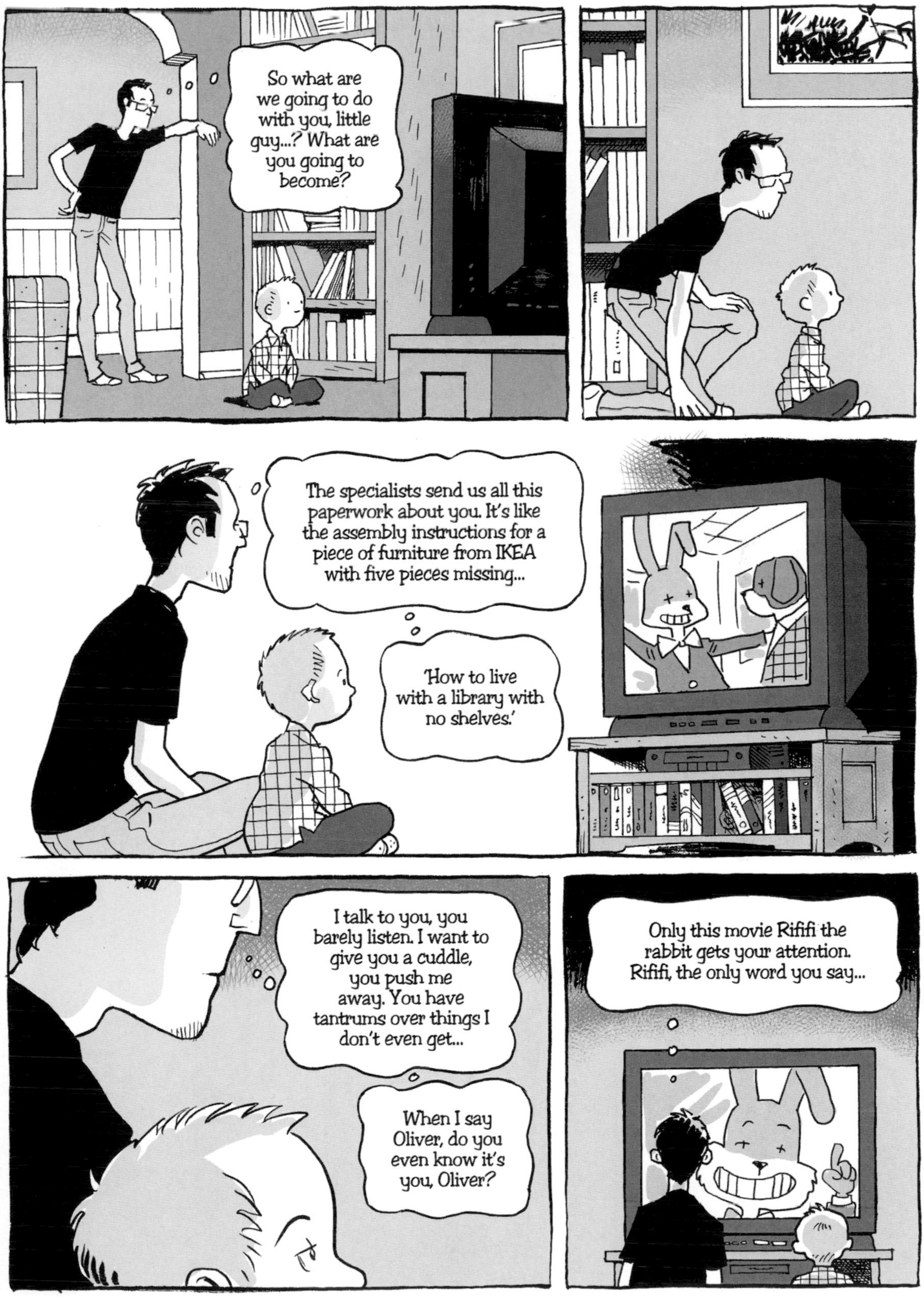
So what are we going to do with you, little guy...? What are you going to become?
The specialists send us all this paperwork about you. It's like the assembly instructions for a piece of furniture from IKEA with five pieces missing...
'How to live with a library with no shelves.'
I talk to you, you barely listen. I want to give you a cuddle, you push me away. You have tantrums over things I don't even get...
When I say Oliver, do you even know it's you, Oliver?
Only this movie Rififi the rabbit gets your attention. Rififi, the only word you say...

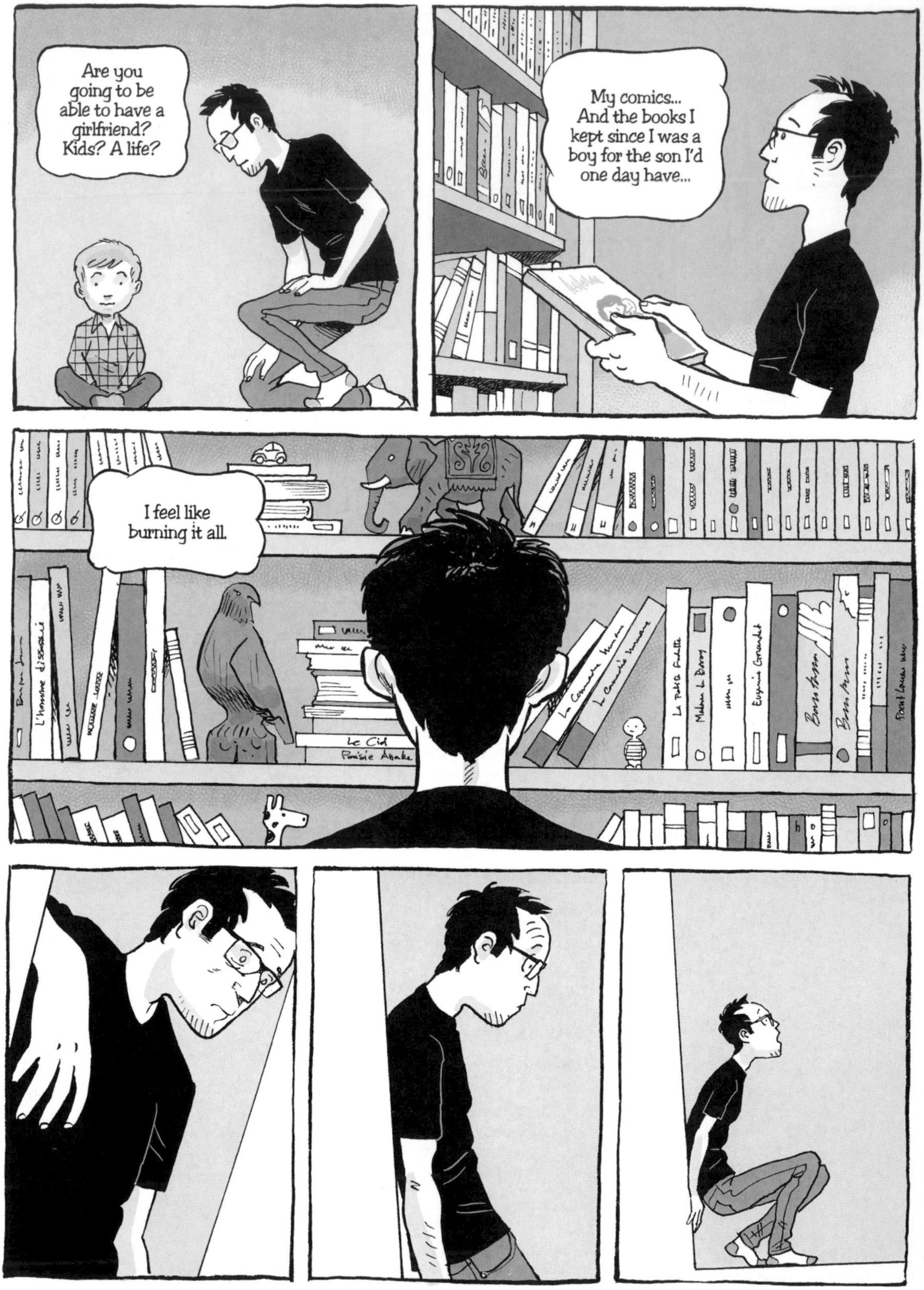
Are you going to be able to have a girlfriend? Kids? A life?
My comics... And the books I kept since I was a boy for the son I'd one day have...
I feel like burning it all.

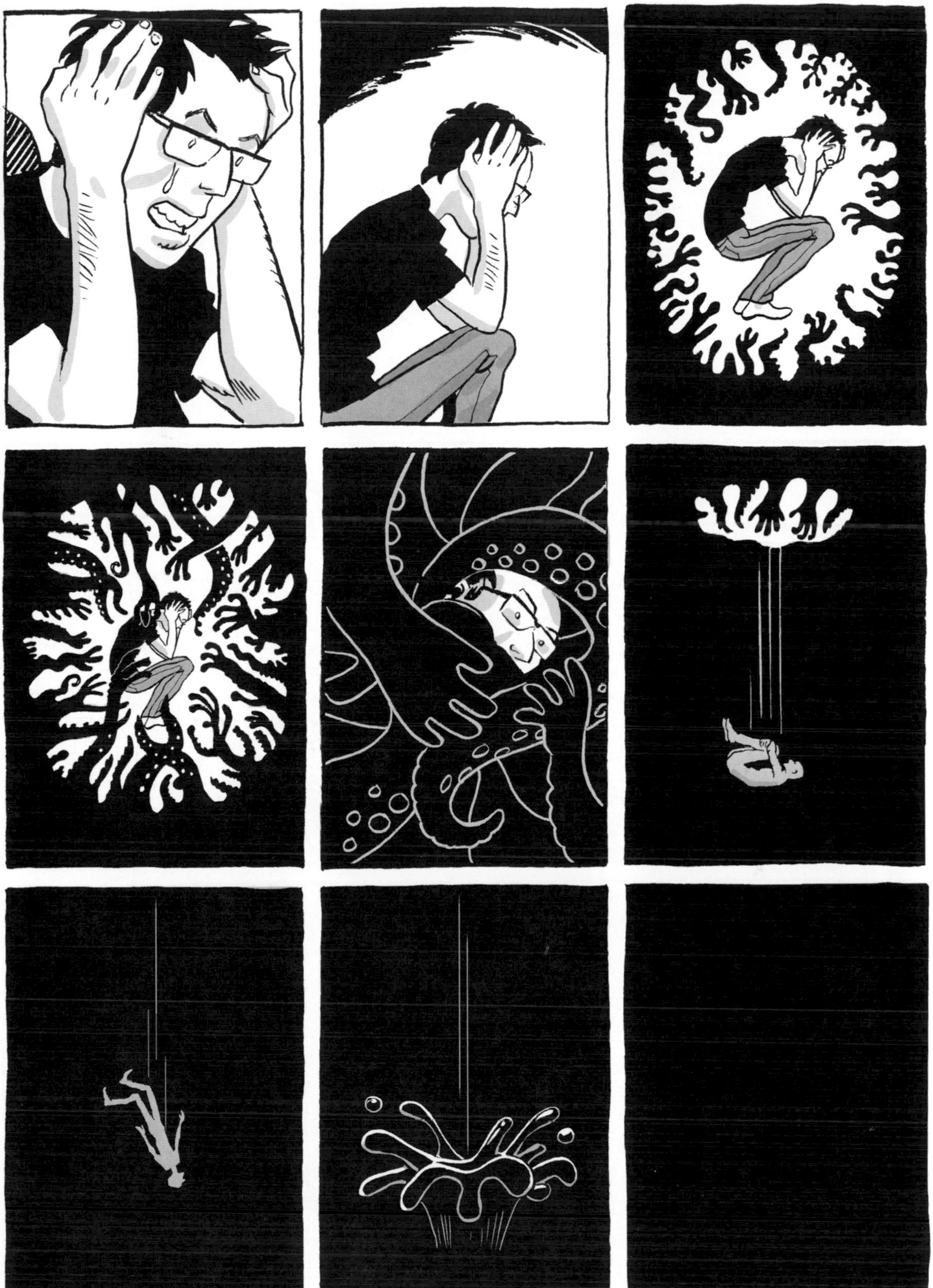

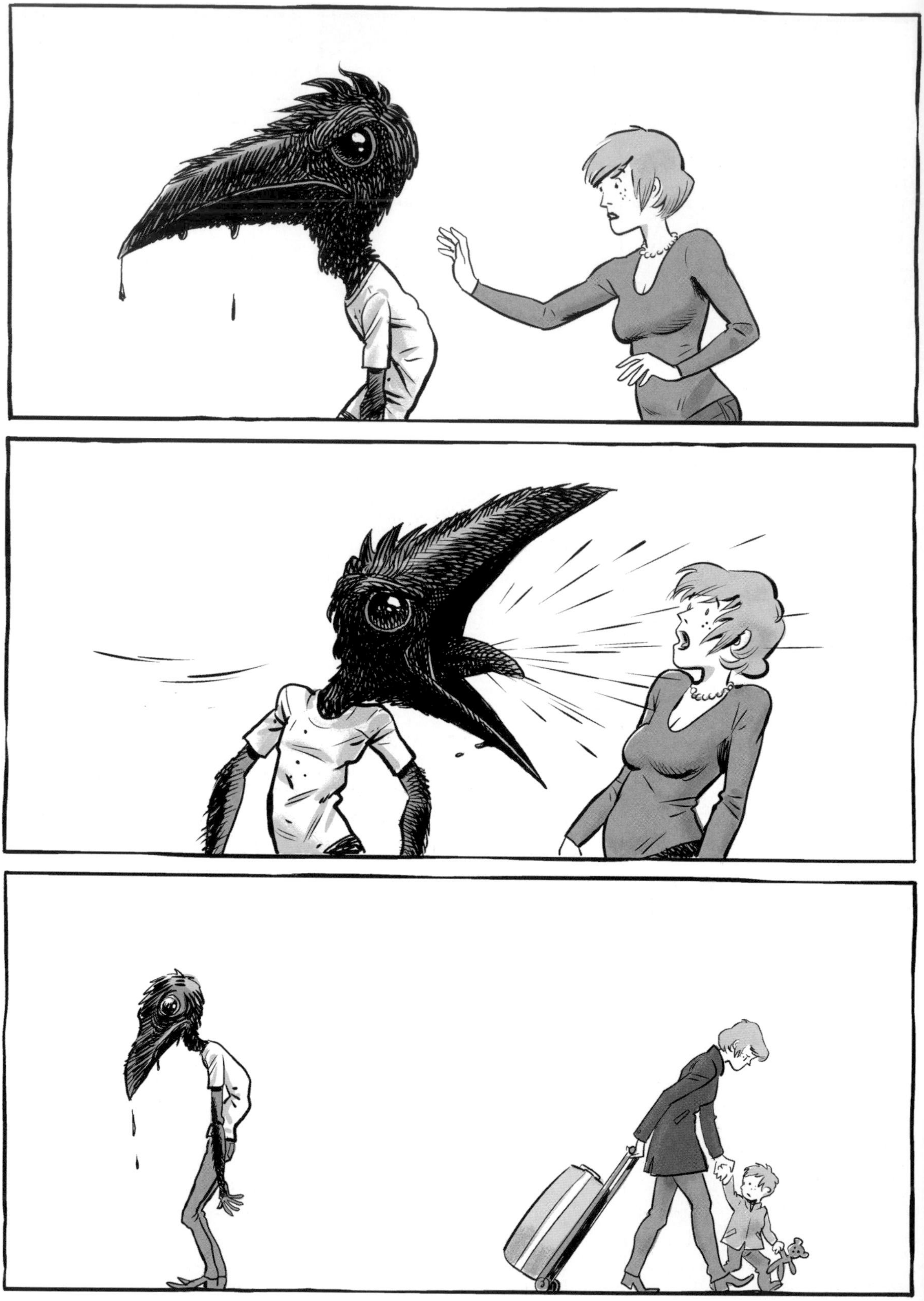

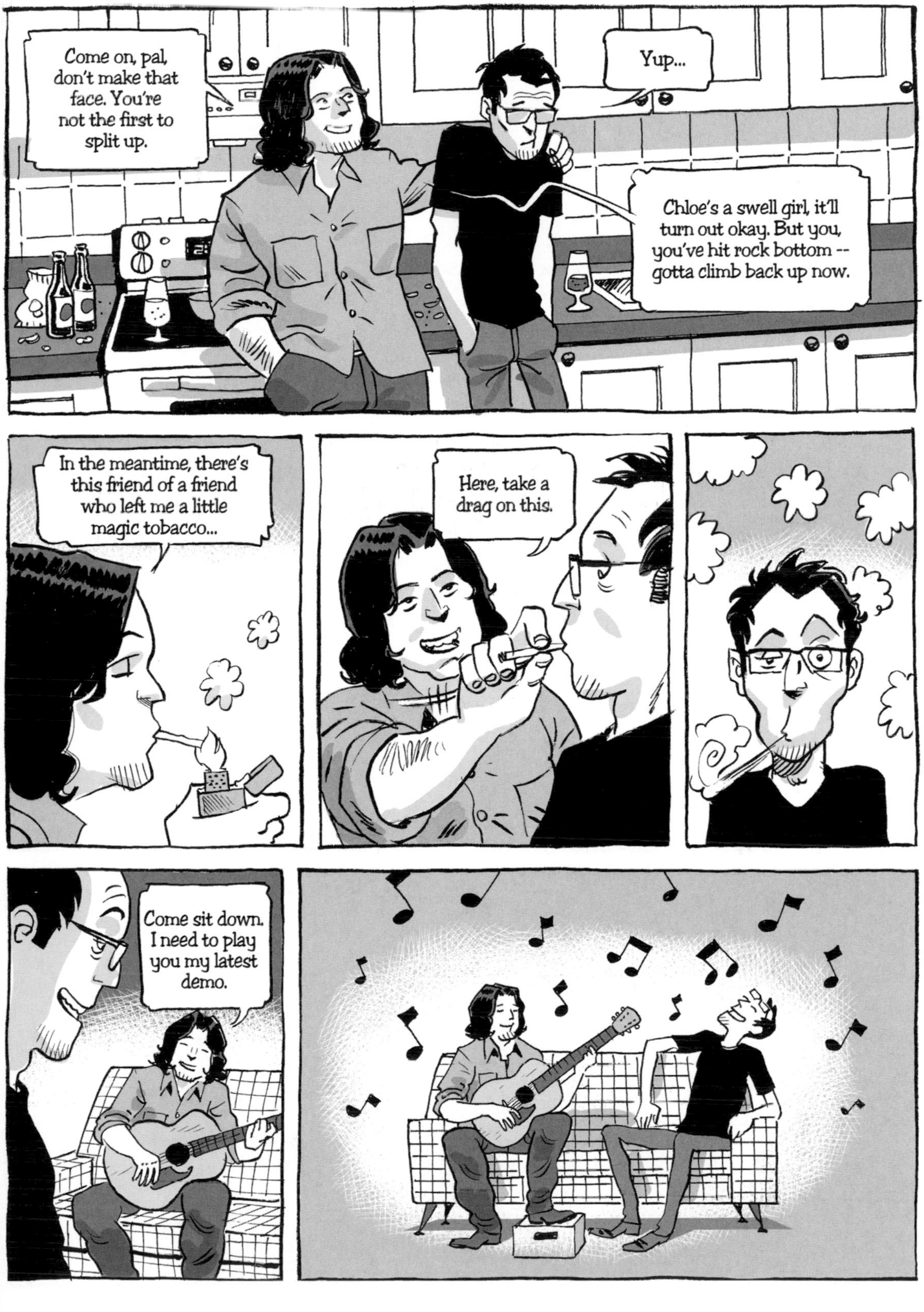
Come on, pal, don't make that face. You're not the first to split up.
Yup...
Chloe's a swell girl, it'll turn out okay. But you, you've hit rock bottom -- gotta climb back up now.
In the meantime, there's this friend of a friend who left me a little magic tobacco...
Here, take a drag on this.
Come sit down. I need to play you my latest demo.

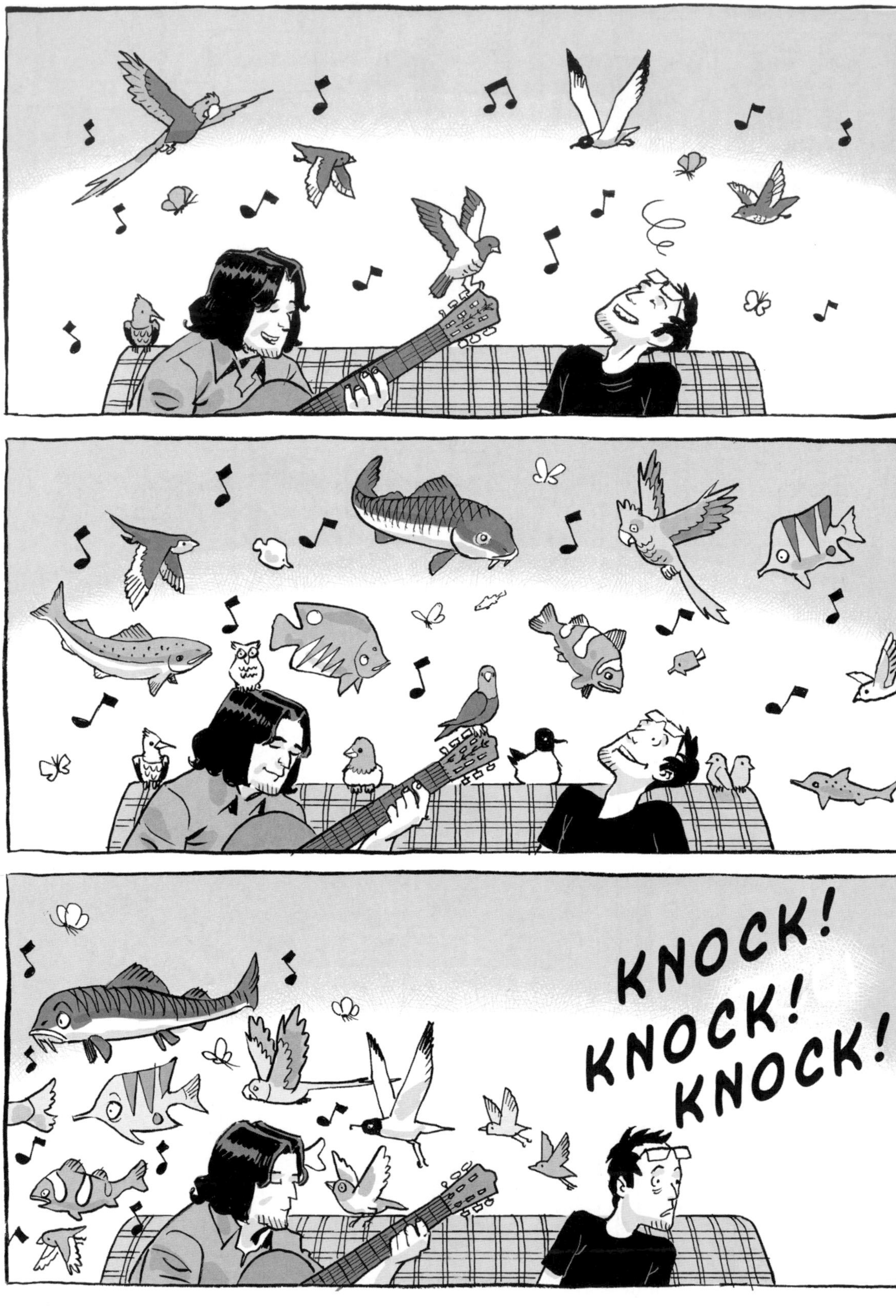
KNOCK!
KNOCK!
KNOCK!

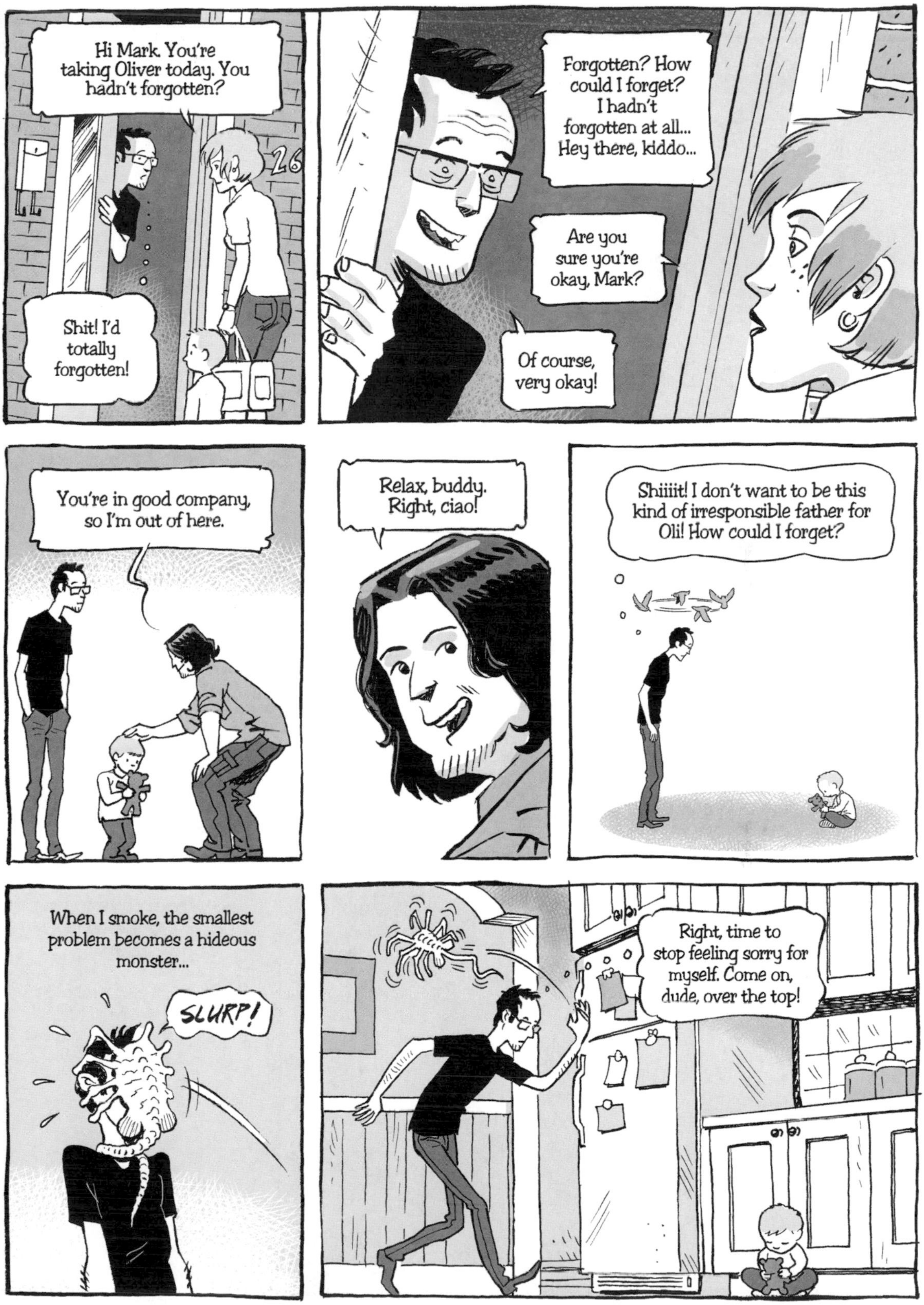
Hi Mark. You're taking Oliver today. You hadn't forgotten?
Shit! I'd totally forgotten!
Forgotten? How could I forget? I hadn't forgotten at all... Hey there, kiddo...
Are you sure you're okay, Mark?
Of course, very okay!
You're in good company, so I'm out of here.
Relax, buddy. Right, ciao!
Shiiiit! I don't want to be this kind of irresponsible father for Oli! How could I forget?
When I smoke, the smallest problem becomes a hideous monster...
SLURP!
Right, time to stop feeling sorry for myself. Come on, dude, over the top!

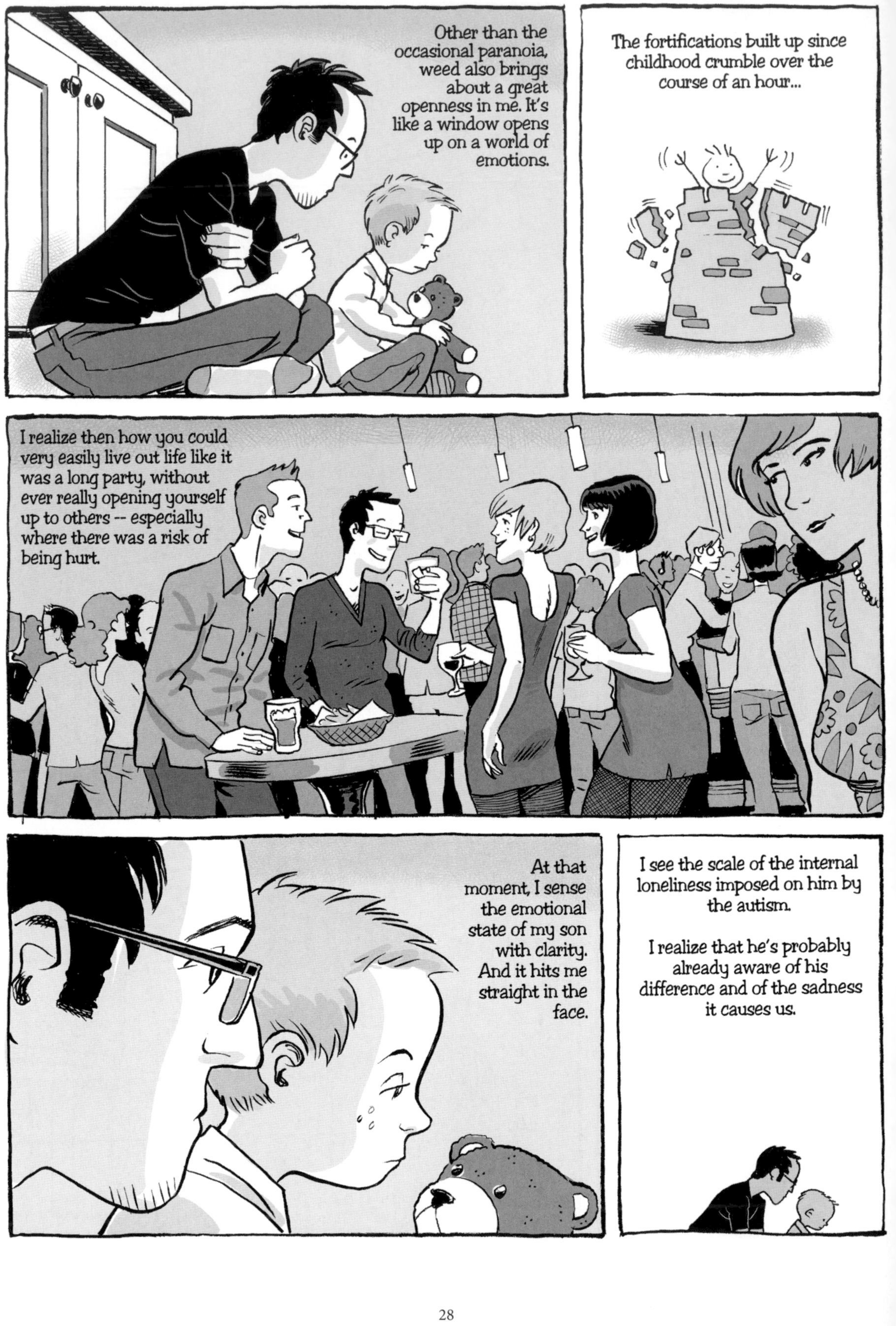
Other than the occasional paranoia, weed also brings about a great openness in me. It's like a window opens up on a world of emotions.
The fortifications built up since childhood crumble over the course of an hour...
I realize then how you could very easily live out life like it was a long party, without ever really opening yourself up to others -- especially where there was a risk of being hurt.
At that moment, I sense the emotional state of my son with clarity. And it hits me straight in the face.
I see the scale of the internal loneliness imposed on him by the autism.
I realize that he's probably already aware of his difference and of the sadness it causes us.

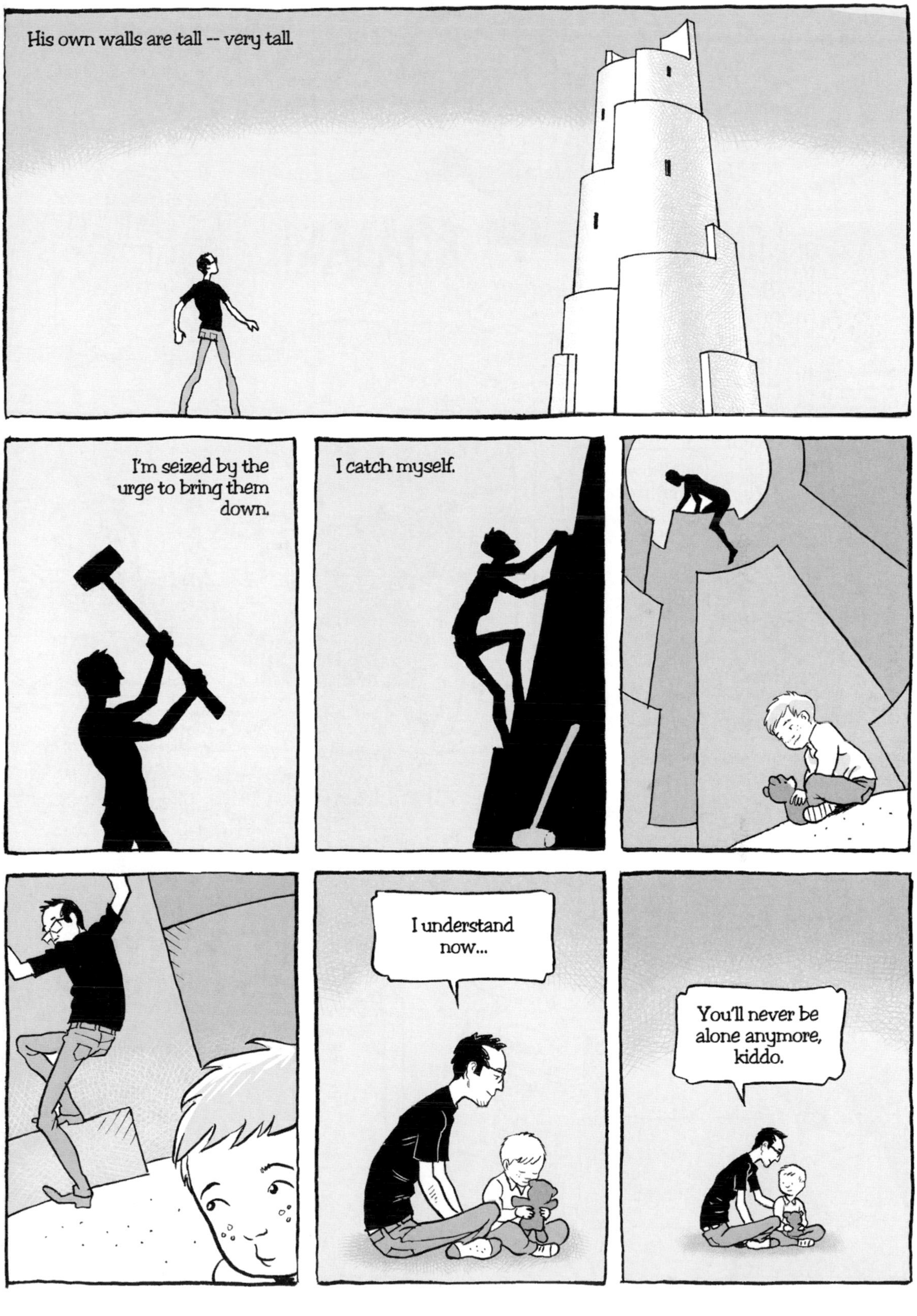
His own walls are tall -- very tall.
I'm seized by the urge to bring them down.
I catch myself.
I understand now...
You'll never be alone anymore, kiddo.

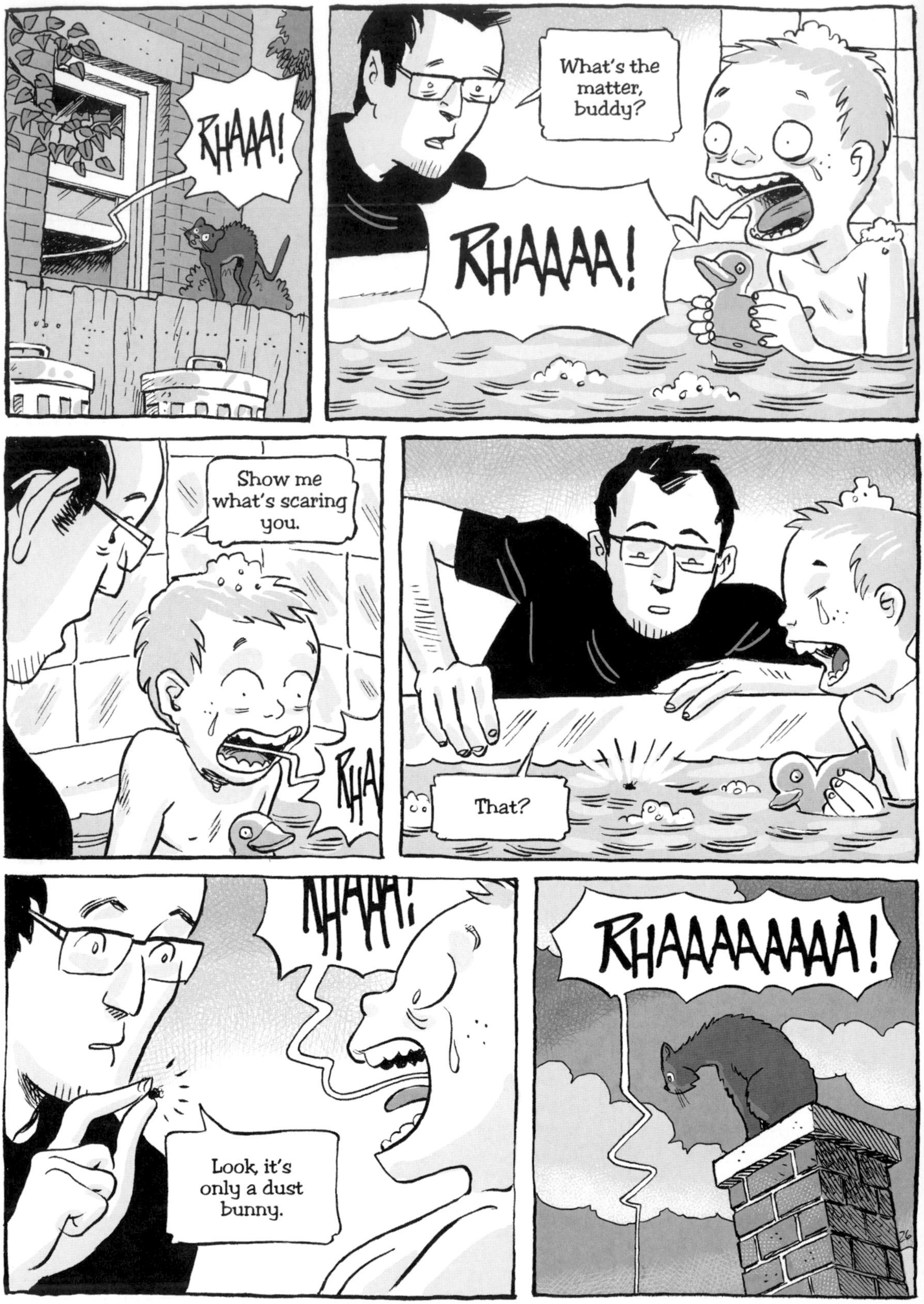
RHAAA!
What's the matter, buddy?
RHAAAA!
Show me what's scaring you.
That?
Look, it's only a dust bunny.
RHAAAAAAAA!

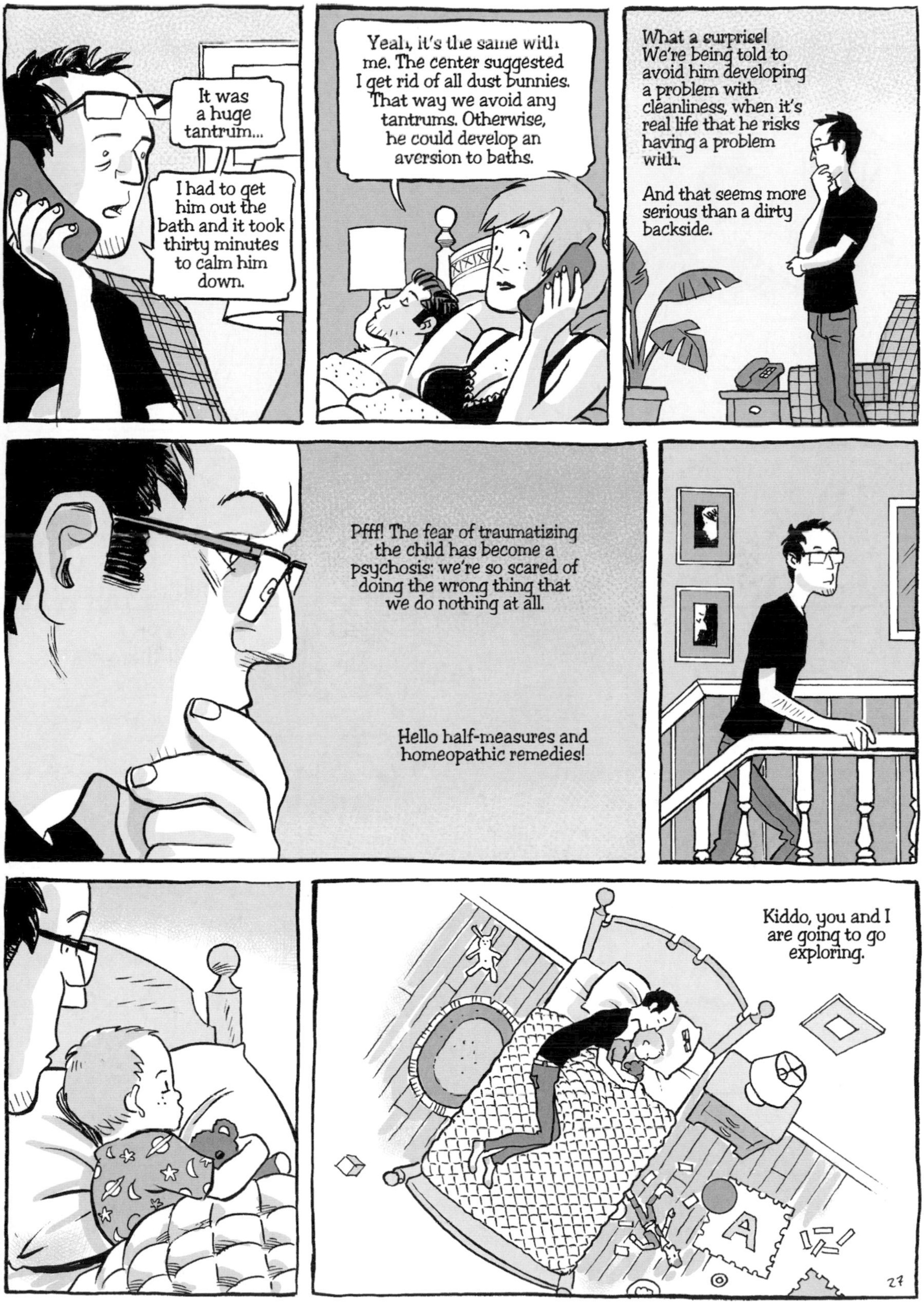
It was a huge tantrum...
I had to get him out the bath and it took thirty minutes to calm him down.
Yeah, it's the same with me. The center suggested I get rid of all dust bunnies. That way we avoid any tantrums. Otherwise, he could develop an aversion to baths.
What a surprise! We're being told to avoid him developing a problem with cleanliness, when it's real life that he risks having a problem with.
And that seems more serious than a dirty backside.
Pfff! The fear of traumatizing the child has become a psychosis: we're so scared of doing the wrong thing that we do nothing at all.
Hello half-measures and homeopathic remedies!
Kiddo, you and I are going to go exploring.
A
27

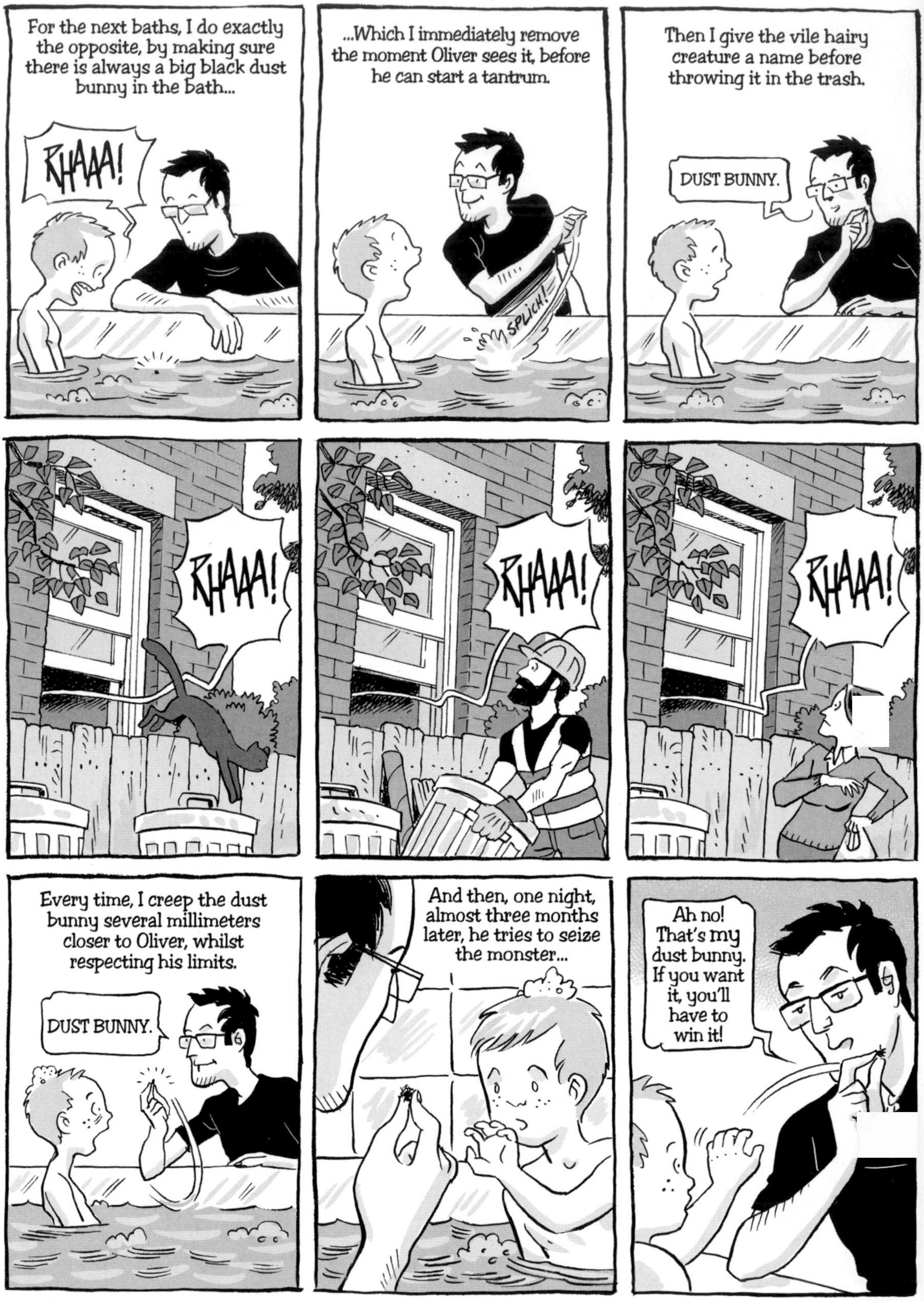
For the next baths, I do exactly the opposite, by making sure there is always a big black dust bunny in the bath...
RHAAA!
...Which I immediately remove the moment Oliver sees it, before he can start a tantrum.
SPLICH!
Then I give the vile hairy creature a name before throwing it in the trash.
DUST BUNNY.
RHAAA!
RHAAA!
RHAAA!
Every time, I creep the dust bunny several millimeters closer to Oliver, whilst respecting his limits.
DUST BUNNY.
And then, one night, almost three months later, he tries to seize the monster...
Ah no! That's my dust bunny. If you want it, you'll have to win it!

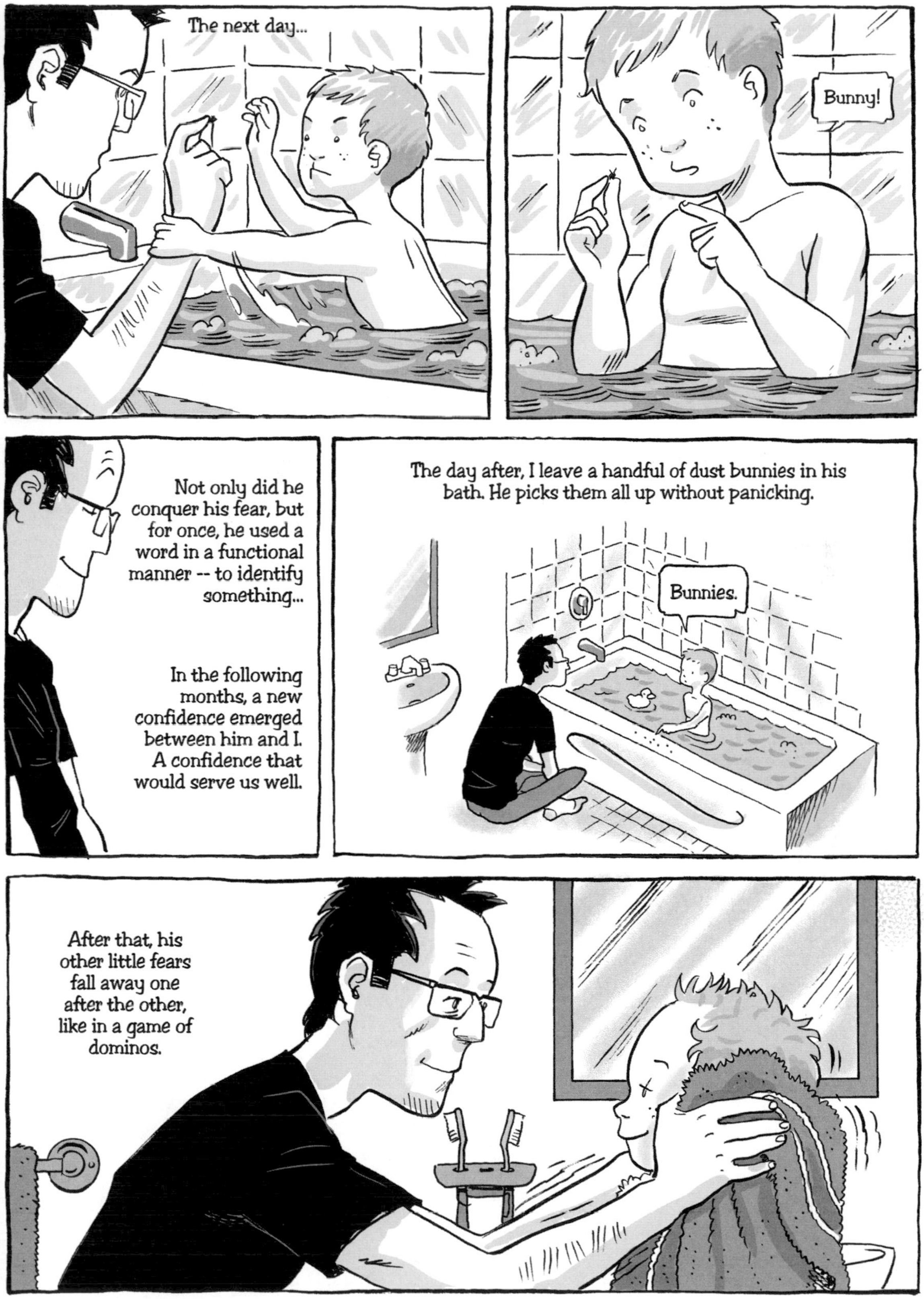

The next day...
Bunny!
Not only did he conquer his fear, but for once, he used a word in a functional manner -- to identify something...
In the following months, a new confidence emerged between him and I. A confidence that would serve us well.
The day after, I leave a handful of dust bunnies in his bath. He picks them all up without panicking.
Bunnies.
After that, his other little fears fall away one after the other, like in a game of dominos.

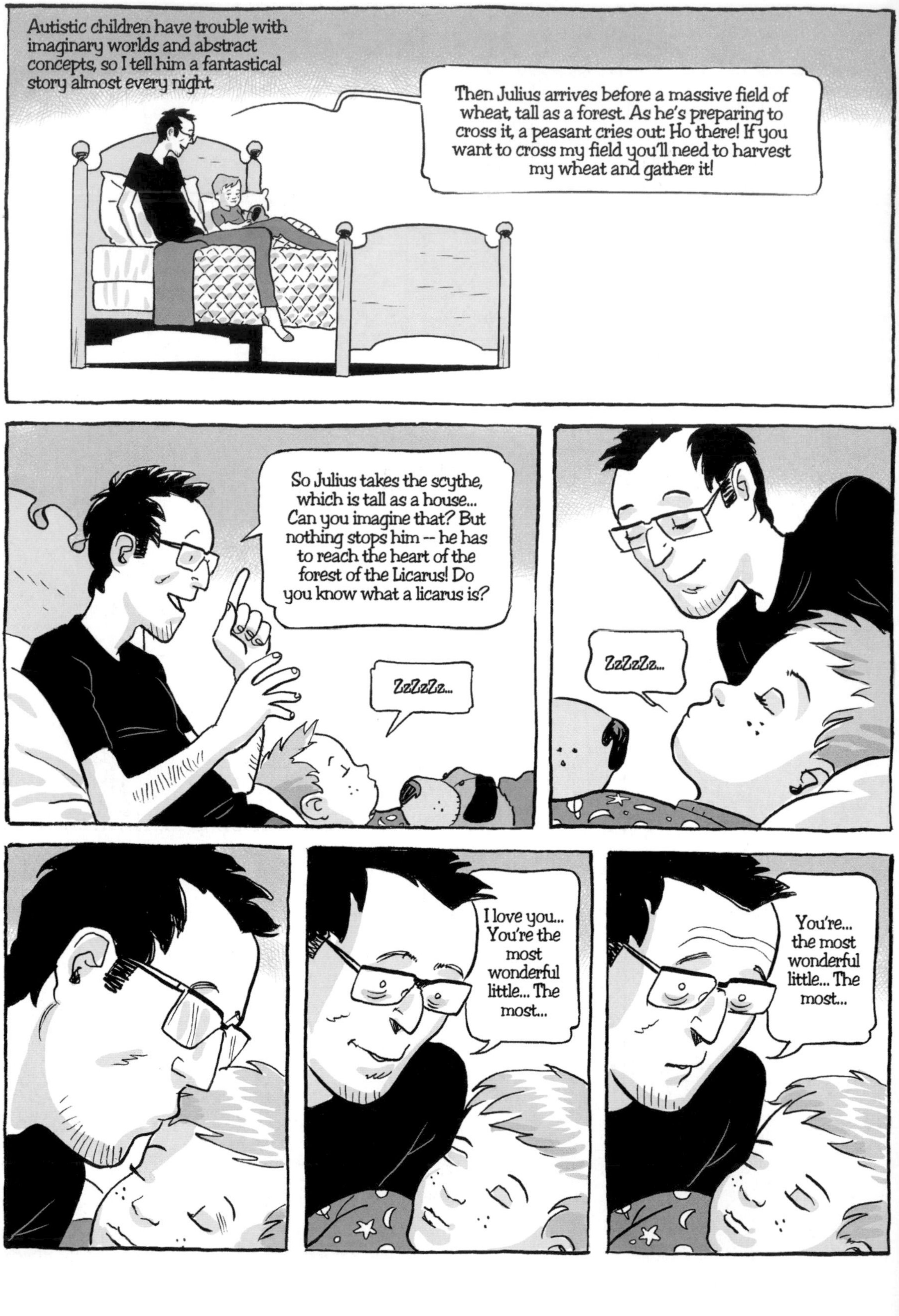
Autistic children have trouble with imaginary worlds and abstract concepts, so I tell him a fantastical story almost every night.
Then Julius arrives before a massive field of wheat, tall as a forest. As he's preparing to cross it, a peasant cries out: Ho there! If you want to cross my field you'll need to harvest my wheat and gather it!
So Julius takes the scythe, which is tall as a house... Can you imagine that? But nothing stops him -- he has to reach the heart of the forest of the Licarus! Do you know what a licarus is?
ZzZzZz...
ZzZzZz...
I love you... You're the most wonderful little... The most...
You're... the most wonderful little... The most...

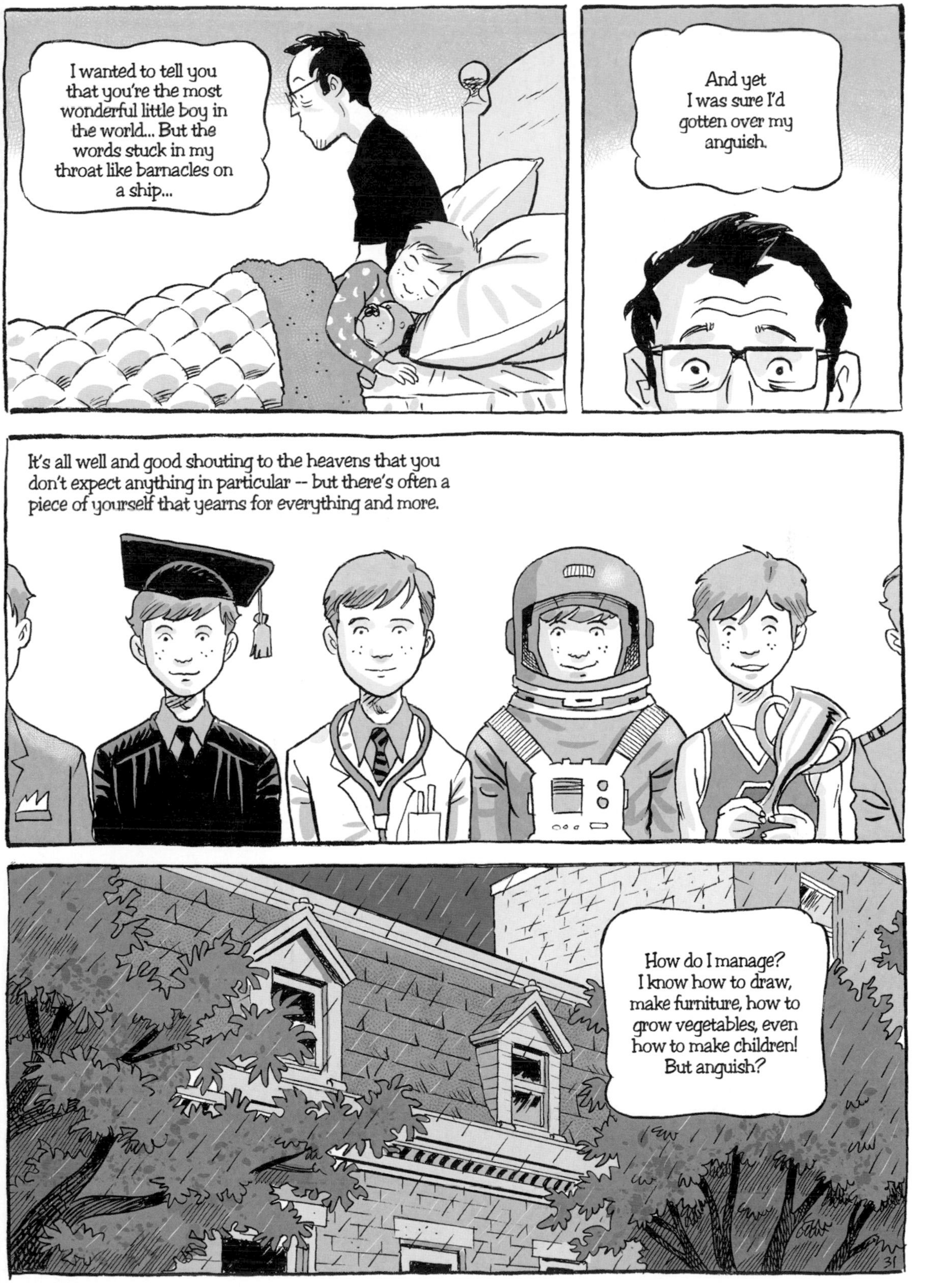

I wanted to tell you that you're the most wonderful little boy in the world... But the words stuck in my throat like barnacles on a ship...
And yet I was sure I'd gotten over my anguish.
It's all well and good shouting to the heavens that you don't expect anything in particular -- but there's often a piece of yourself that yearns for everything and more.
How do I manage? I know how to draw, make furniture, how to grow vegetables, even how to make children! But anguish?
31

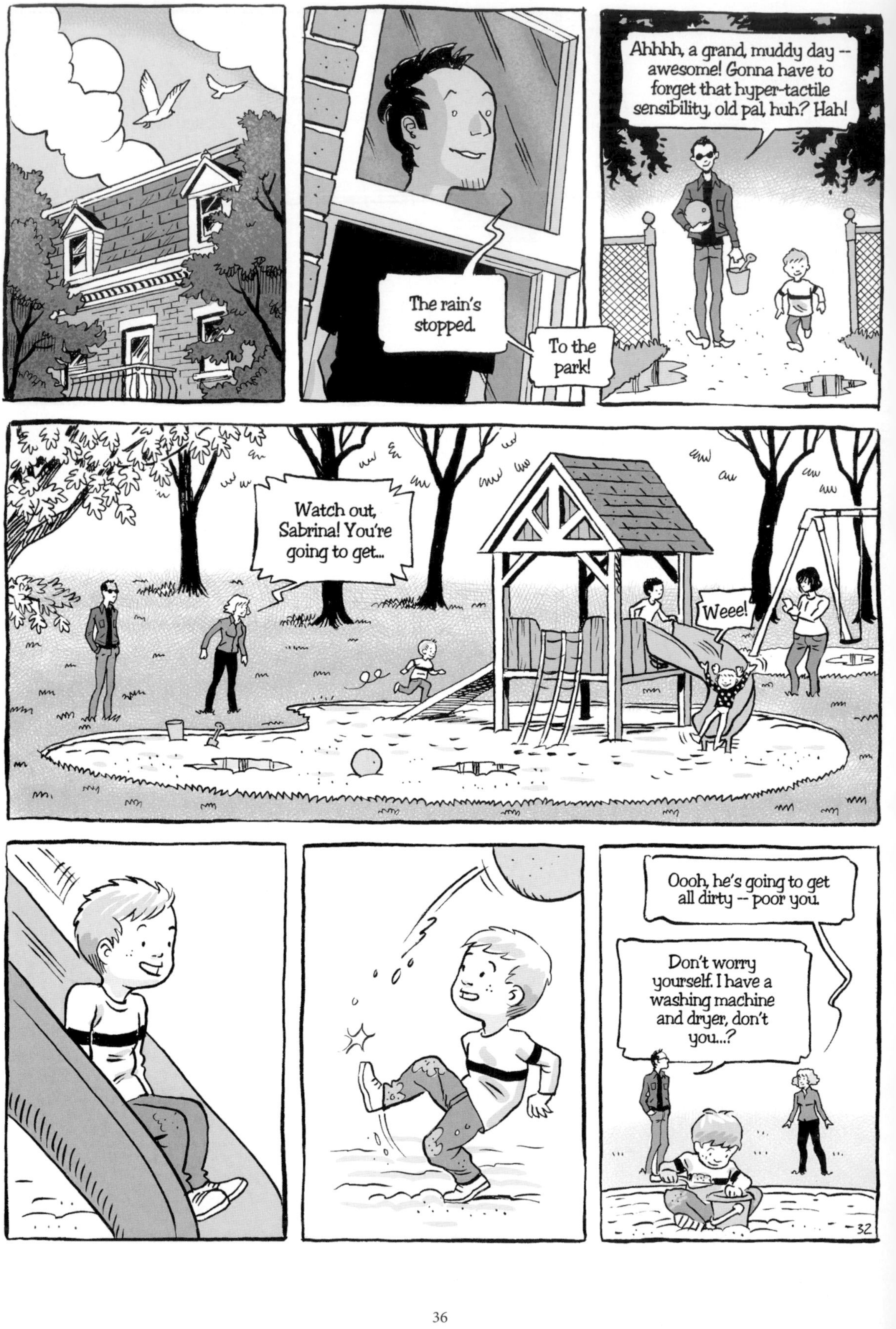
The rain's stopped.
To the park!
Ahhhh, a grand, muddy day -- awesome! Gonna have to forget that hyper-tactile sensibility, old pal, huh? Hah!
Watch out, Sabrina! You're going to get...
Weee!
Oooh, he's going to get all dirty -- poor you.
Don't worry yourself. I have a washing machine and dryer, don't you...?
32

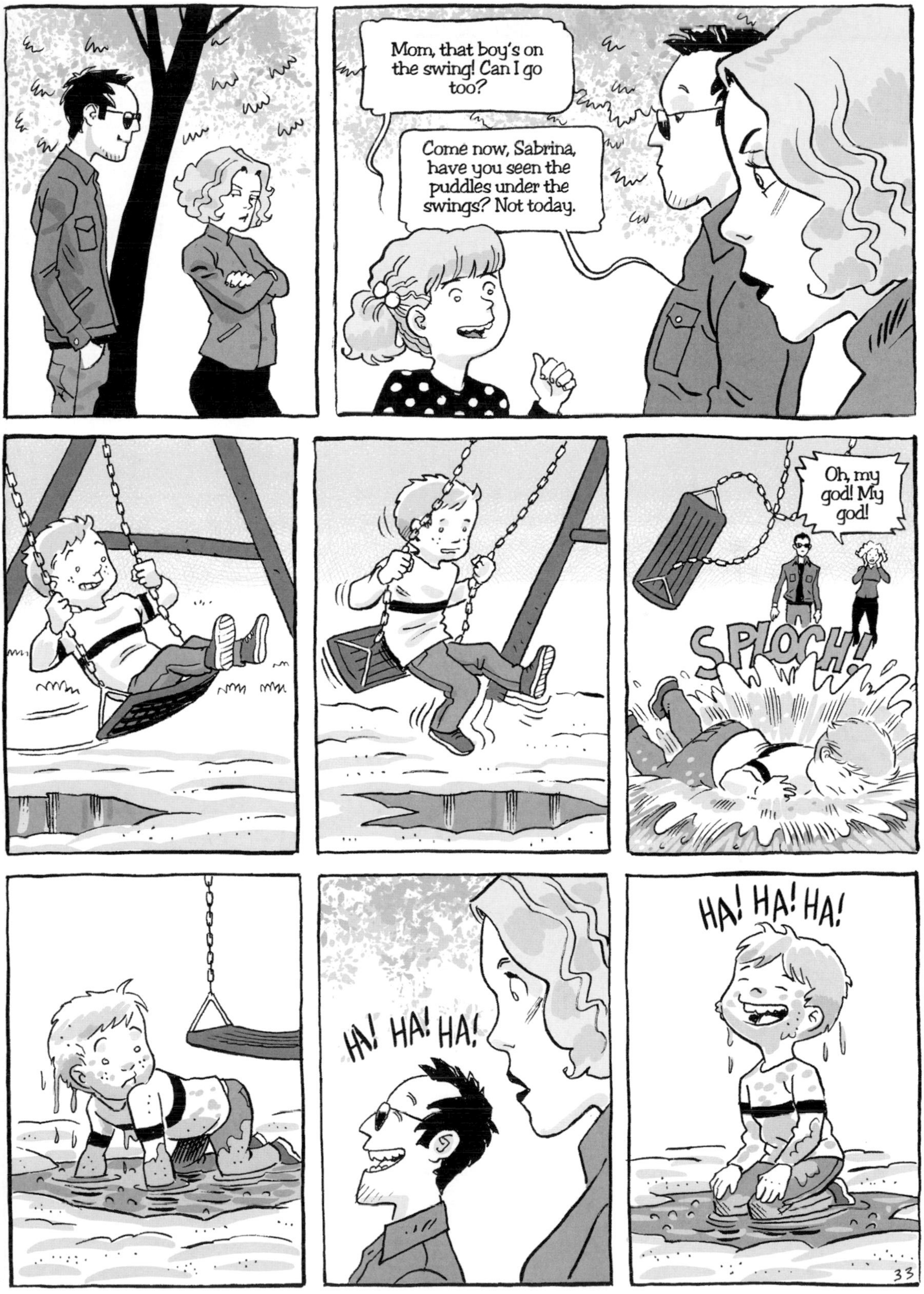
Mom, that boy's on the swing! Can I go too?
Come now, Sabrina, have you seen the puddles under the swings? Not today.
Oh, my god! My god!
SPLOCH!
HA! HA! HA!
HA! HA! HA!
33

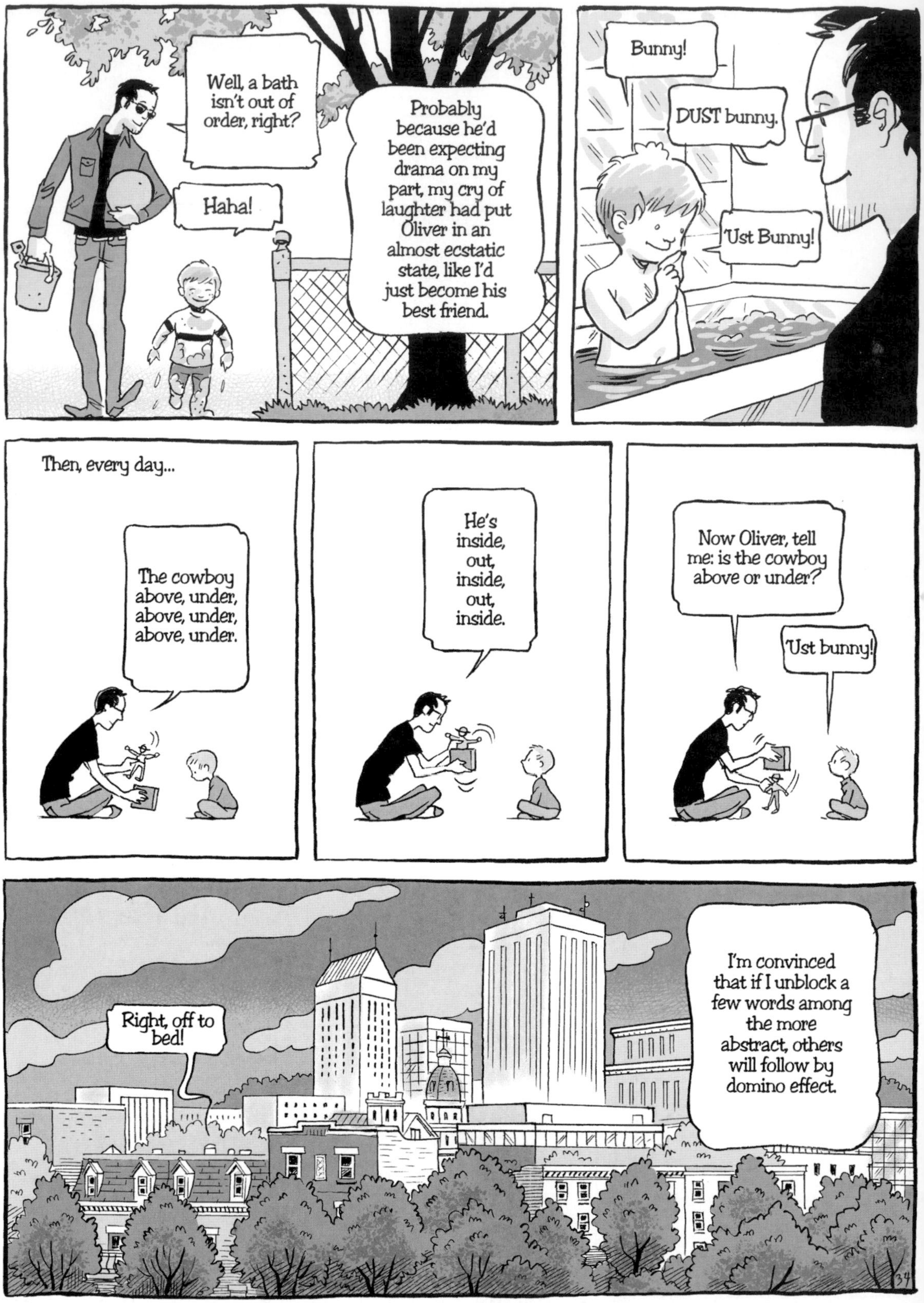
Well, a bath isn't out of order, right?
Haha!
Probably because he'd been expecting drama on my part, my cry of laughter had put Oliver in an almost ecstatic state, like I'd just become his best friend.
Bunny!
DUST bunny.
'Ust Bunny!
Then, every day...
The cowboy above, under, above, under, above, under.
He's inside, out, inside, out, inside.
Now Oliver, tell me: is the cowboy above or under?
'Ust bunny!
Right, off to bed!
I'm convinced that if I unblock a few words among the more abstract, others will follow by domino effect.

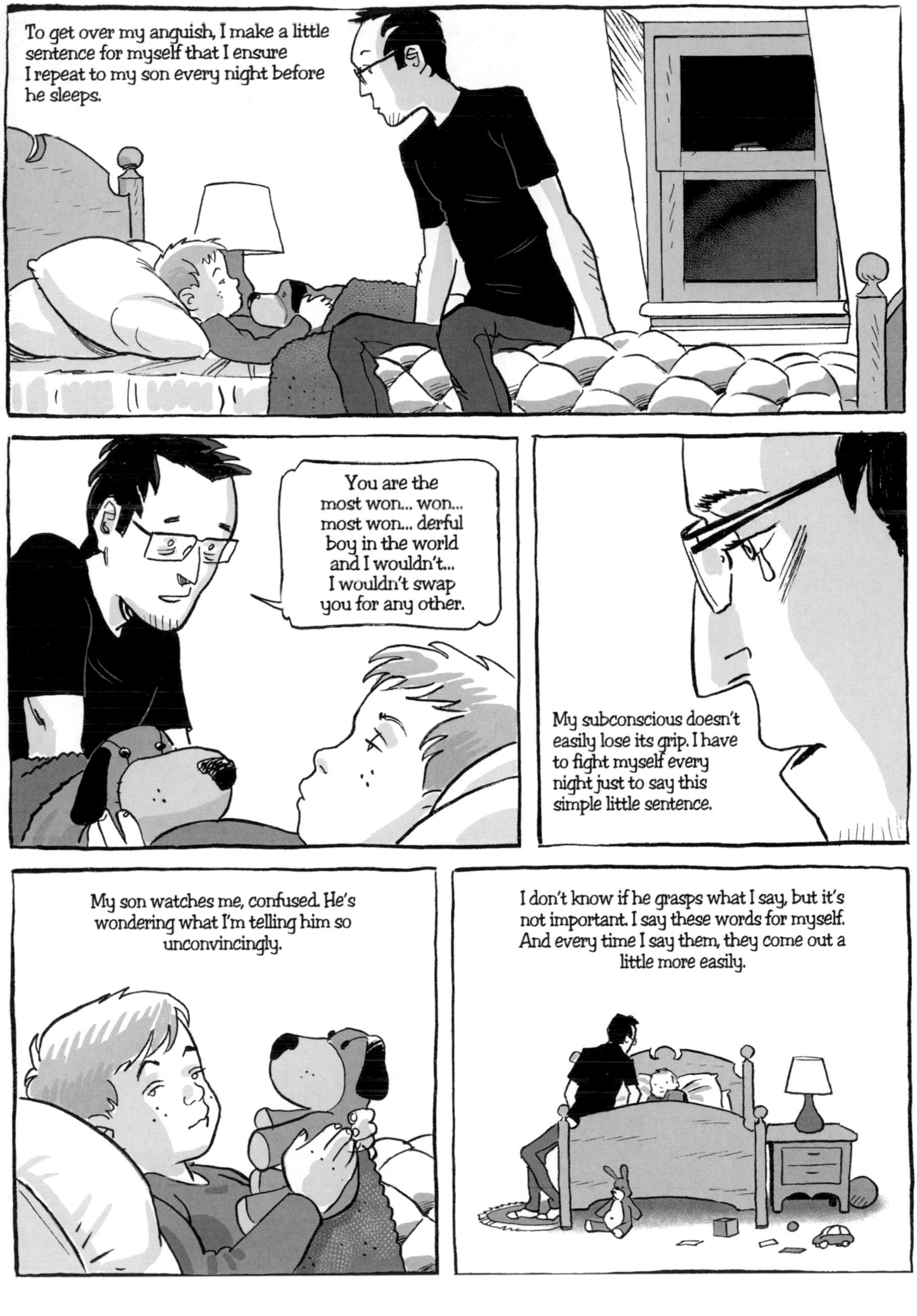
To get over my anguish, I make a little sentence for myself that I ensure I repeat to my son every night before he sleeps.
You are the most won... won... most won... derful boy in the world and I wouldn't... I wouldn't swap you for any other.
My subconscious doesn't easily lose its grip. I have to fight myself every night just to say this simple little sentence.
My son watches me, confused. He's wondering what I'm telling him so unconvincingly.
I don't know if he grasps what I say, but it's not important. I say these words for myself. And every time I say them, they come out a little more easily.

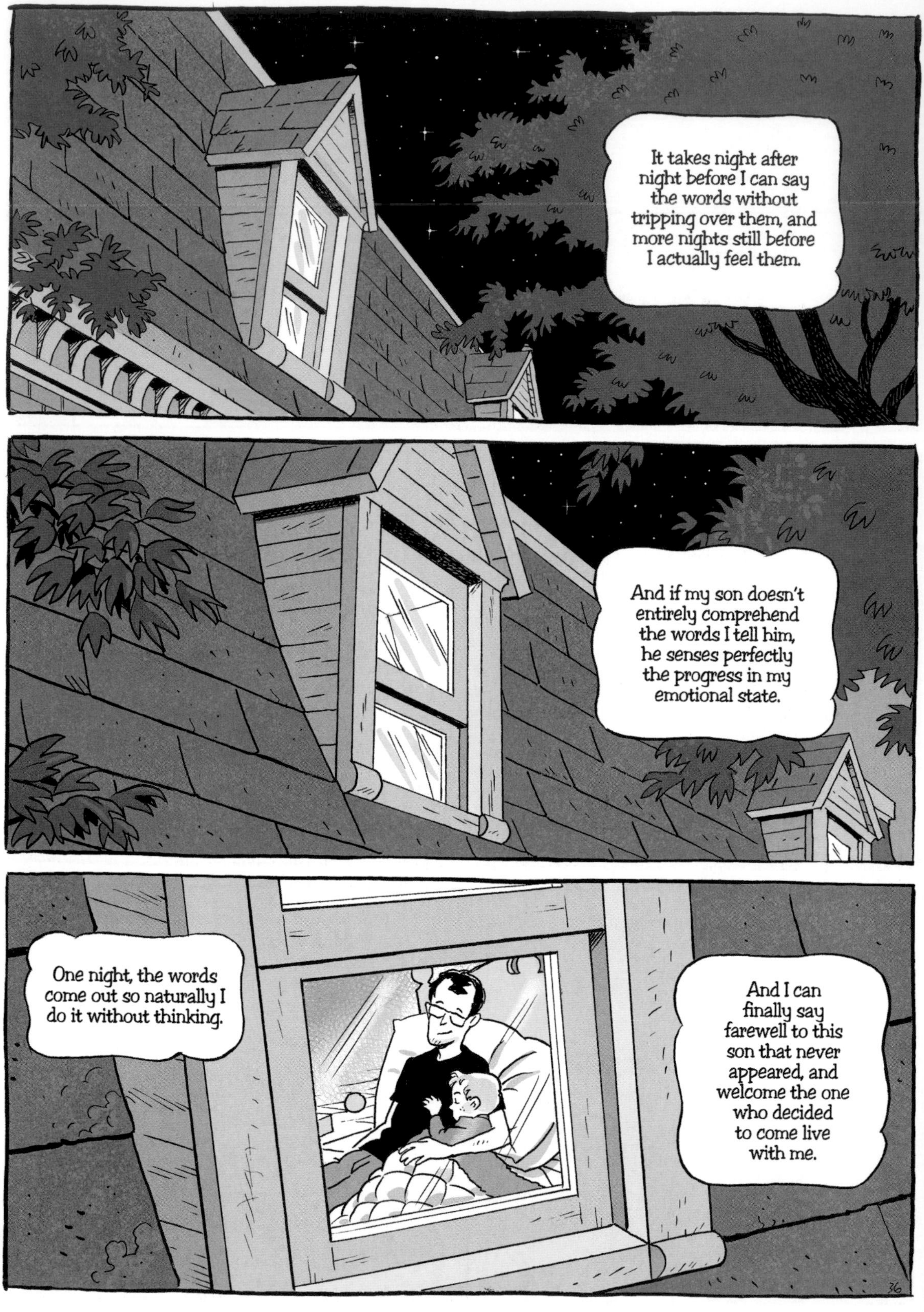
It takes night after night before I can say the words without tripping over them, and more nights still before I actually feel them.
And if my son doesn't entirely comprehend the words I tell him, he senses perfectly the progress in my emotional state.
One night, the words come out so naturally I do it without thinking.
And I can finally say farewell to this son that never appeared, and welcome the one who decided to come live with me.
36

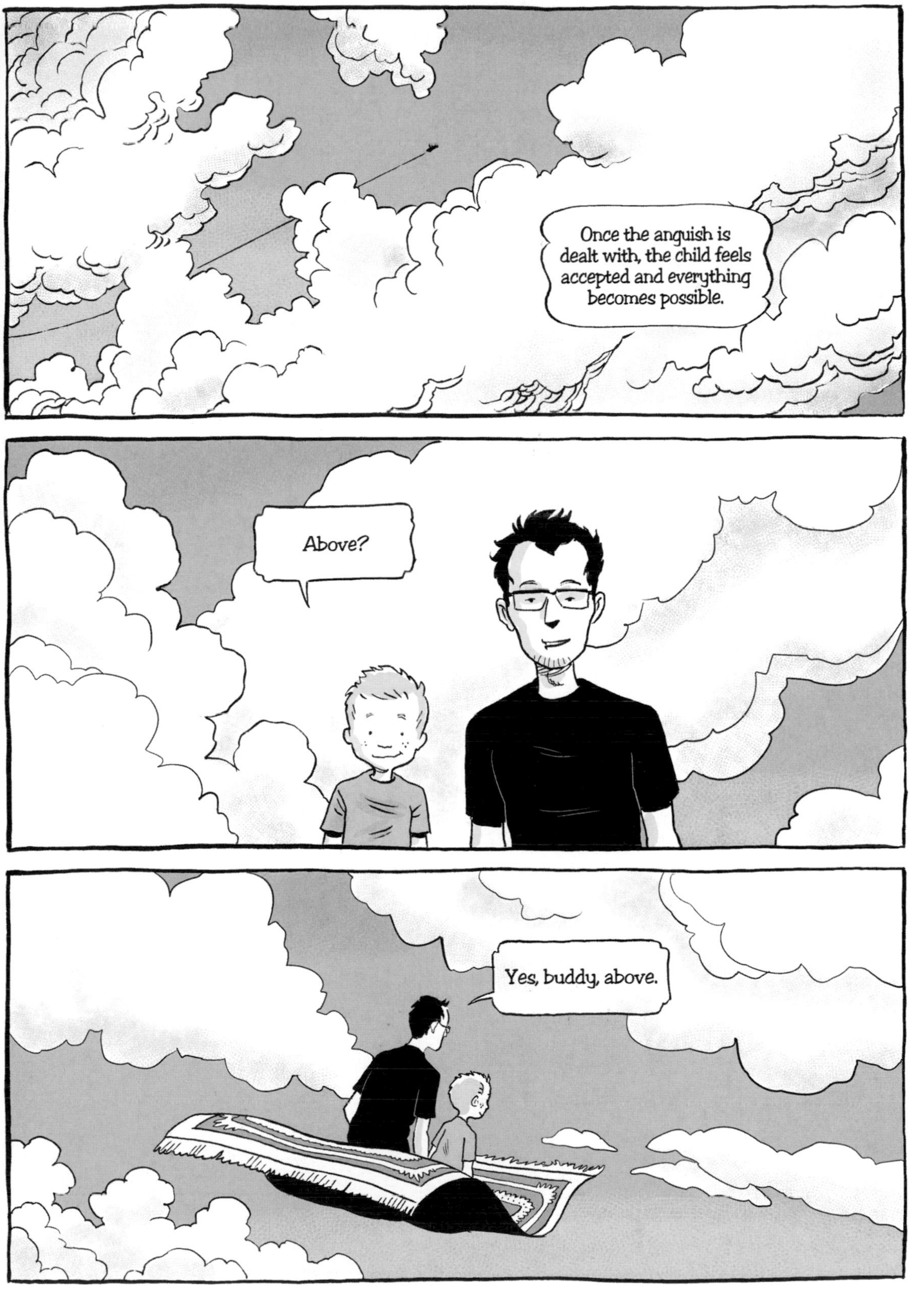
Once the anguish is dealt with, the child feels accepted and everything becomes possible.
Above?
Yes, buddy, above.

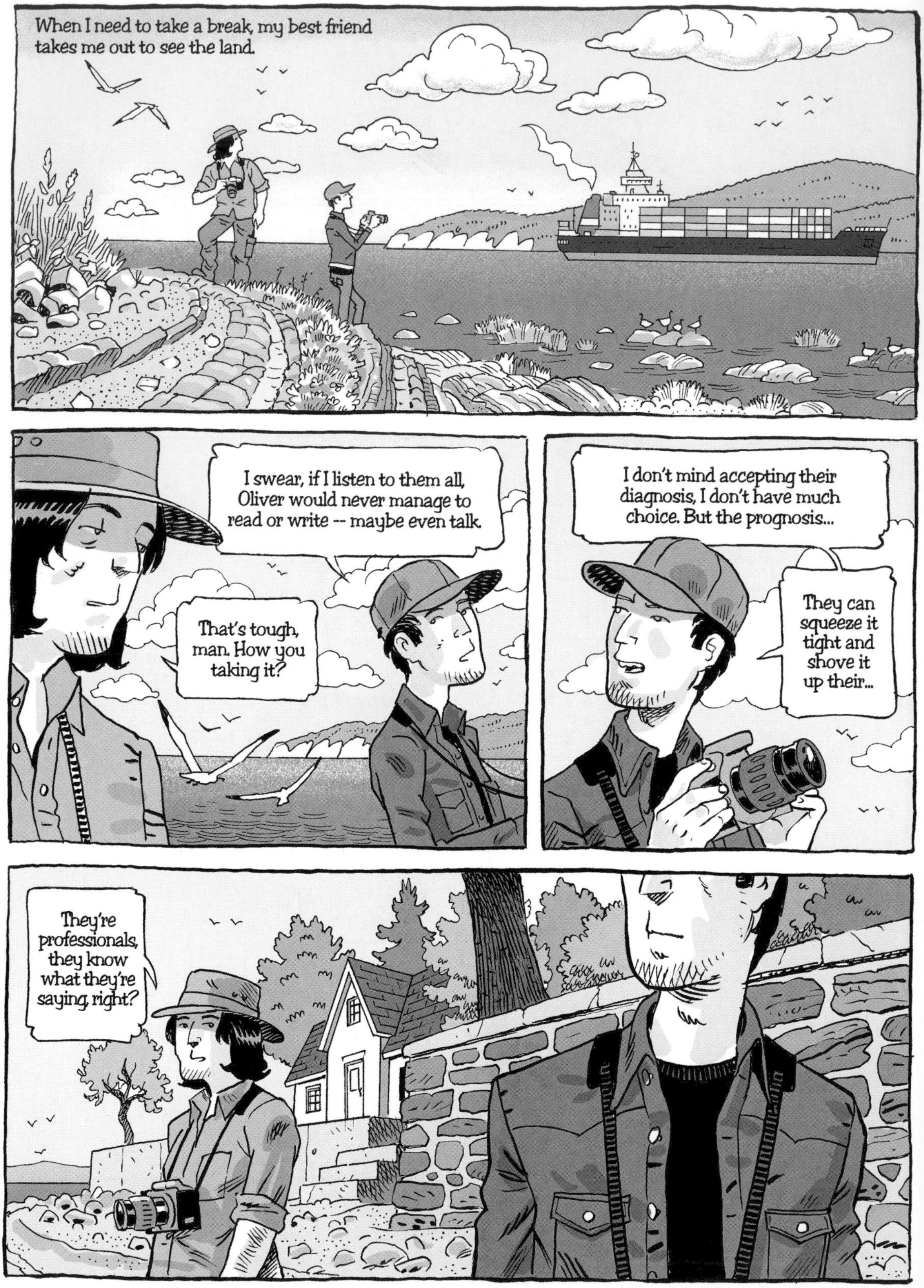
When I need to take a break, my best friend takes me out to see the land.
I swear, if I listen to them all, Oliver would never manage to read or write -- maybe even talk.
That's tough, man. How you taking it?
I don't mind accepting their diagnosis, I don't have much choice. But the prognosis...
They can squeeze it tight and shove it up their...
They're professionals, they know what they're saying, right?

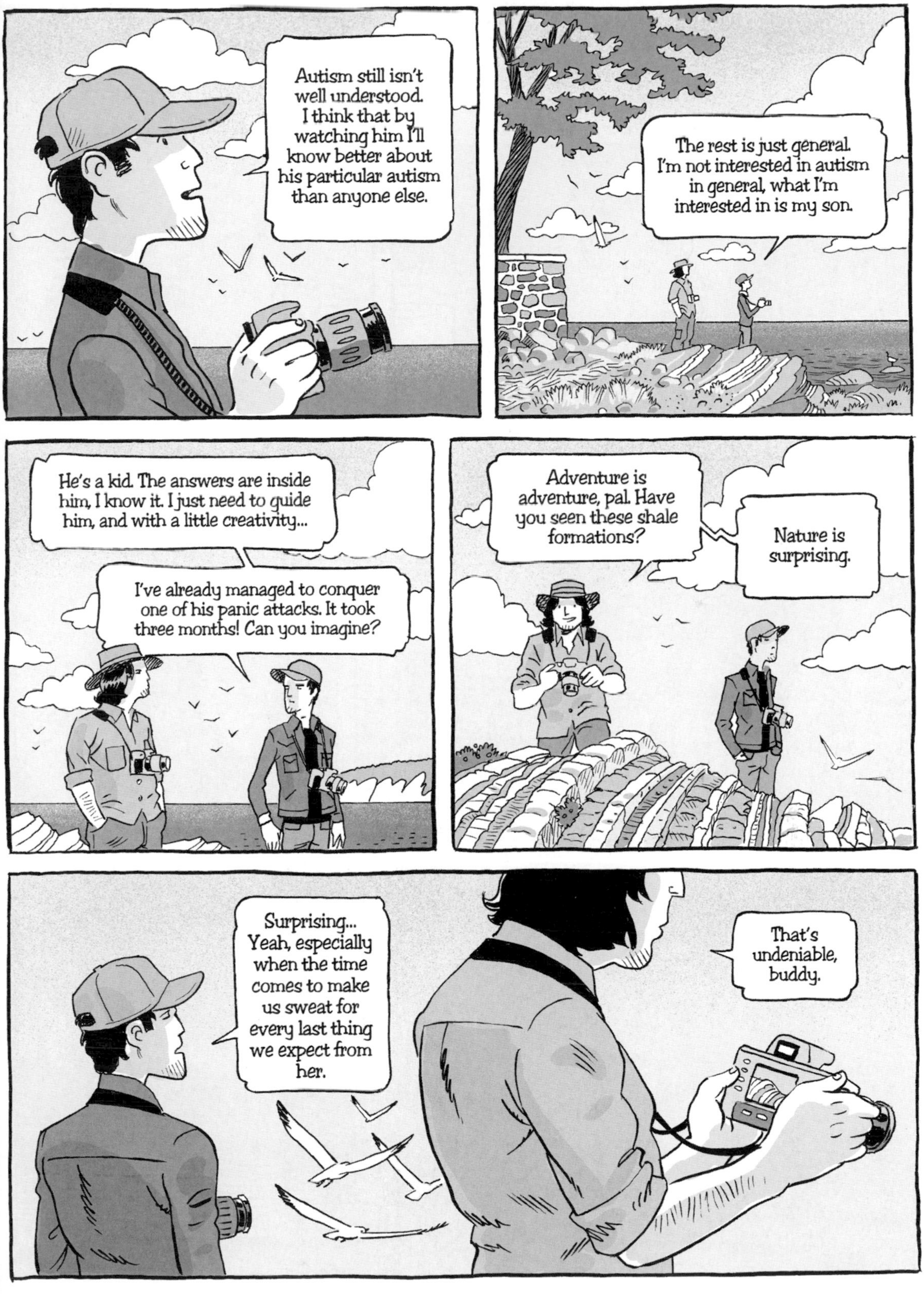
Autism still isn't well understood. I think that by watching him I'll know better about his particular autism than anyone else.
The rest is just general. I'm not interested in autism in general, what I'm interested in is my son.
He's a kid. The answers are inside him, I know it. I just need to guide him, and with a little creativity...
I've already managed to conquer one of his panic attacks. It took three months! Can you imagine?
Adventure is adventure, pal. Have you seen these shale formations?
Nature is surprising.
Surprising... Yeah, especially when the time comes to make us sweat for every last thing we expect from her.
That's undeniable, buddy.

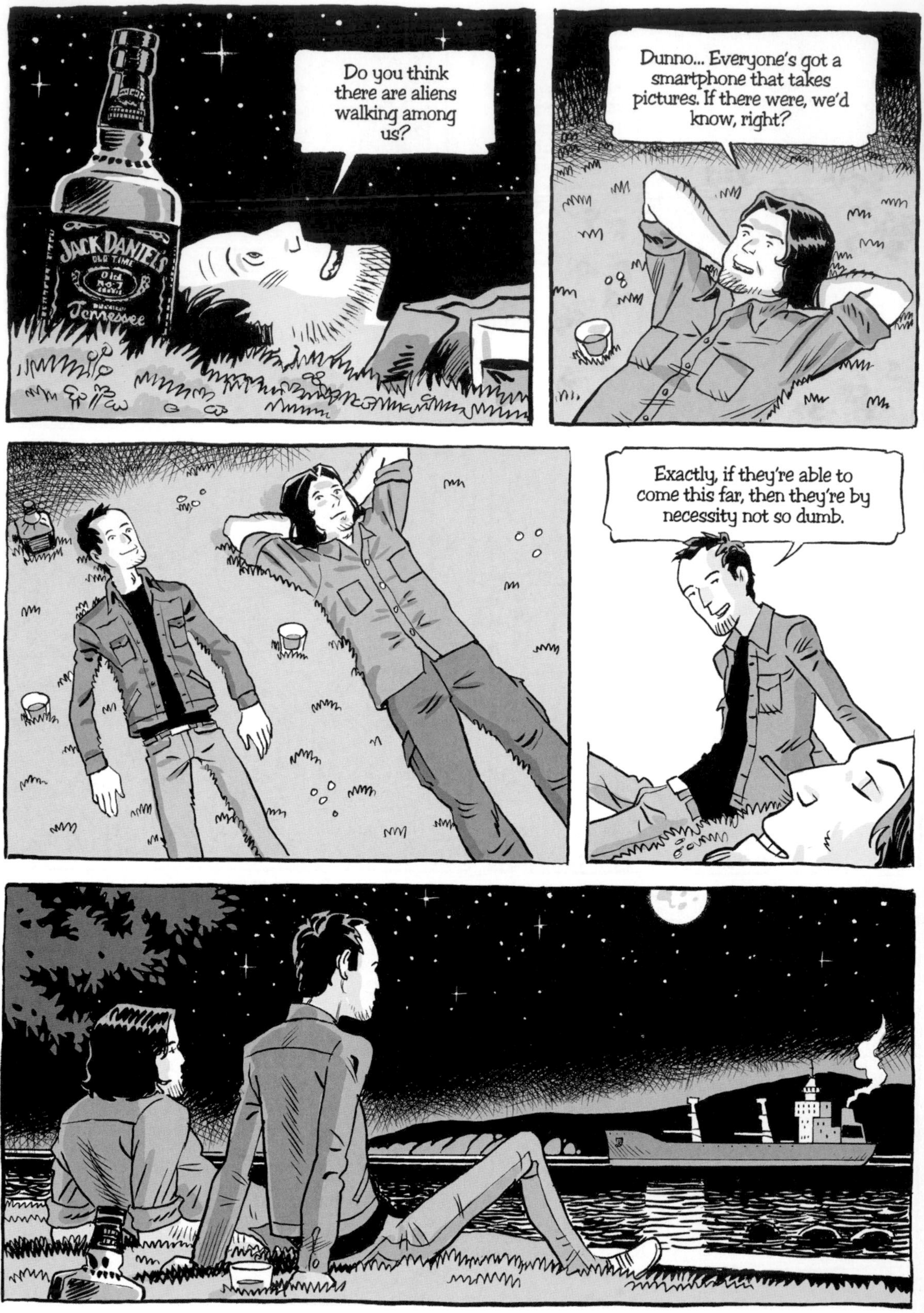
JACK DANIELS
Tennessee
Do you think there are aliens walking among us?
Dunno... Everyone's got a smartphone that takes pictures. If there were, we'd know, right?
Exactly, if they're able to come this far, then they're by necessity not so dumb.

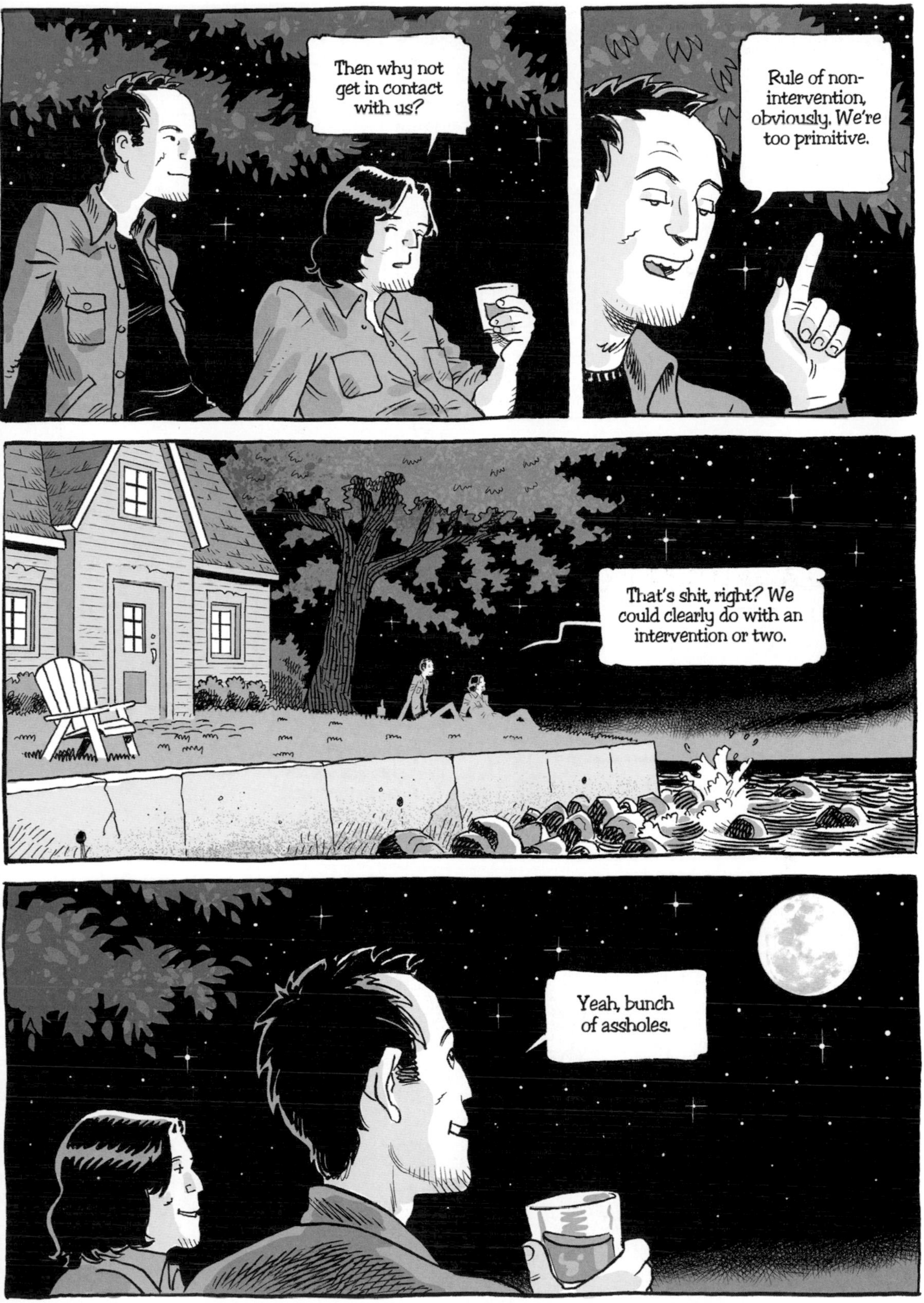
Then why not get in contact with us?
Rule of non-intervention, obviously. We're too primitive.
That's shit, right? We could clearly do with an intervention or two.
Yeah, bunch of assholes.

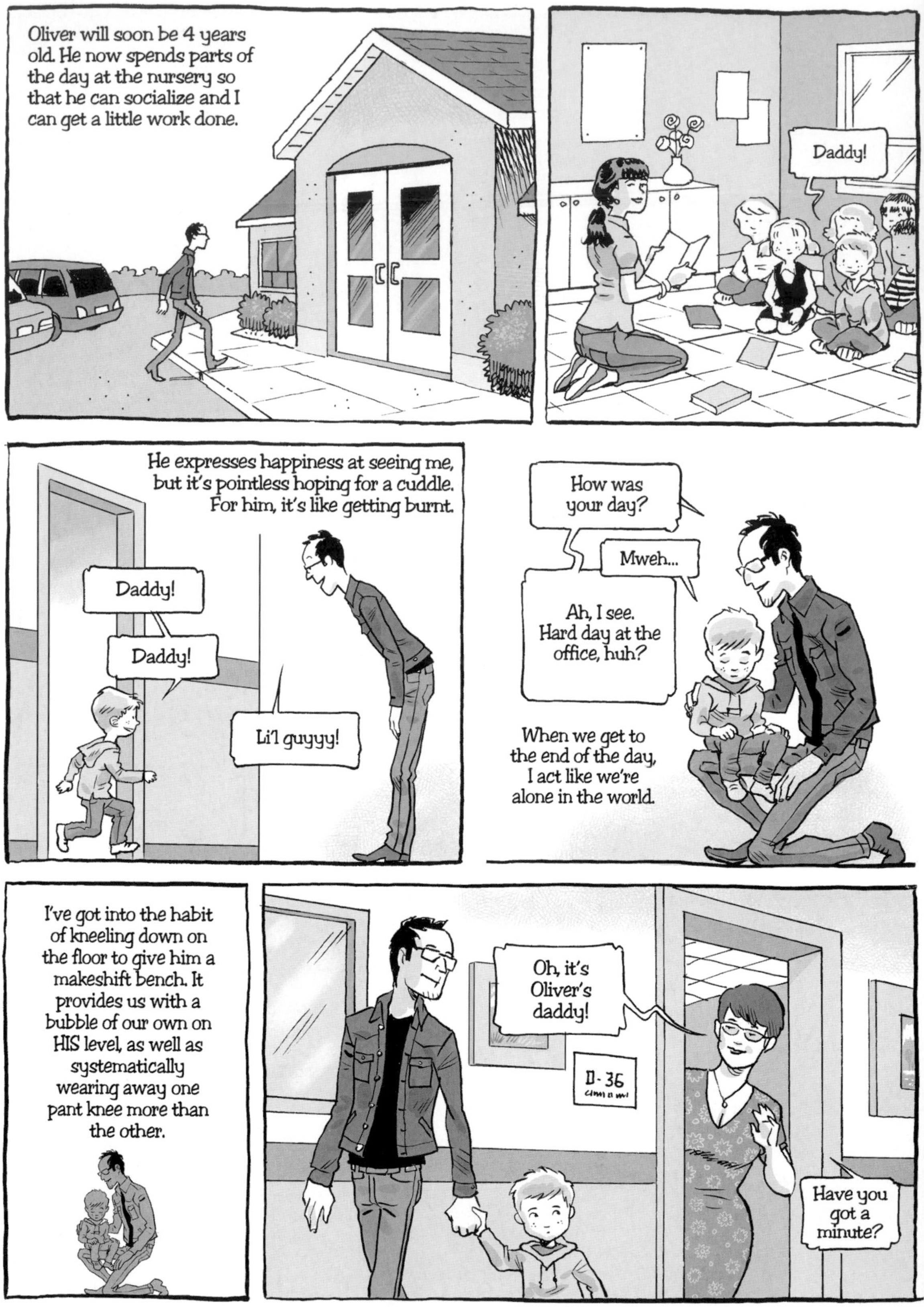
Oliver will soon be 4 years old. He now spends parts of the day at the nursery so that he can socialize and I can get a little work done.
Daddy!
He expresses happiness at seeing me, but it's pointless hoping for a cuddle. For him, it's like getting burnt.
Daddy!
Daddy!
Li'l guyyy!
How was your day?
Mweh...
Ah, I see. Hard day at the office, huh?
When we get to the end of the day, I act like we're alone in the world.
I've got into the habit of kneeling down on the floor to give him a makeshift bench. It provides us with a bubble of our own on HIS level, as well as systematically wearing away one pant knee more than the other.
Oh, it's Oliver's daddy!
D-36
Have you got a minute?

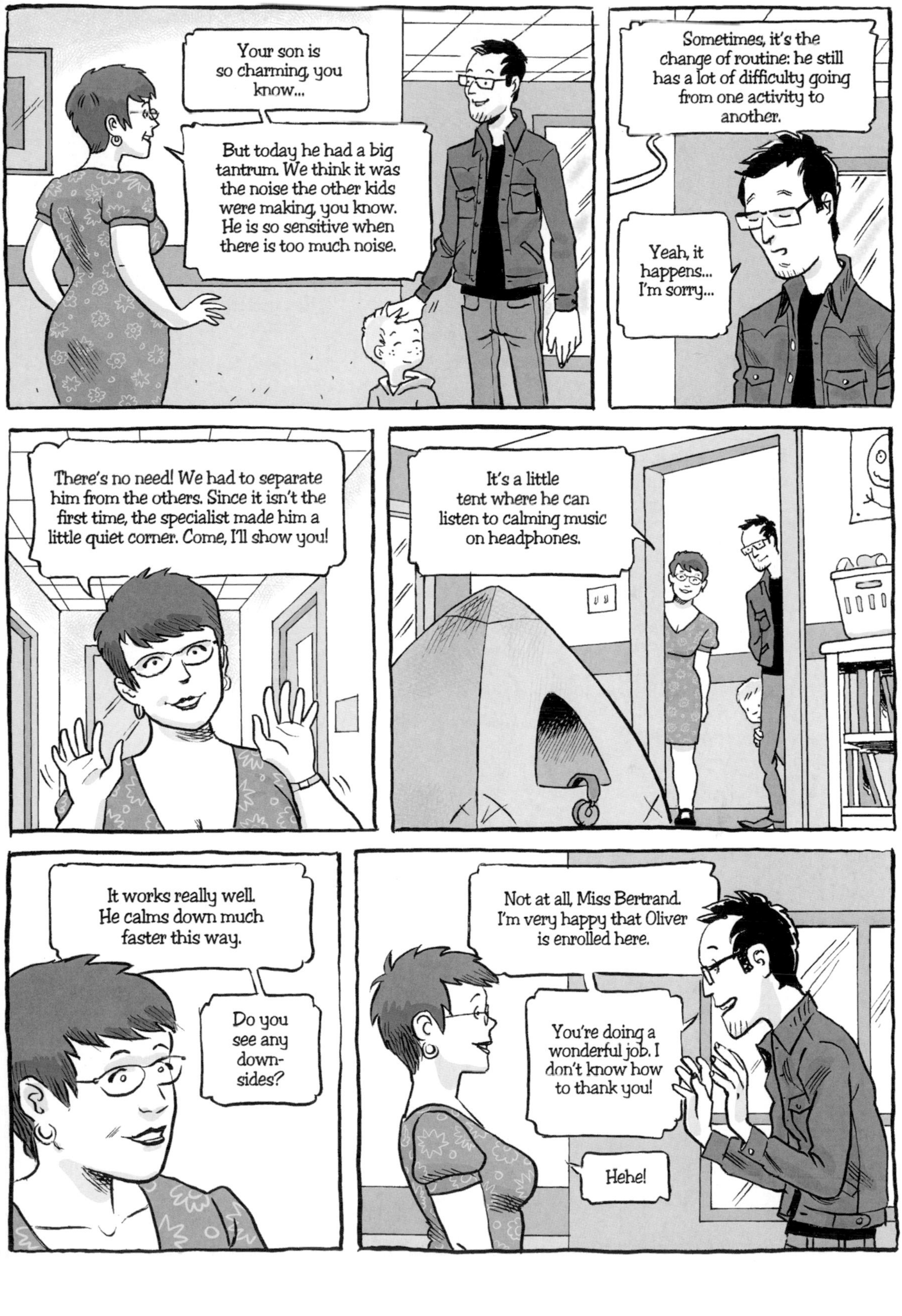

Your son is so charming, you know...
But today he had a big tantrum. We think it was the noise the other kids were making, you know. He is so sensitive when there is too much noise.
Sometimes, it's the change of routine: he still has a lot of difficulty going from one activity to another.
Yeah, it happens... I'm sorry...
There's no need! We had to separate him from the others. Since it isn't the first time, the specialist made him a little quiet corner. Come, I'll show you!
It's a little tent where he can listen to calming music on headphones.
It works really well. He calms down much faster this way.
Do you see any down-sides?
Not at all, Miss Bertrand. I'm very happy that Oliver is enrolled here.
You're doing a wonderful job. I don't know how to thank you!
Hehe!

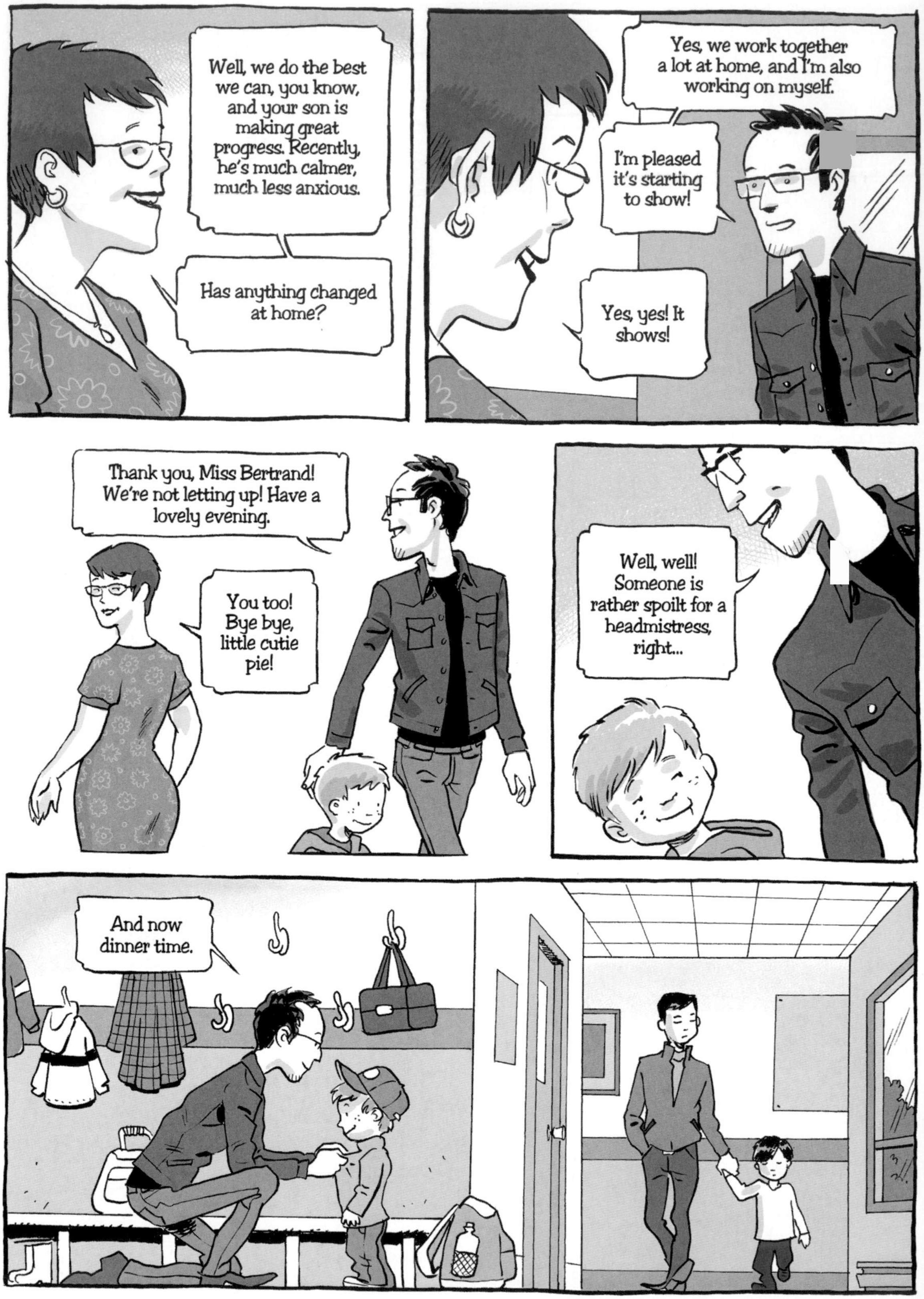
Well, we do the best we can, you know, and your son is making great progress. Recently, he's much calmer, much less anxious.
Has anything changed at home?
Yes, we work together a lot at home, and I'm also working on myself.
I'm pleased it's starting to show!
Yes, yes! It shows!
Thank you, Miss Bertrand! We're not letting up! Have a lovely evening.
You too! Bye bye, little cutie pie!
Well, well! Someone is rather spoilt for a headmistress, right...
And now dinner time.

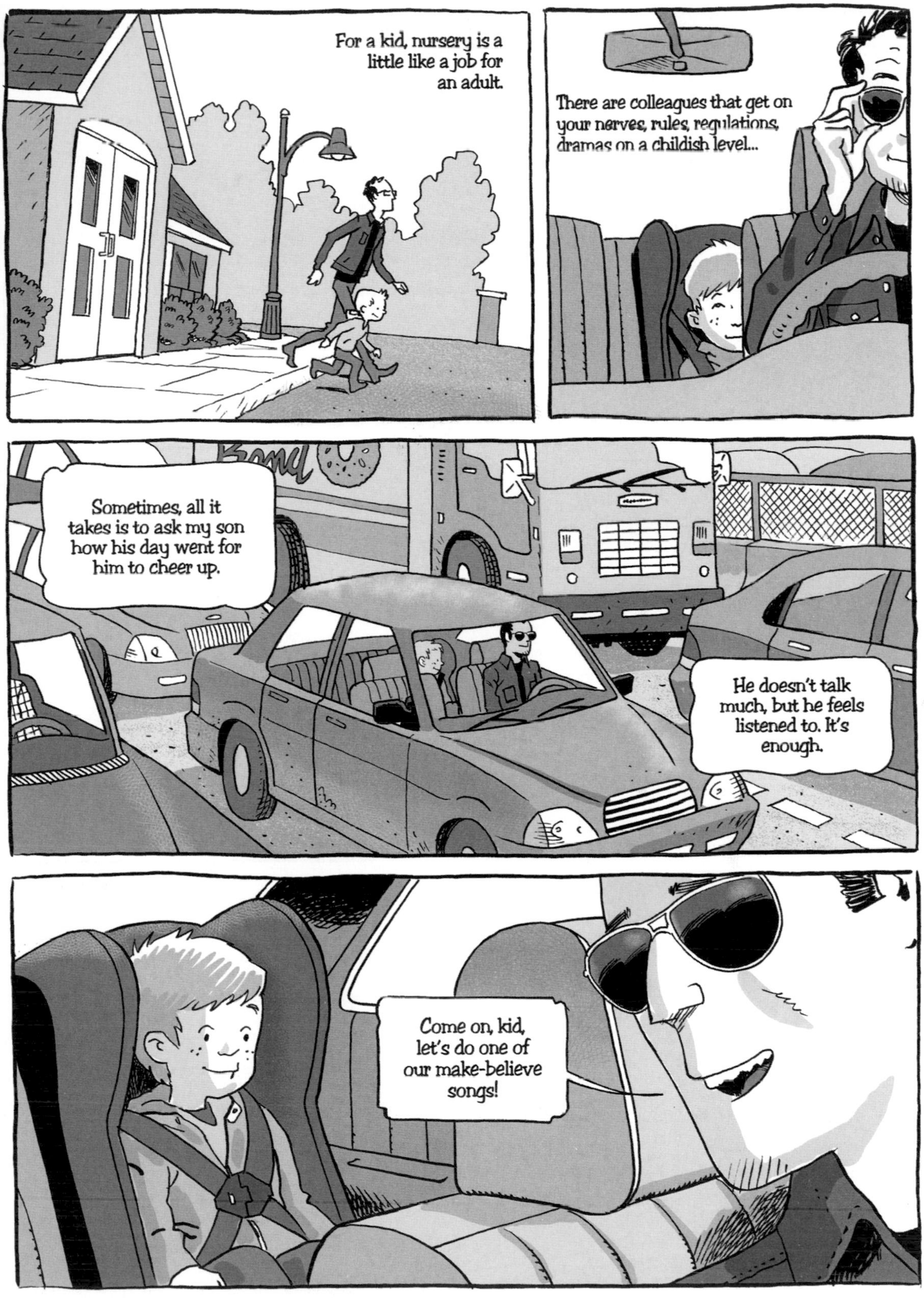
For a kid, nursery is a little like a job for an adult.
There are colleagues that get on your nerves, rules, regulations, dramas on a childish level...
Sometimes, all it takes is to ask my son how his day went for him to cheer up.
He doesn't talk much, but he feels listened to. It's enough.
Come on, kid, let's do one of our make-believe songs!

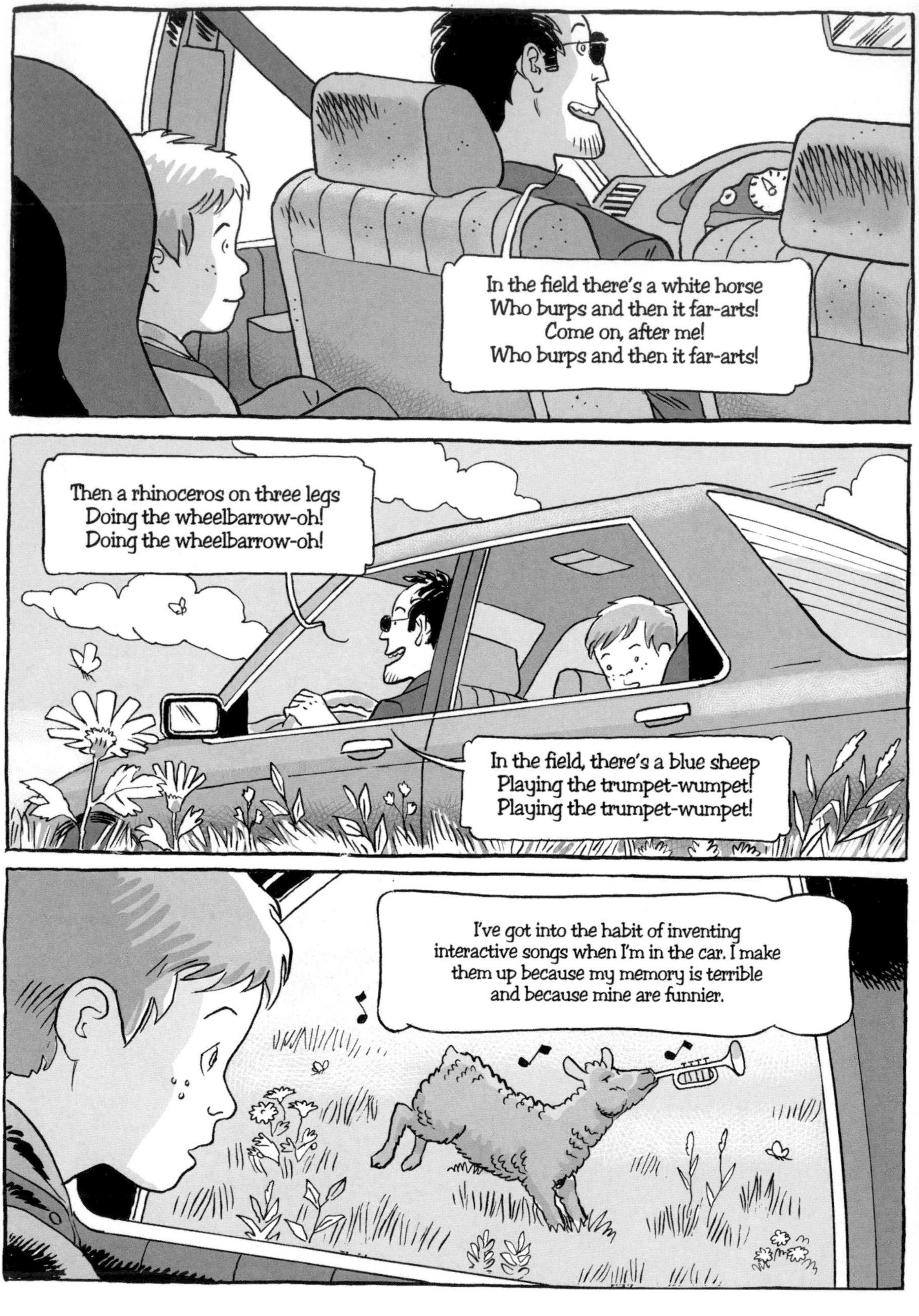
In the field there's a white horse
Who burps and then it far-arts!
Come on, after me!
Who burps and then it far-arts!
Then a rhinoceros on three legs
Doing the wheelbarrow-oh!
Doing the wheelbarrow-oh!
In the field, there's a blue sheep
Playing the trumpet-wumpet!
Playing the trumpet-wumpet!
I've got into the habit of inventing interactive songs when I'm in the car. I make them up because my memory is terrible and because mine are funnier.

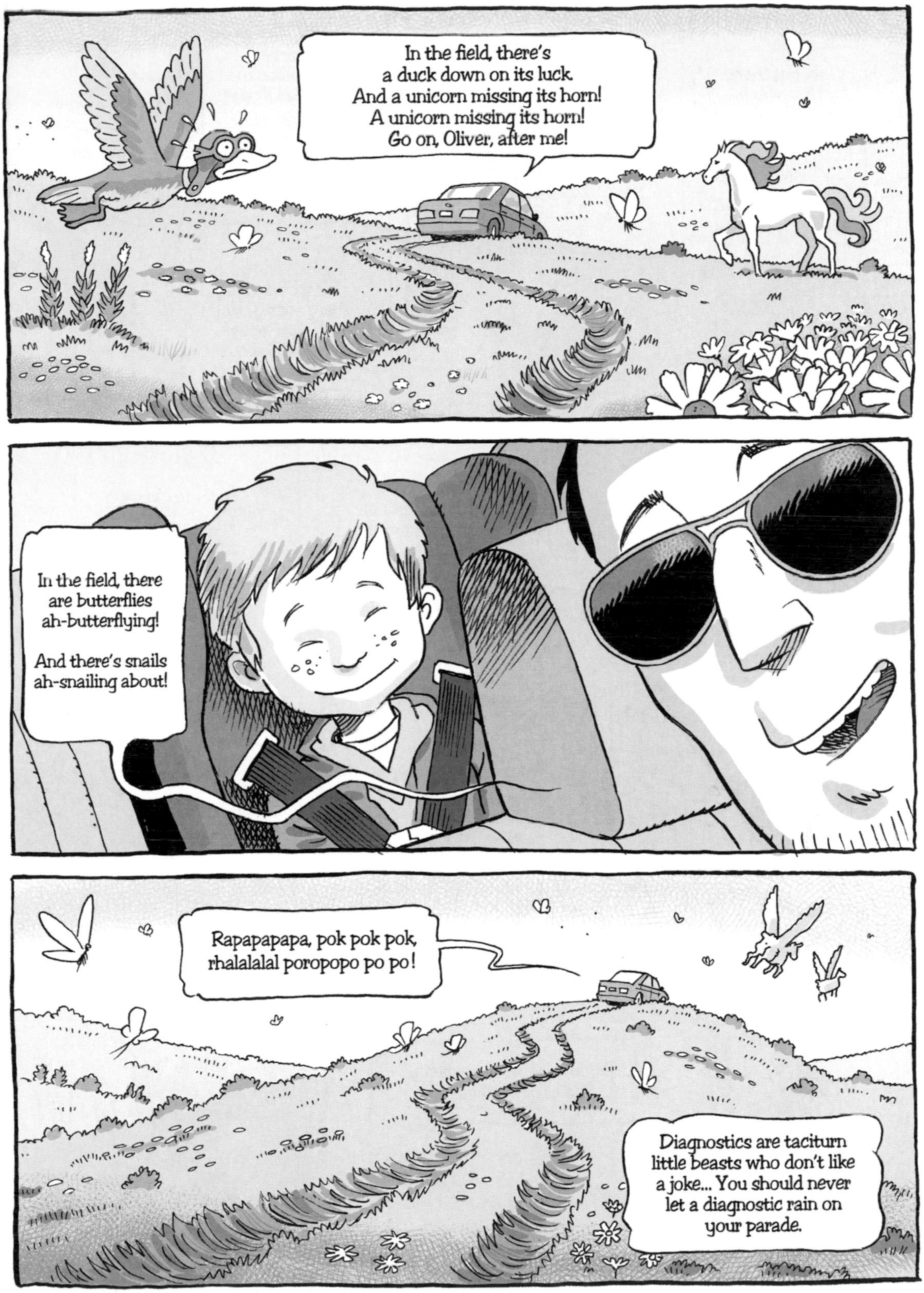
In the field, there's a duck down on its luck. And a unicorn missing its horn! A unicorn missing its horn! Go on, Oliver, after me!
In the field, there are butterflies ah-butterflying! And there's snails ah-snailing about!
Rapapapapa, pok pok pok, rhalalalal poropopo po po!
Diagnostics are taciturn little beasts who don't like a joke... You should never let a diagnostic rain on your parade.

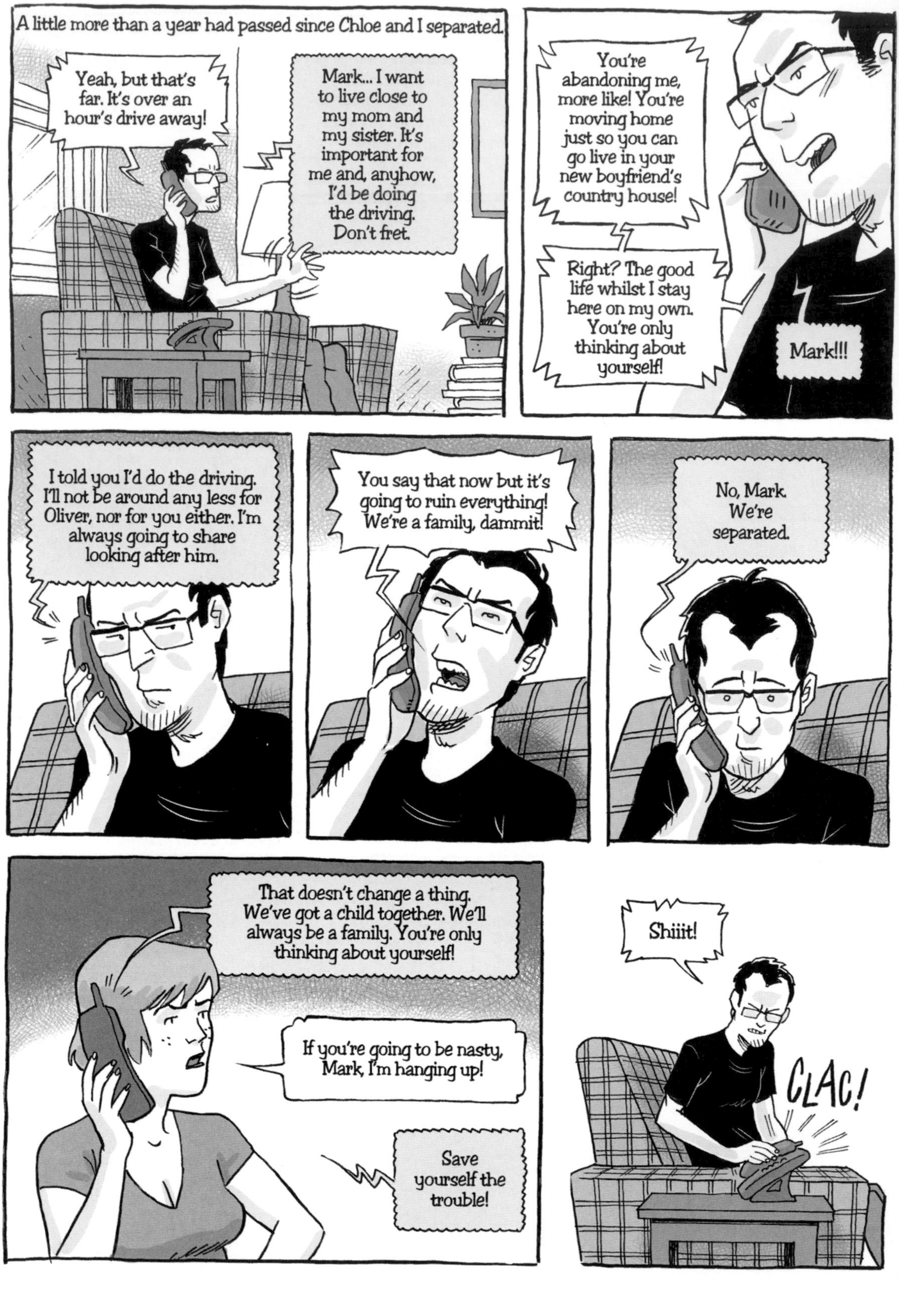

A little more than a year had passed since Chloe and I separated.
Yeah, but that's far. It's over an hour's drive away!
Mark... I want to live close to my mom and my sister. It's important for me and, anyhow, I'd be doing the driving. Don't fret.
You're abandoning me, more like! You're moving home just so you can go live in your new boyfriend's country house!
Right? The good life whilst I stay here on my own. You're only thinking about yourself!
Mark!!!
I told you I'd do the driving. I'll not be around any less for Oliver, nor for you either. I'm always going to share looking after him.
You say that now but it's going to ruin everything! We're a family, dammit!
No, Mark. We're separated.
That doesn't change a thing. We've got a child together. We'll always be a family. You're only thinking about yourself!
If you're going to be nasty, Mark, I'm hanging up!
Save yourself the trouble!
Shiiit!
CLAC!

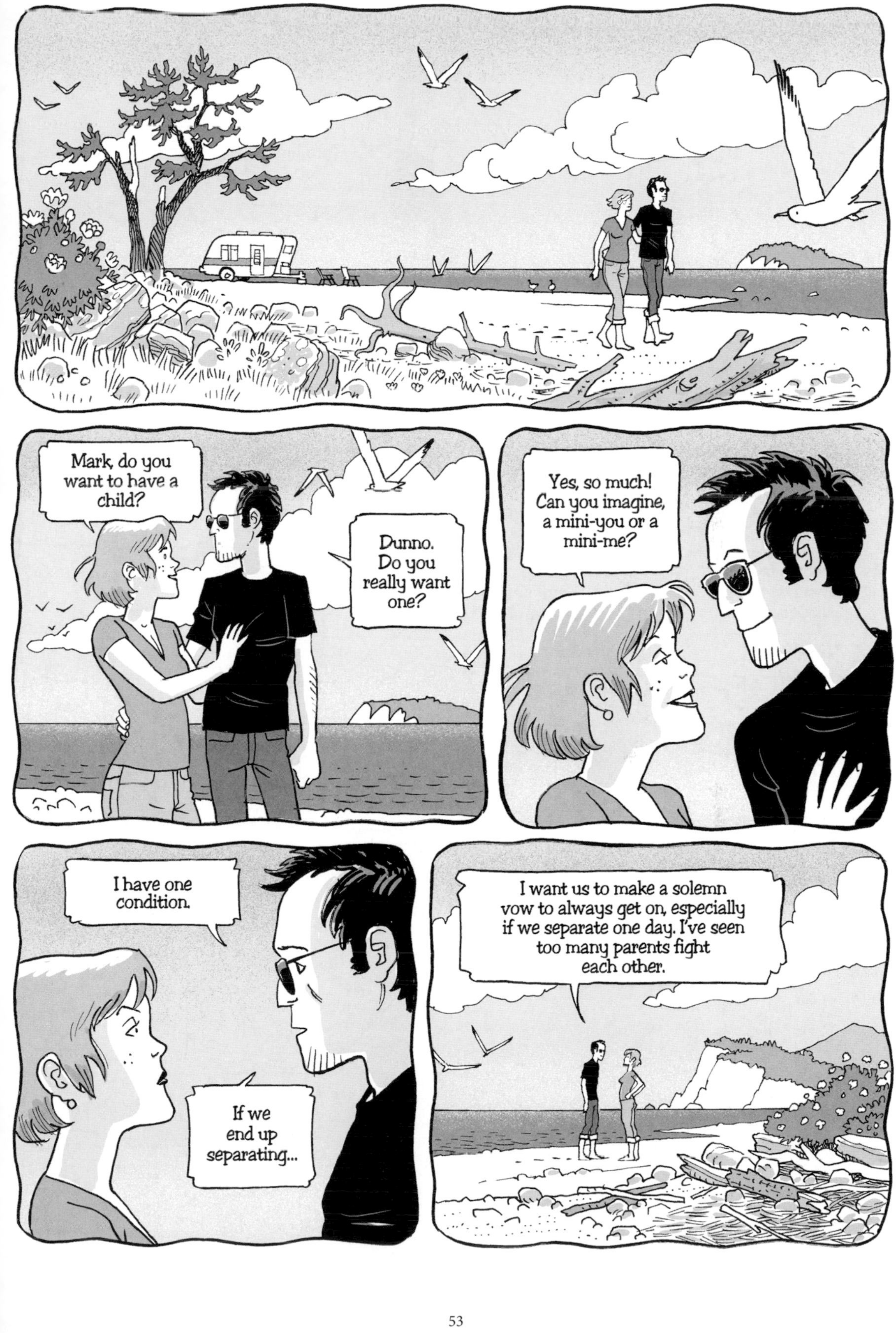
Mark, do you want to have a child?
Dunno. Do you really want one?
Yes, so much! Can you imagine, a mini-you or a mini-me?
I have one condition.
If we end up separating...
I want us to make a solemn vow to always get on, especially if we separate one day. I've seen too many parents fight each other.

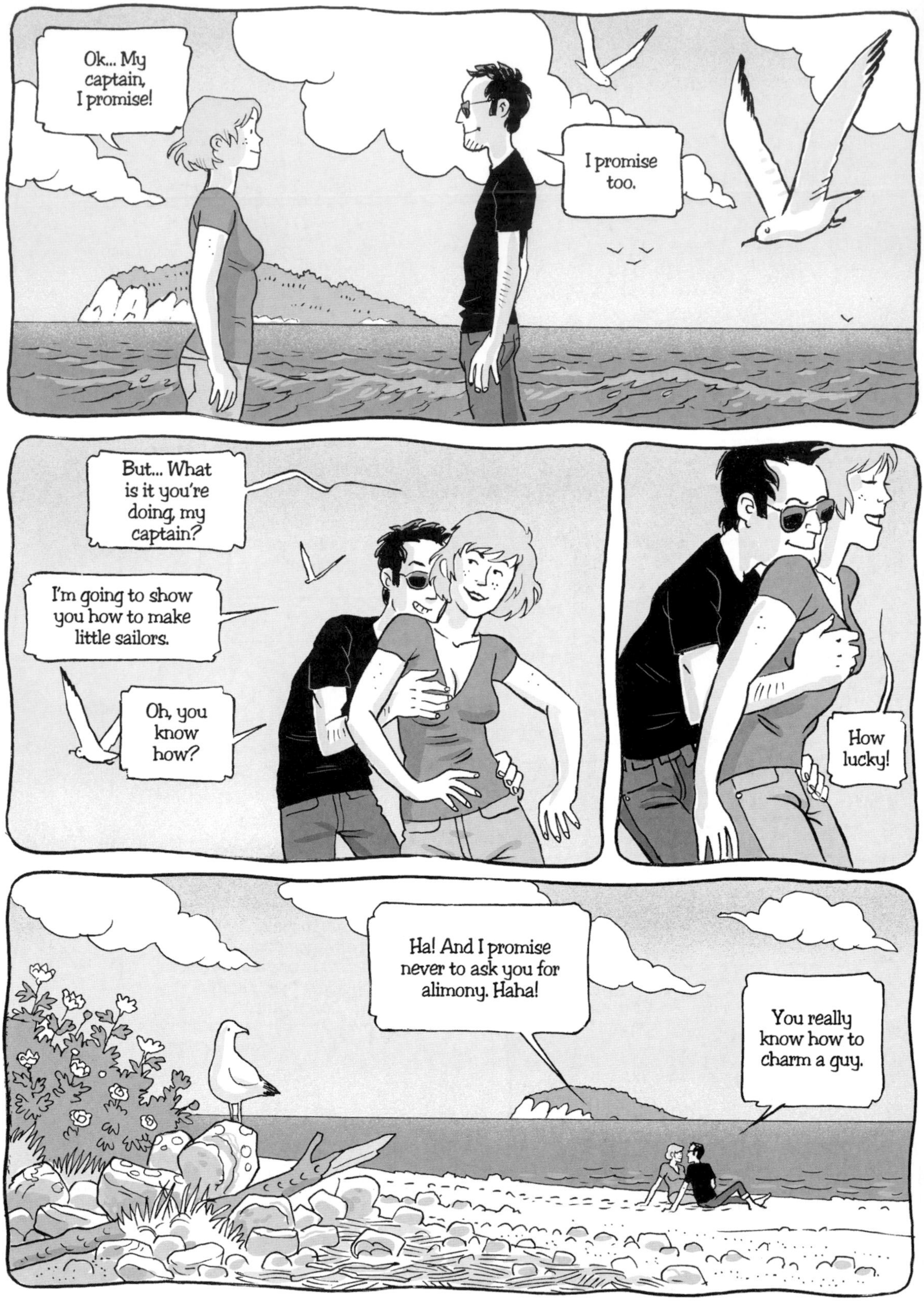
Ok... My captain, I promise!
I promise too.
But... What is it you're doing, my captain?
I'm going to show you how to make little sailors.
Oh, you know how?
How lucky!
Ha! And I promise never to ask you for alimony. Haha!
You really know how to charm a guy.

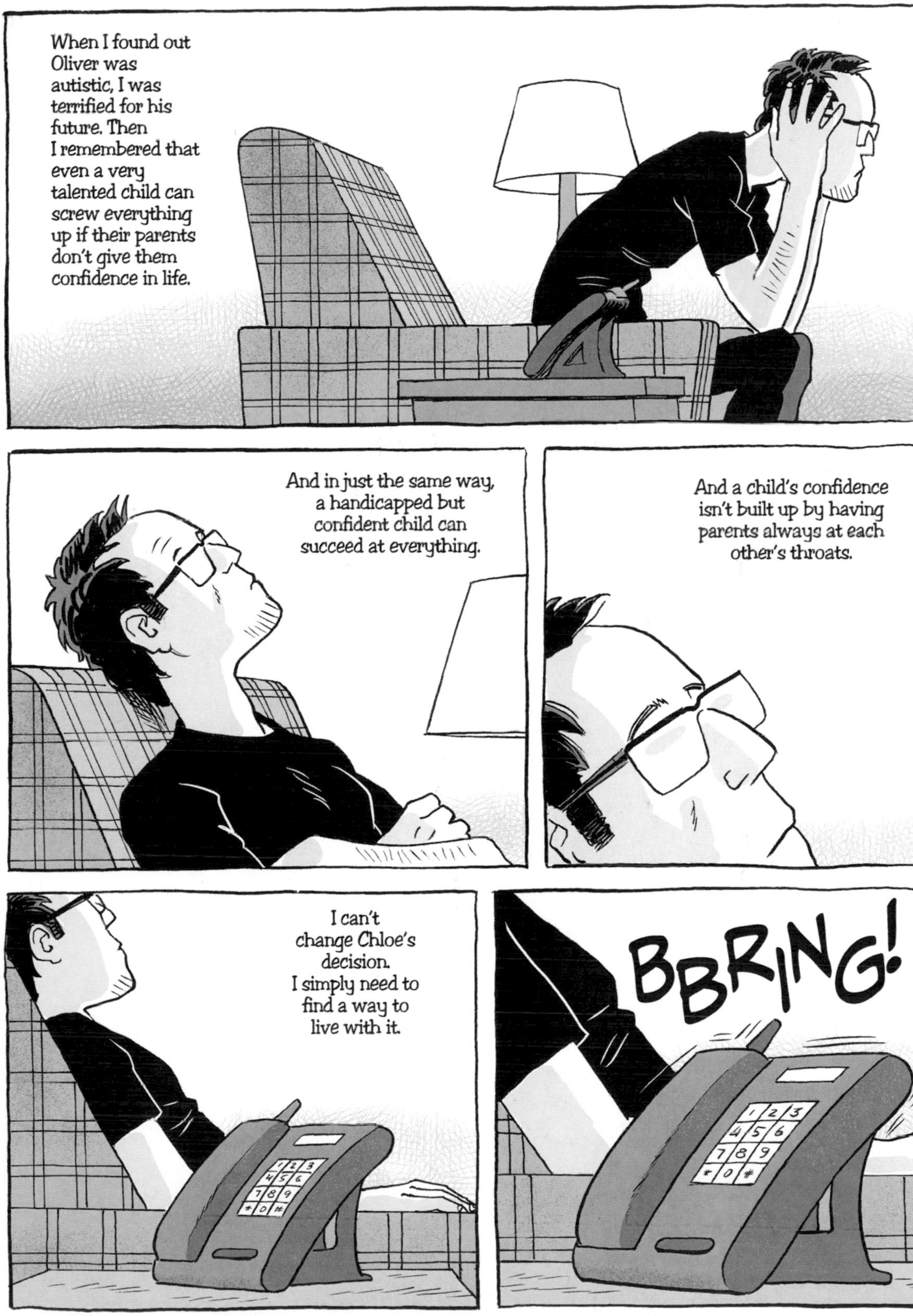
When I found out Oliver was autistic, I was terrified for his future. Then I remembered that even a very talented child can screw everything up if their parents don't give them confidence in life.
And in just the same way, a handicapped but confident child can succeed at everything.
And a child's confidence isn't built up by having parents always at each other's throats.
I can't change Chloe's decision. I simply need to find a way to live with it.
BBRING!

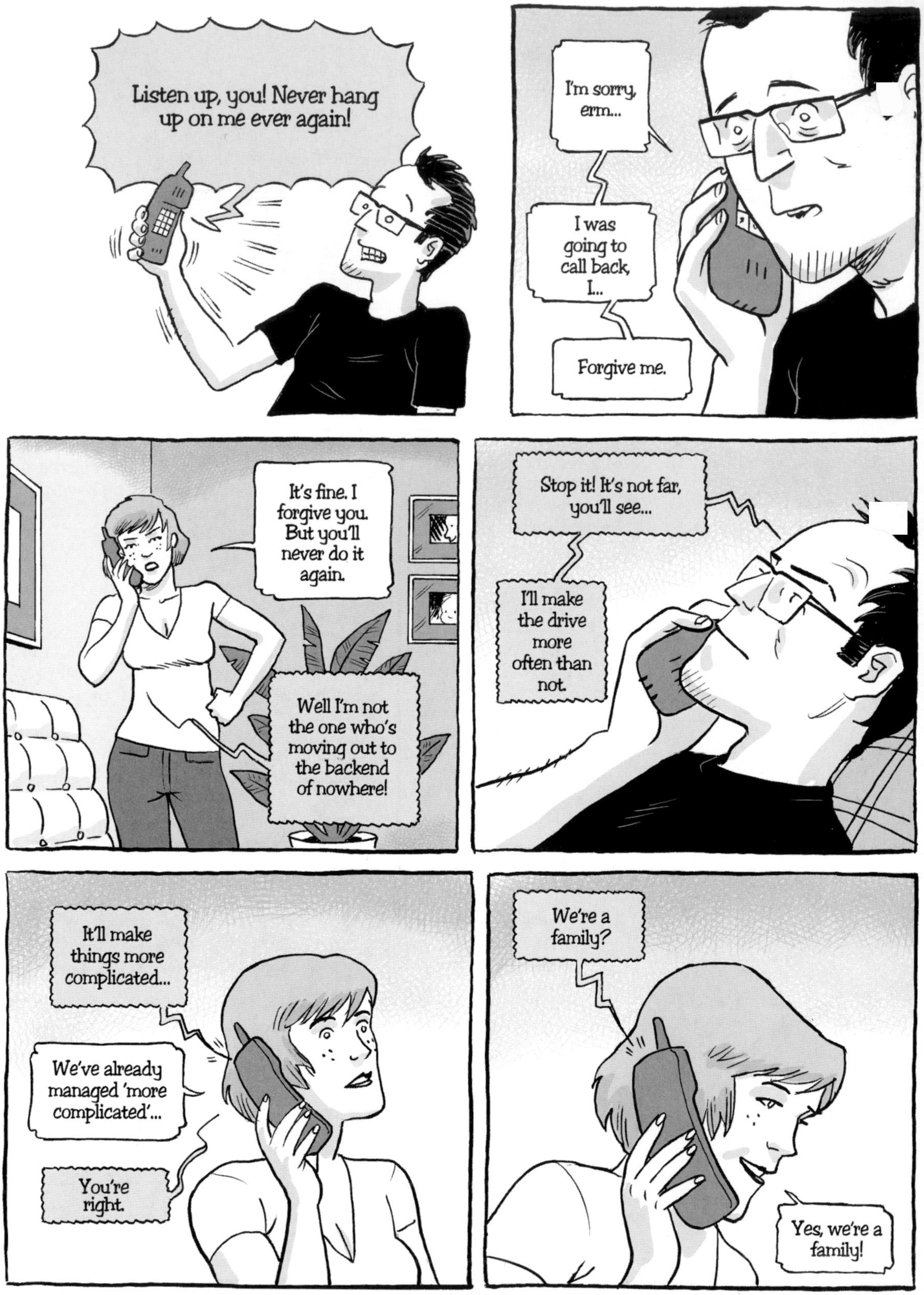
Listen up, you! Never hang up on me ever again!
I'm sorry, erm...
I was going to call back, I...
Forgive me.
It's fine. I forgive you. But you'll never do it again.
Well I'm not the one who's moving out to the backend of nowhere!
Stop it! It's not far, you'll see...
I'll make the drive more often than not.
It'll make things more complicated...
We've already managed 'more complicated'...
You're right.
We're a family?
Yes, we're a family!

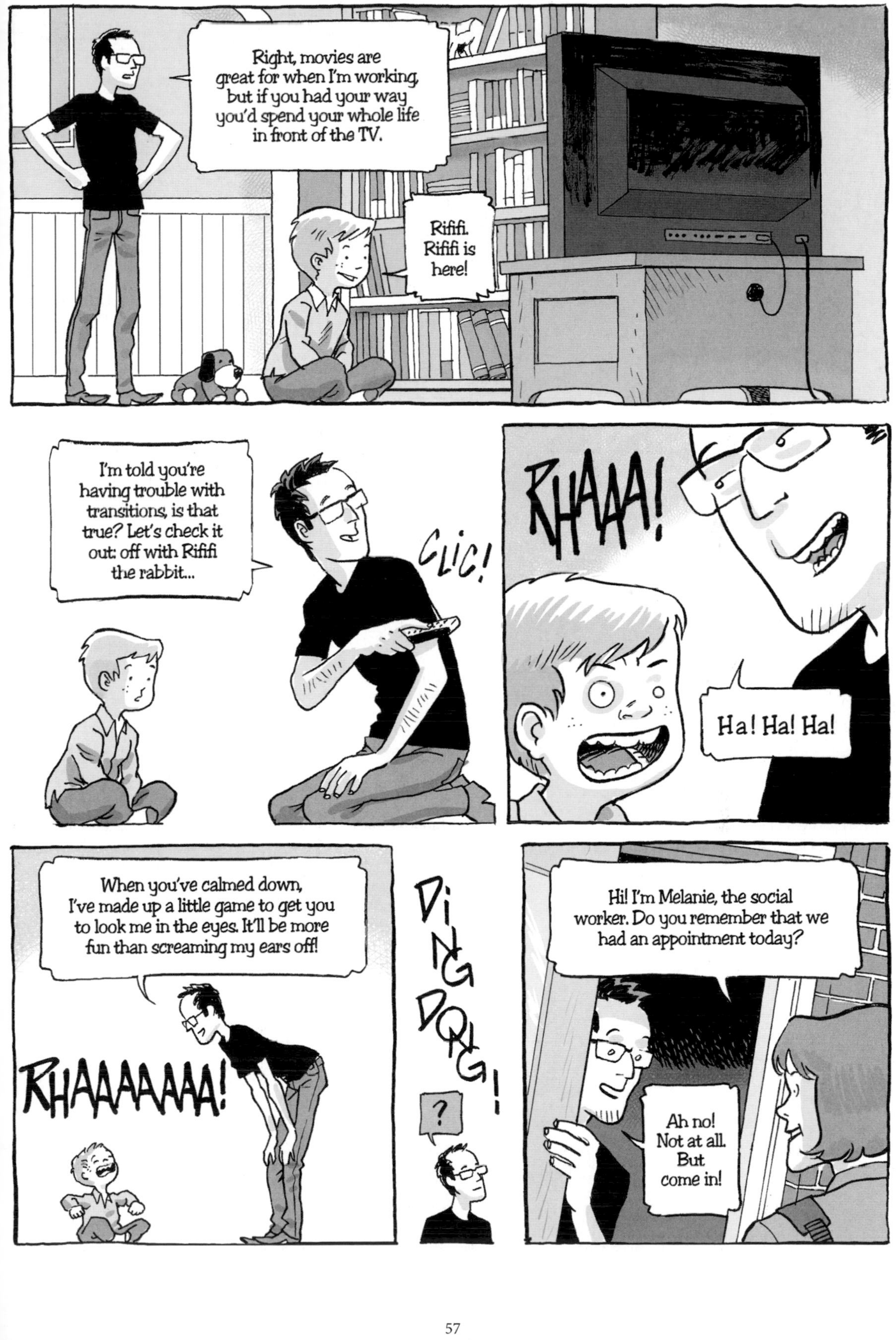
Right, movies are great for when I'm working, but if you had your way you'd spend your whole life in front of the TV.
Rififi. Rififi is here!
I'm told you're having trouble with transitions, is that true? Let's check it out: off with Rififi the rabbit...
CLIC!
RHAAA!
Ha! Ha! Ha!
When you've calmed down, I've made up a little game to get you to look me in the eyes. It'll be more fun than screaming my ears off!
RHAAAAAAA!
DING DONG!
?
Hi! I'm Melanie, the social worker. Do you remember that we had an appointment today?
Ah no! Not at all. But come in!

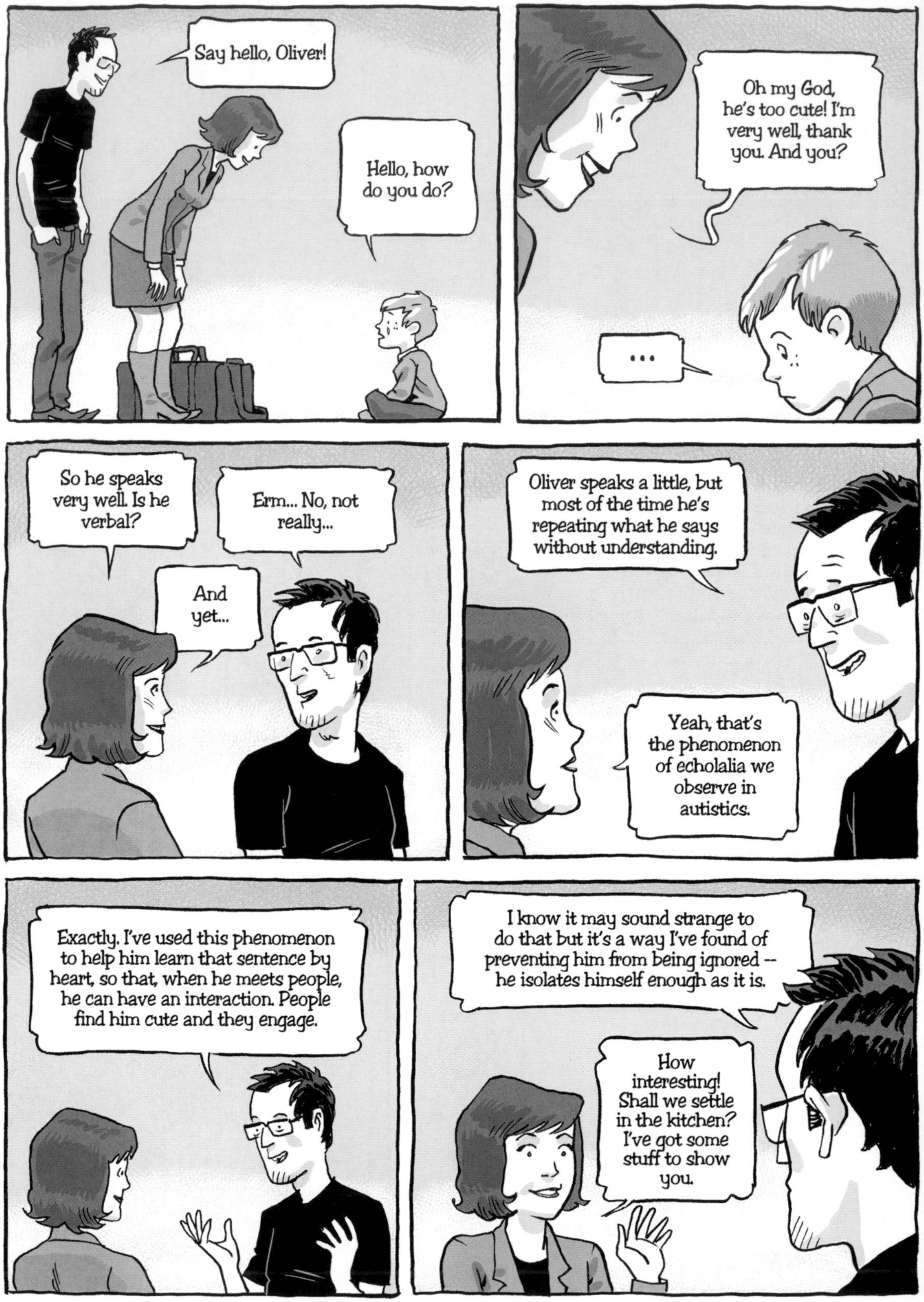
Say hello, Oliver!
Hello, how do you do?
Oh my God, he's too cute! I'm very well, thank you. And you?
...
So he speaks very well. Is he verbal?
Erm... No, not really...
And yet...
Oliver speaks a little, but most of the time he's repeating what he says without understanding.
Yeah, that's the phenomenon of echolalia we observe in autistics.
Exactly. I've used this phenomenon to help him learn that sentence by heart, so that, when he meets people, he can have an interaction. People find him cute and they engage.
I know it may sound strange to do that but it's a way I've found of preventing him from being ignored -- he isolates himself enough as it is.
How interesting! Shall we settle in the kitchen? I've got some stuff to show you.

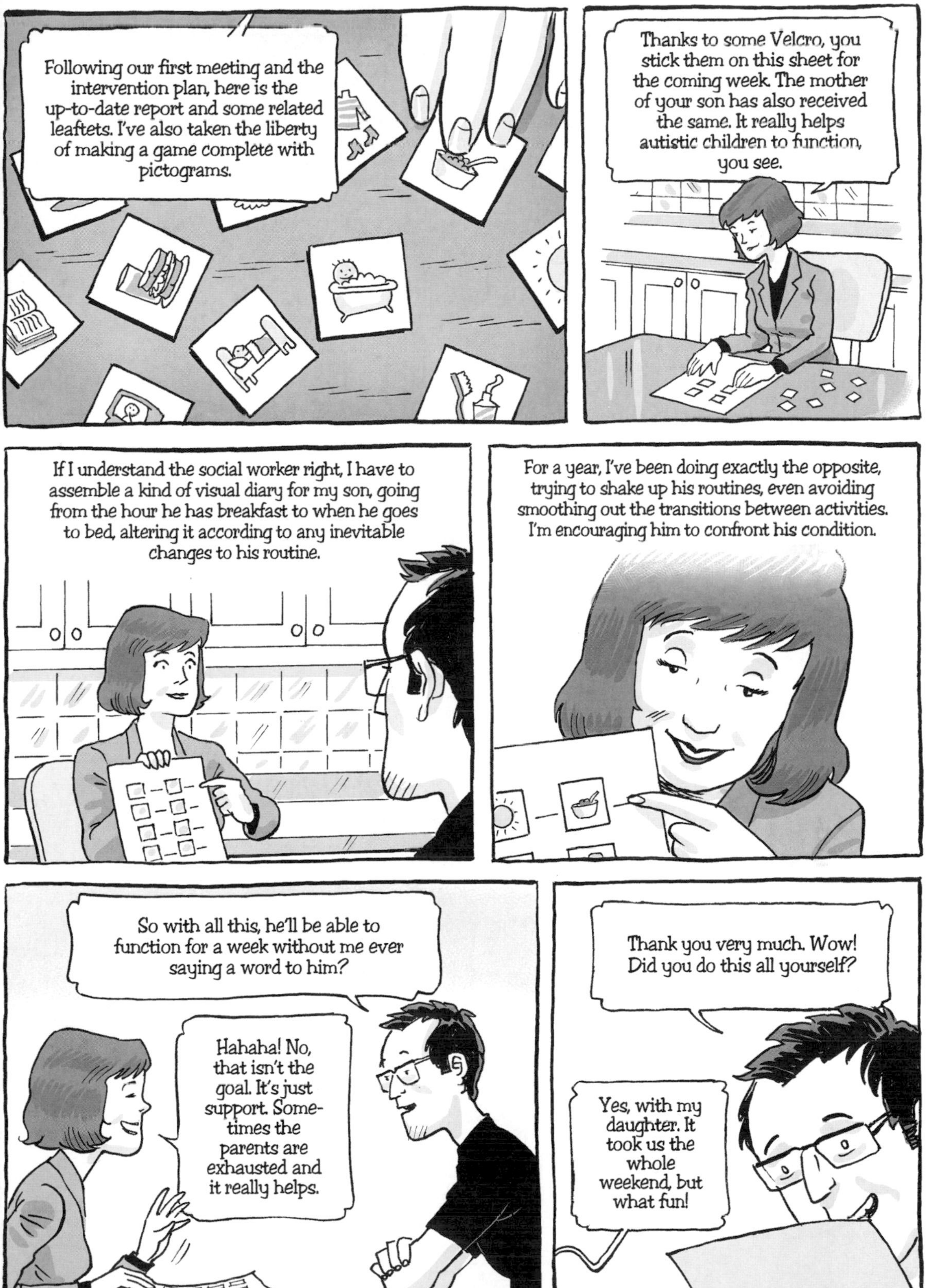
Following our first meeting and the intervention plan, here is the up-to-date report and some related leaftets. I've also taken the liberty of making a game complete with pictograms.
Thanks to some Velcro, you stick them on this sheet for the coming week. The mother of your son has also received the same. It really helps autistic children to function, you see.
If I understand the social worker right, I have to assemble a kind of visual diary for my son, going from the hour he has breakfast to when he goes to bed, altering it according to any inevitable changes to his routine.
For a year, I've been doing exactly the opposite, trying to shake up his routines, even avoiding smoothing out the transitions between activities. I'm encouraging him to confront his condition.
So with all this, he'll be able to function for a week without me ever saying a word to him?
Hahaha! No, that isn't the goal. It's just support. Sometimes the parents are exhausted and it really helps.
Thank you very much. Wow! Did you do this all yourself?
Yes, with my daughter. It took us the whole weekend, but what fun!

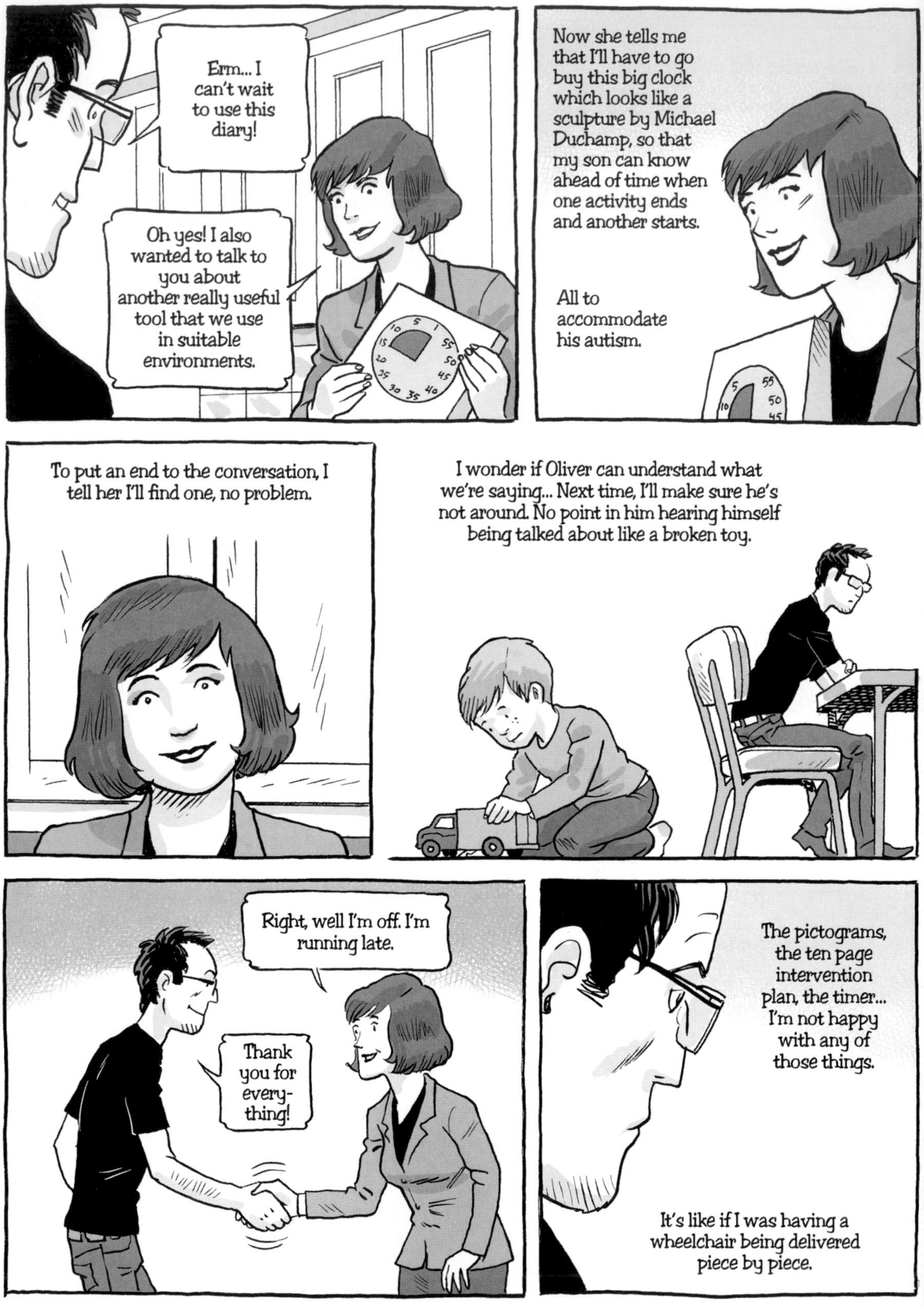
Erm... I can't wait to use this diary!
Oh yes! I also wanted to talk to you about another really useful tool that we use in suitable environments.
Now she tells me that I'll have to go buy this big clock which looks like a sculpture by Michael Duchamp, so that my son can know ahead of time when one activity ends and another starts.
All to accommodate his autism.
To put an end to the conversation, I tell her I'll find one, no problem.
I wonder if Oliver can understand what we're saying... Next time, I'll make sure he's not around. No point in him hearing himself being talked about like a broken toy.
Right, well I'm off. I'm running late.
Thank you for every-thing!
The pictograms, the ten page intervention plan, the timer... I'm not happy with any of those things.
It's like if I was having a wheelchair being delivered piece by piece.

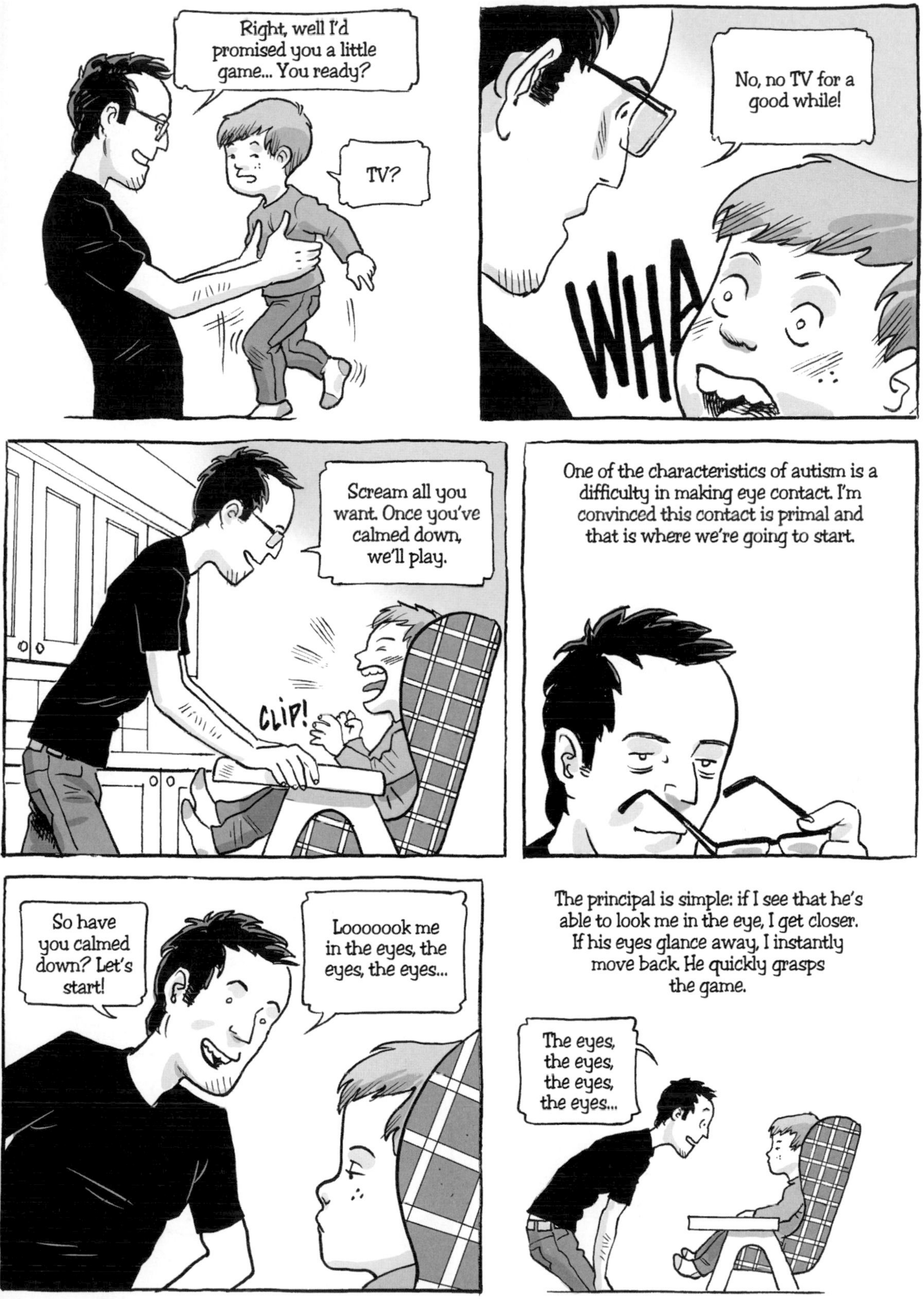
Right, well I'd promised you a little game... You ready?
TV?
No, no TV for a good while!
WHA
Scream all you want. Once you've calmed down, we'll play.
CLIP!
One of the characteristics of autism is a difficulty in making eye contact. I'm convinced this contact is primal and that is where we're going to start.
So have you calmed down? Let's start!
Loooooook me in the eyes, the eyes, the eyes...
The principal is simple: if I see that he's able to look me in the eye, I get closer. If his eyes glance away, I instantly move back. He quickly grasps the game.
The eyes, the eyes, the eyes, the eyes...

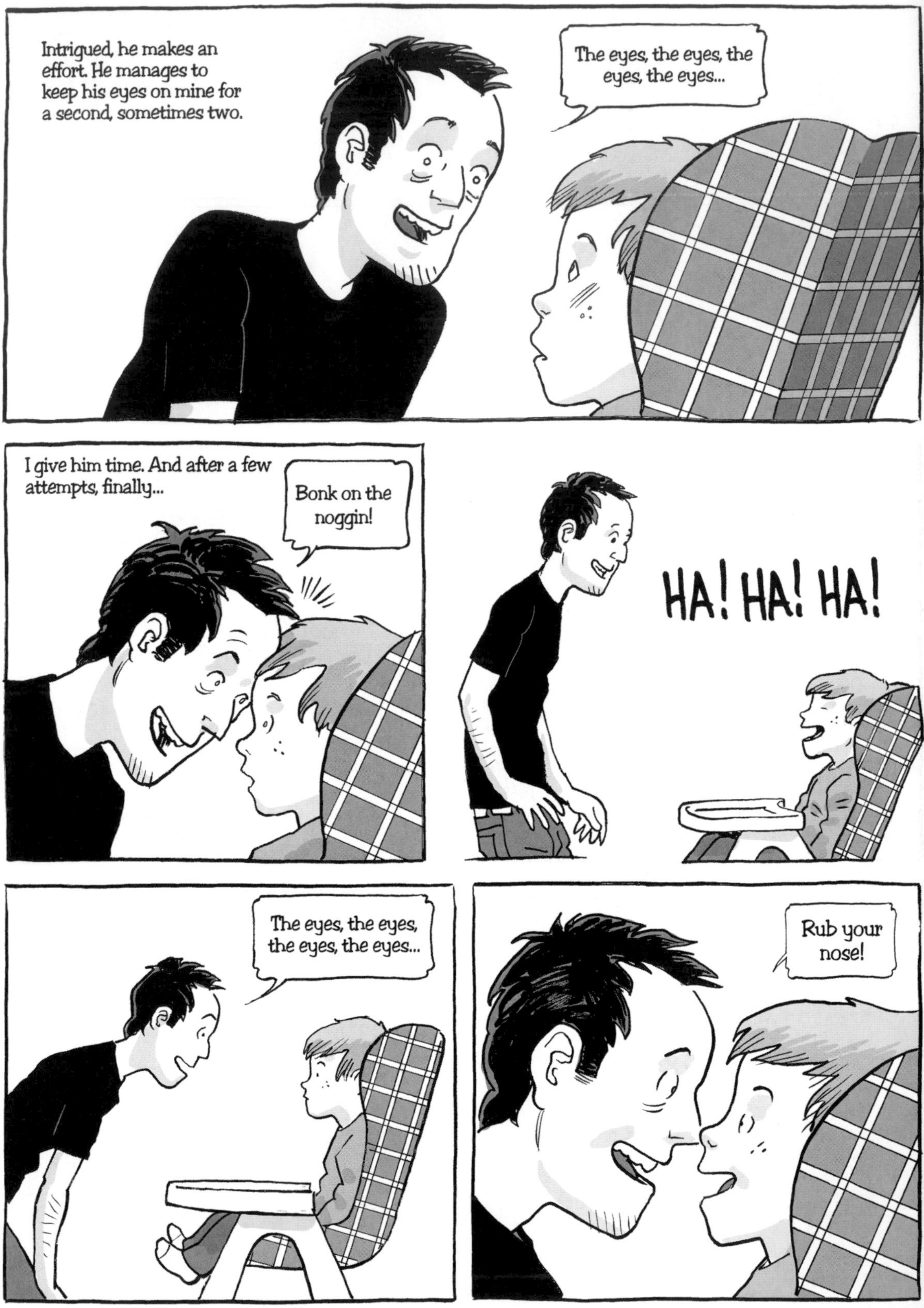
Intrigued, he makes an effort. He manages to keep his eyes on mine for a second, sometimes two.
The eyes, the eyes, the eyes, the eyes...
I give him time. And after a few attempts, finally...
Bonk on the noggin!
HA! HA! HA!
The eyes, the eyes, the eyes, the eyes...
Rub your nose!

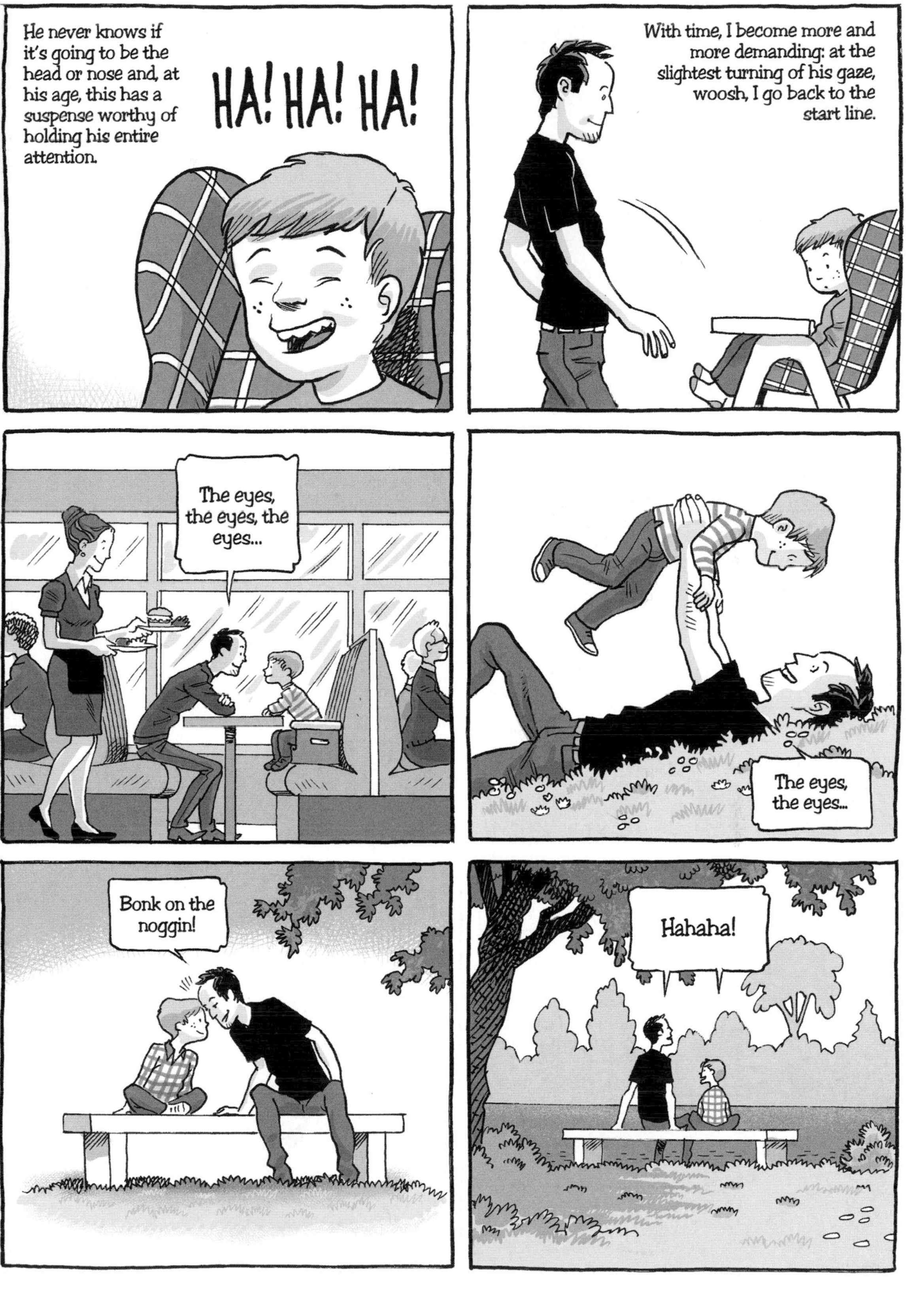

He never knows if it's going to be the head or nose and, at his age, this has a suspense worthy of holding his entire attention.
HA! HA! HA!
With time, I become more and more demanding: at the slightest turning of his gaze, woosh, I go back to the start line.
The eyes, the eyes, the eyes...
The eyes, the eyes...
Bonk on the noggin!
Hahaha!

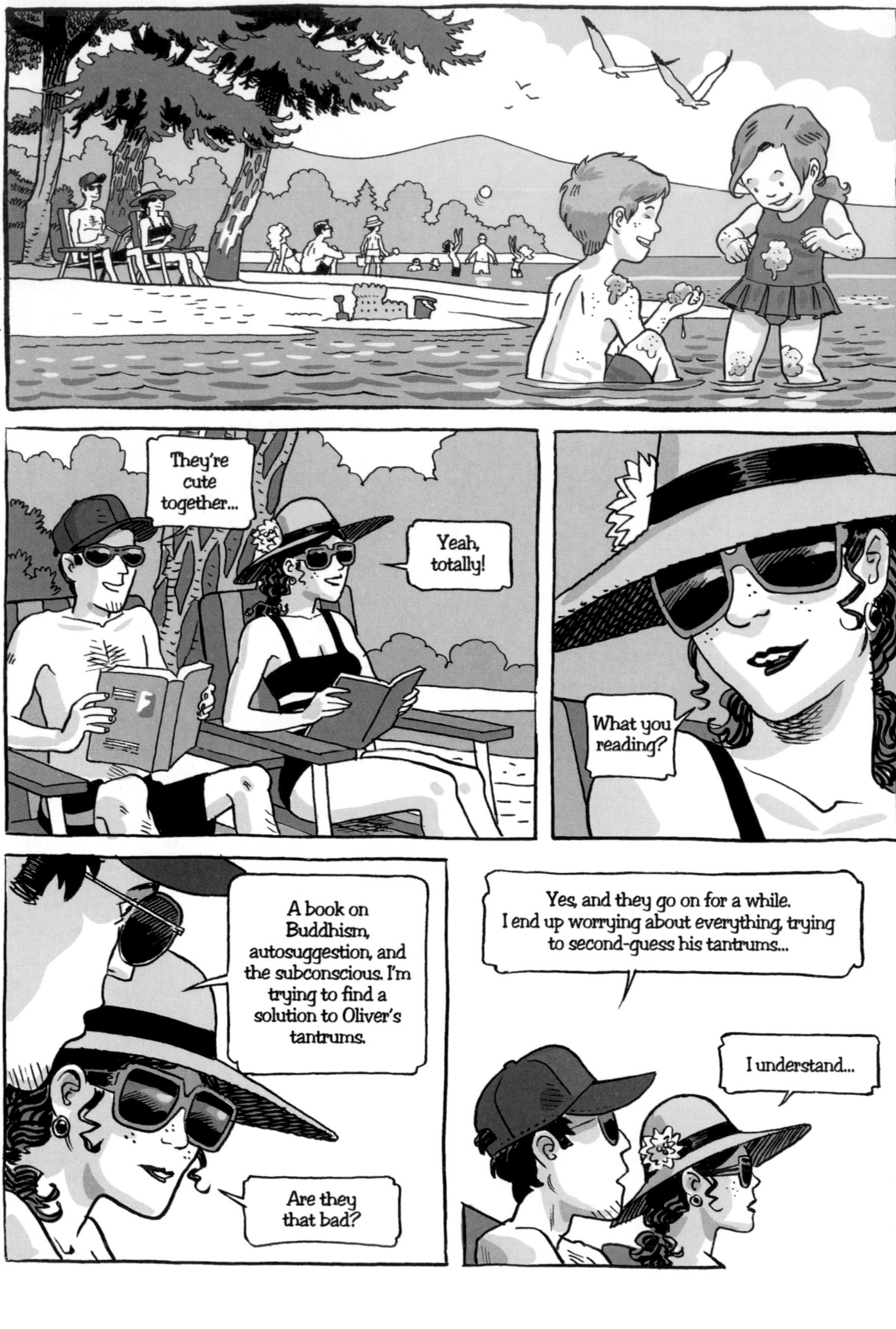
They're cute together...
Yeah, totally!
What you reading?
A book on Buddhism, autosuggestion, and the subconscious. I'm trying to find a solution to Oliver's tantrums.
Are they that bad?
Yes, and they go on for a while. I end up worrying about everything, trying to second-guess his tantrums...
I understand...

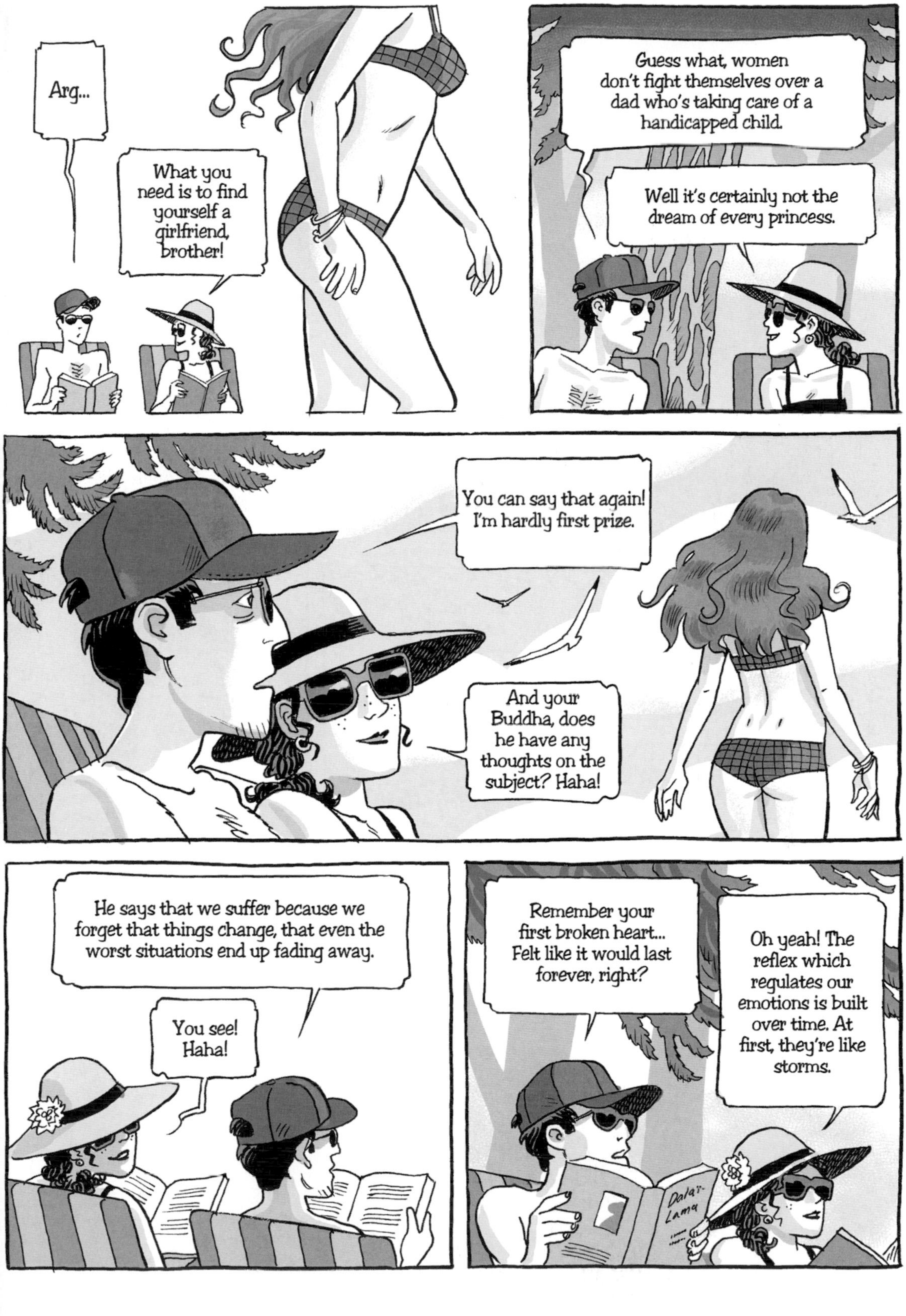
Arg...
What you need is to find yourself a girlfriend, brother!
Guess what, women don't fight themselves over a dad who's taking care of a handicapped child.
Well it's certainly not the dream of every princess.
You can say that again! I'm hardly first prize.
And your Buddha, does he have any thoughts on the subject? Haha!
He says that we suffer because we forget that things change, that even the worst situations end up fading away.
You see! Haha!
Remember your first broken heart... Felt like it would last forever, right?
Oh yeah! The reflex which regulates our emotions is built over time. At first, they're like storms.
Dalaï-Lama

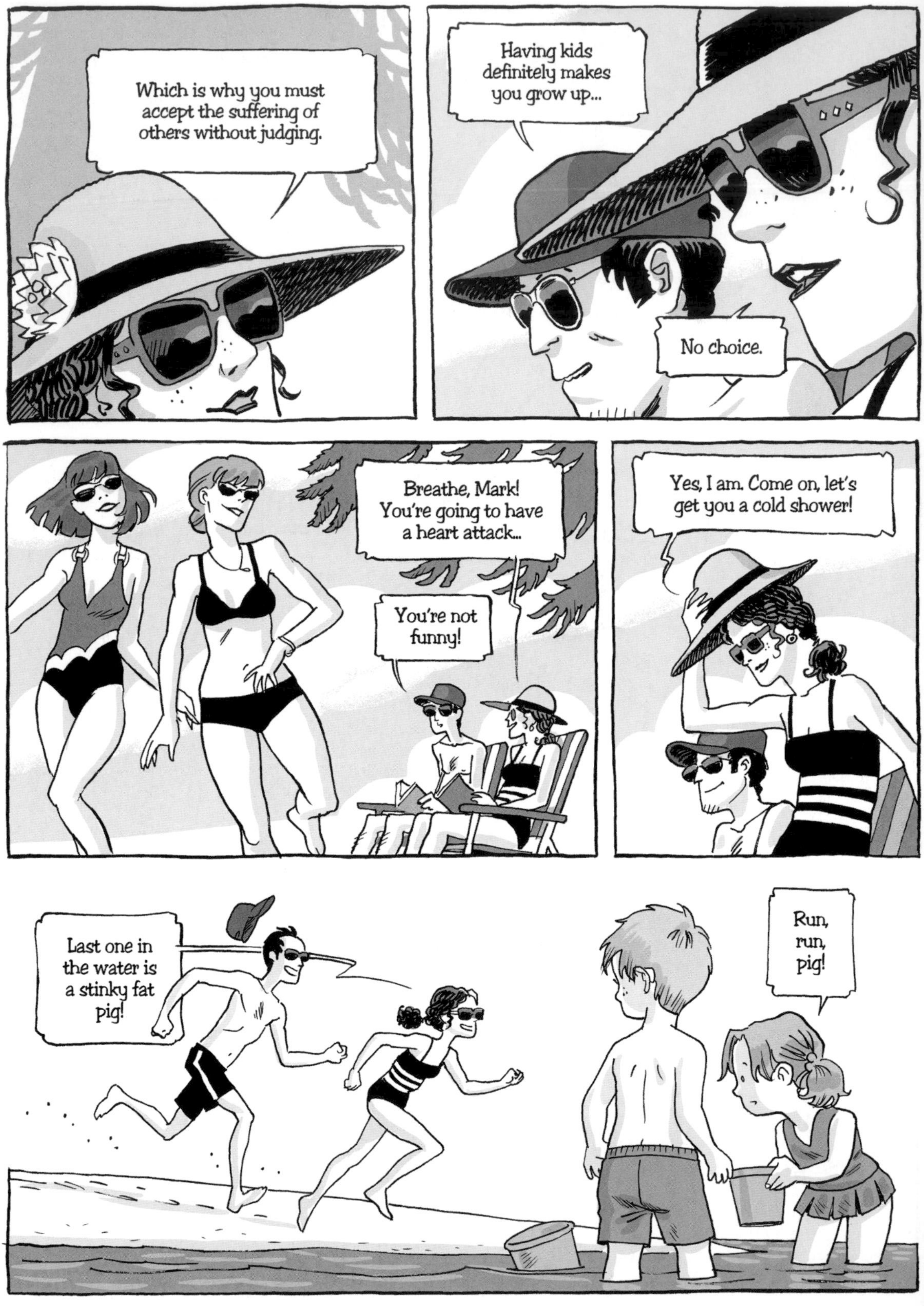
Which is why you must accept the suffering of others without judging.
Having kids definitely makes you grow up...
No choice.
Breathe, Mark! You're going to have a heart attack...
You're not funny!
Yes, I am. Come on, let's get you a cold shower!
Last one in the water is a stinky fat pig!
Run, run, pig!

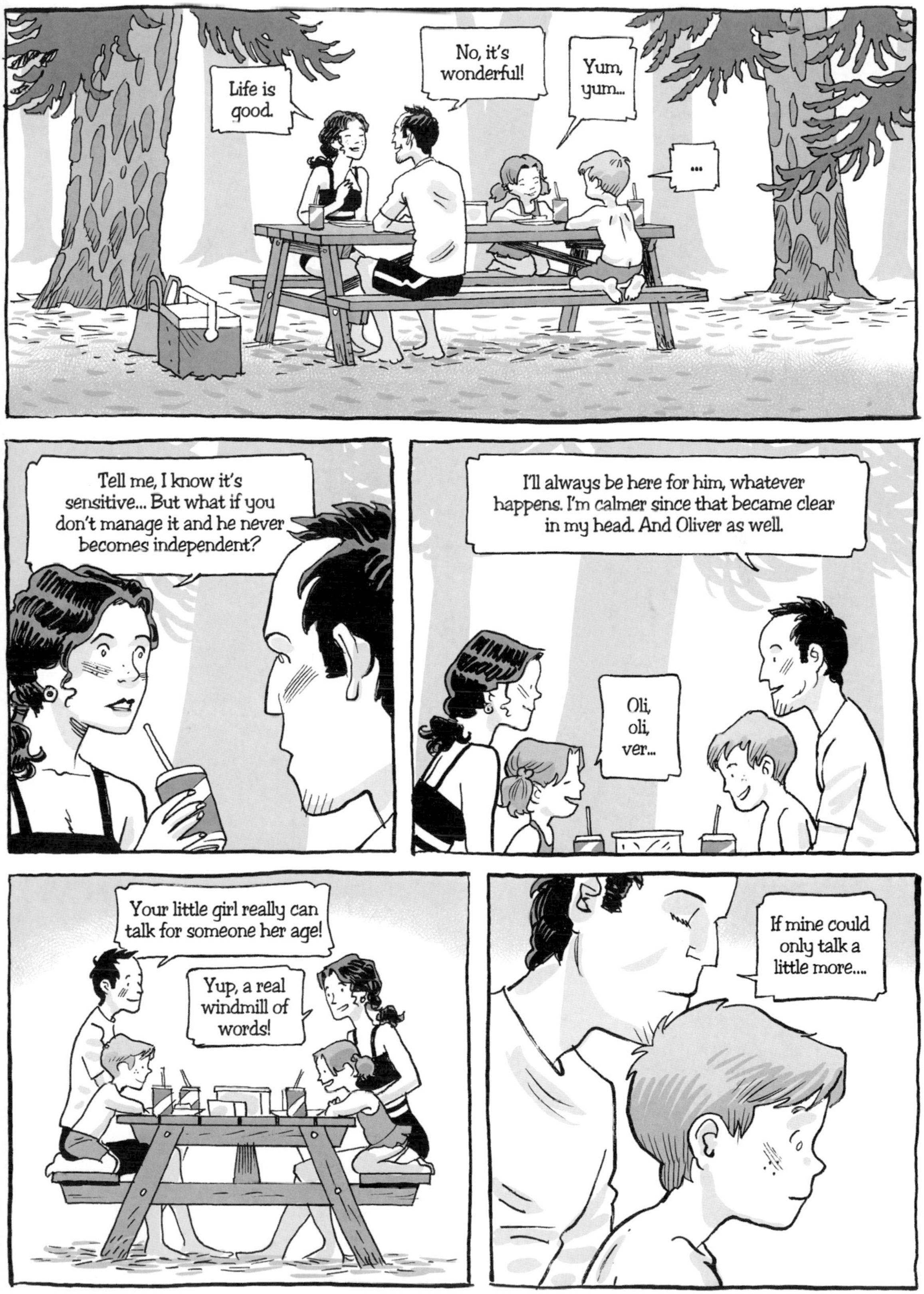
Life is good.
No, it's wonderful!
Yum, yum...
...
Tell me, I know it's sensitive... But what if you don't manage it and he never becomes independent?
I'll always be here for him, whatever happens. I'm calmer since that became clear in my head. And Oliver as well.
Oli, oli, ver...
Your little girl really can talk for someone her age!
Yup, a real windmill of words!
If mine could only talk a little more....

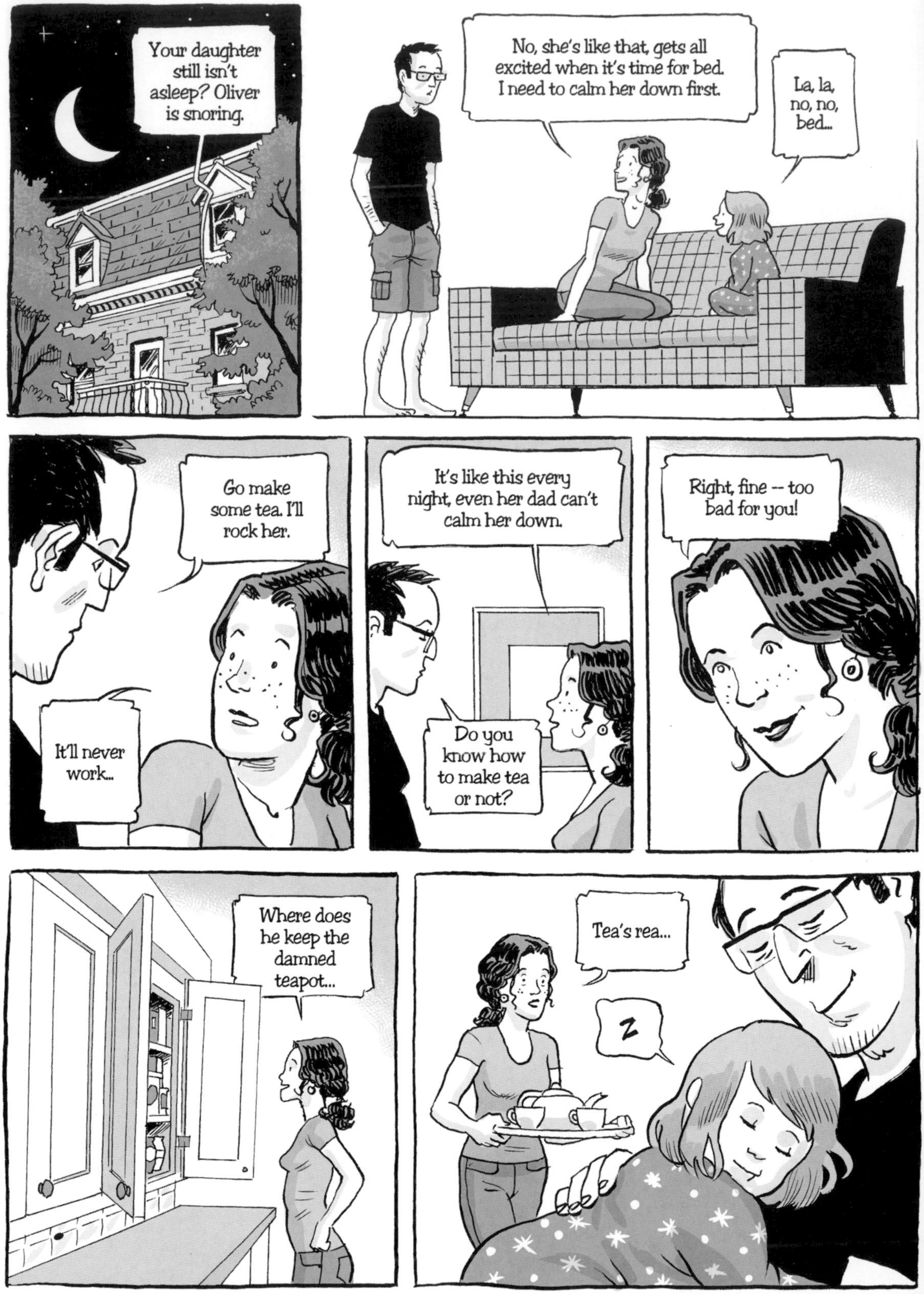
Your daughter still isn't asleep? Oliver is snoring.
No, she's like that, gets all excited when it's time for bed. I need to calm her down first.
La, la, no, no, bed...
Go make some tea. I'll rock her.
It'll never work...
It's like this every night, even her dad can't calm her down.
Do you know how to make tea or not?
Right, fine -- too bad for you!
Where does he keep the damned teapot...
Tea's rea...
Z

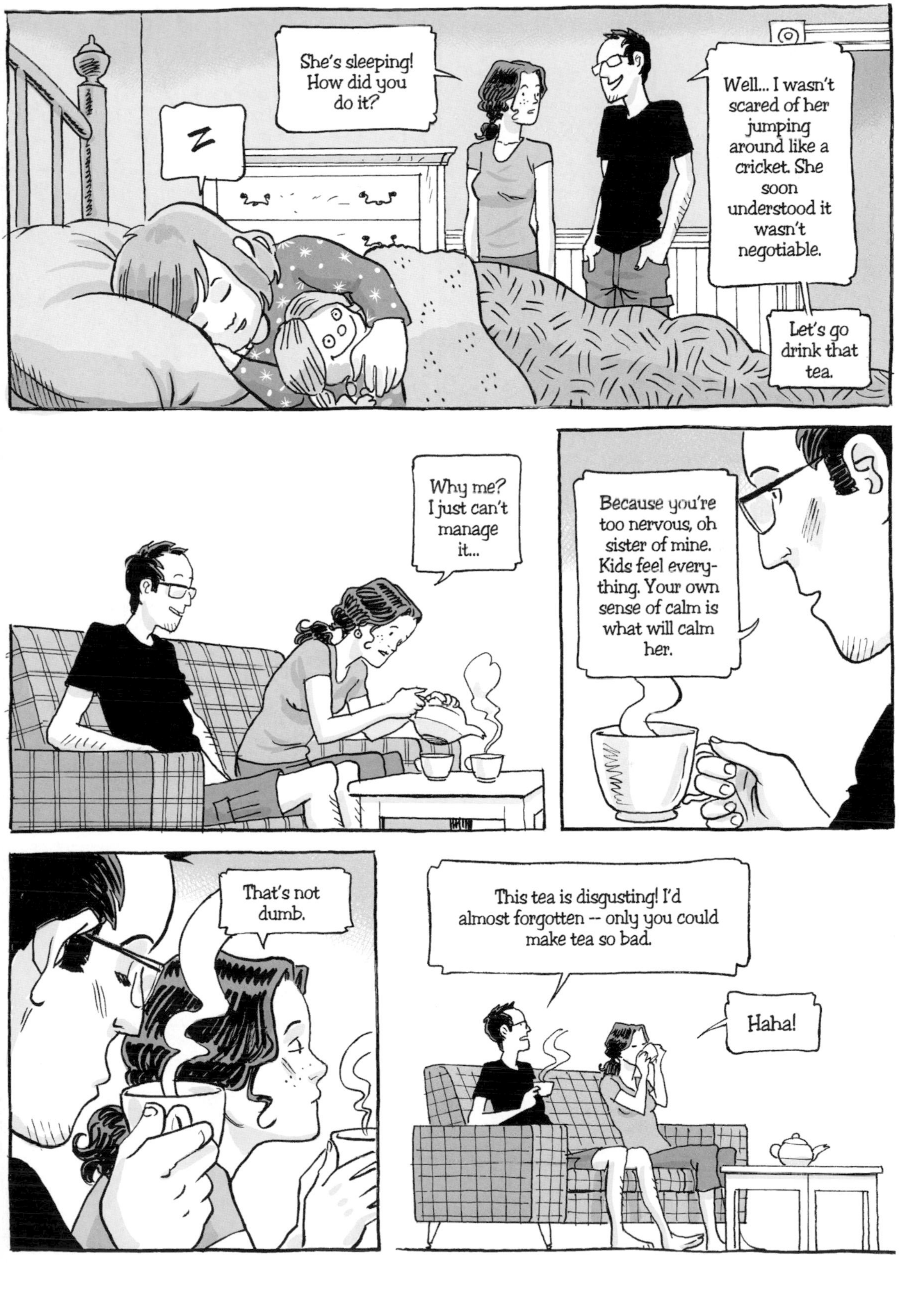
Z
She's sleeping! How did you do it?
Well... I wasn't scared of her jumping around like a cricket. She soon understood it wasn't negotiable.
Let's go drink that tea.
Why me? I just can't manage it...
Because you're too nervous, oh sister of mine. Kids feel everything. Your own sense of calm is what will calm her.
That's not dumb.
This tea is disgusting! I'd almost forgotten -- only you could make tea so bad.
Haha!

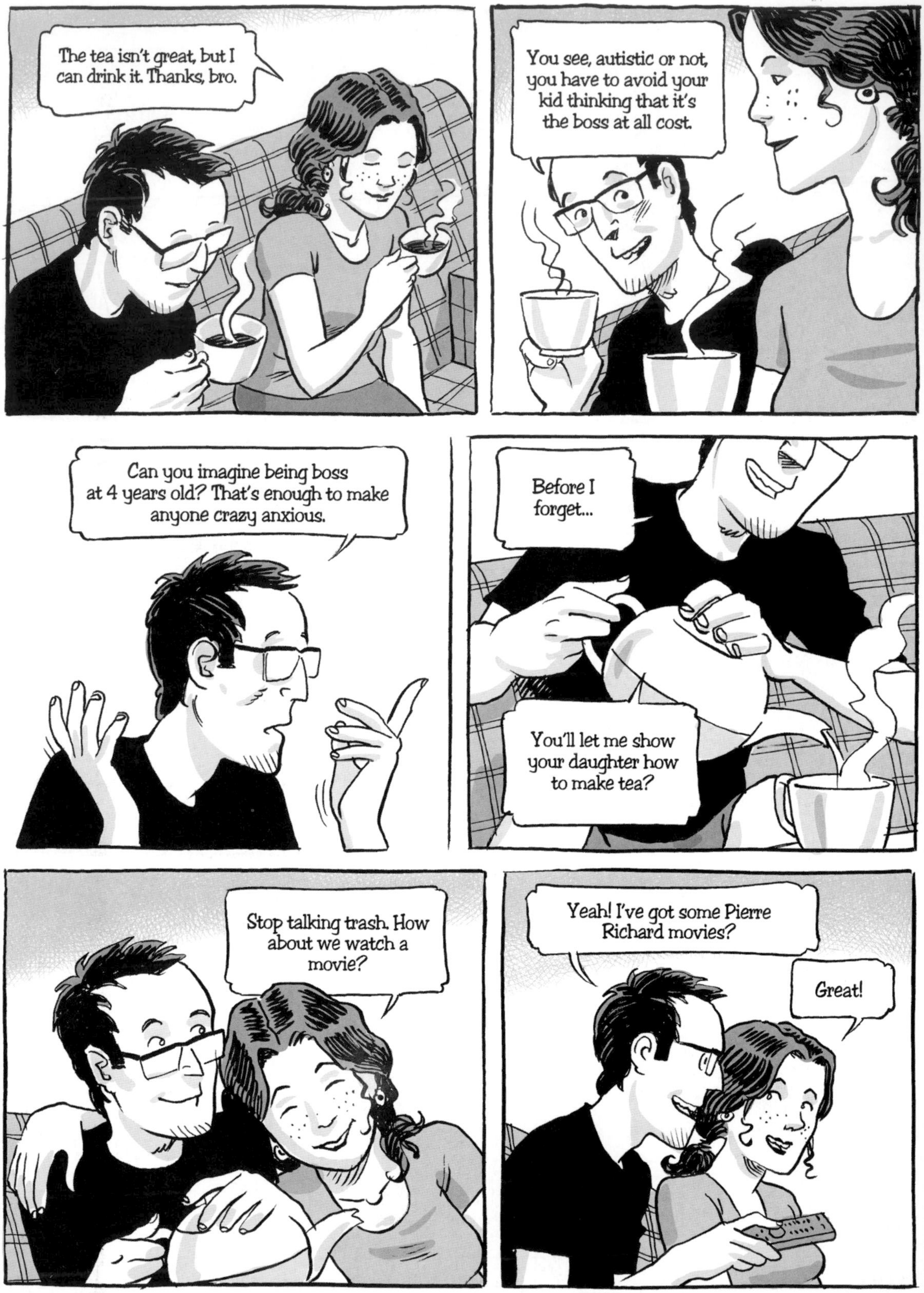
The tea isn't great, but I can drink it. Thanks, bro.
You see, autistic or not, you have to avoid your kid thinking that it's the boss at all cost.
Can you imagine being boss at 4 years old? That's enough to make anyone crazy anxious.
Before I forget...
You'll let me show your daughter how to make tea?
Stop talking trash. How about we watch a movie?
Yeah! I've got some Pierre Richard movies?
Great!

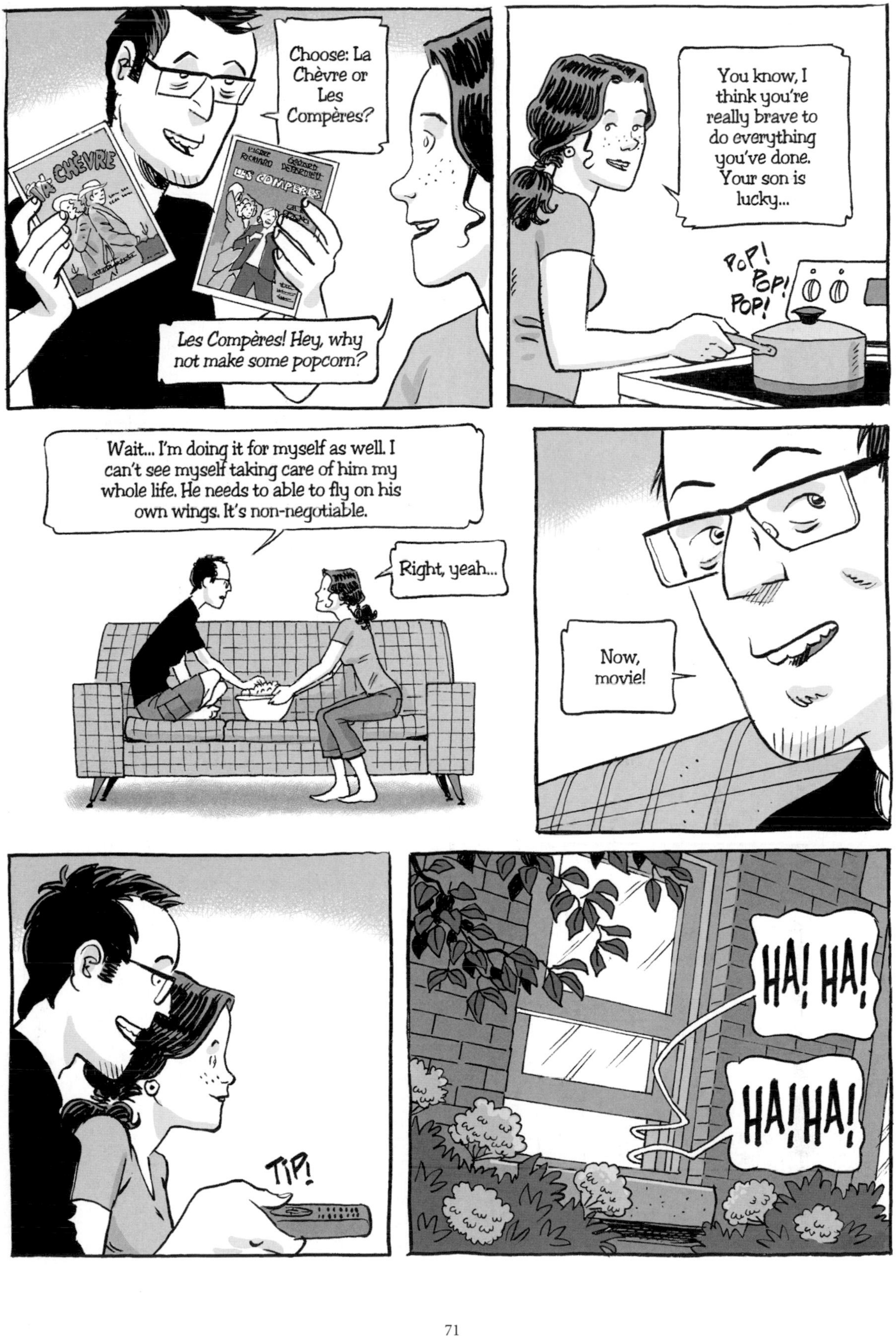
Choose: La Chèvre or Les Compères?
LA CHÈVRE
LES COMPÈRES
Les Compères! Hey, why not make some popcorn?
You know, I think you're really brave to do everything you've done. Your son is lucky...
POP! POP! POP!
Wait... I'm doing it for myself as well. I can't see myself taking care of him my whole life. He needs to able to fly on his own wings. It's non-negotiable.
Right, yeah...
Now, movie!
TIP!
HA! HA!
HA! HA!

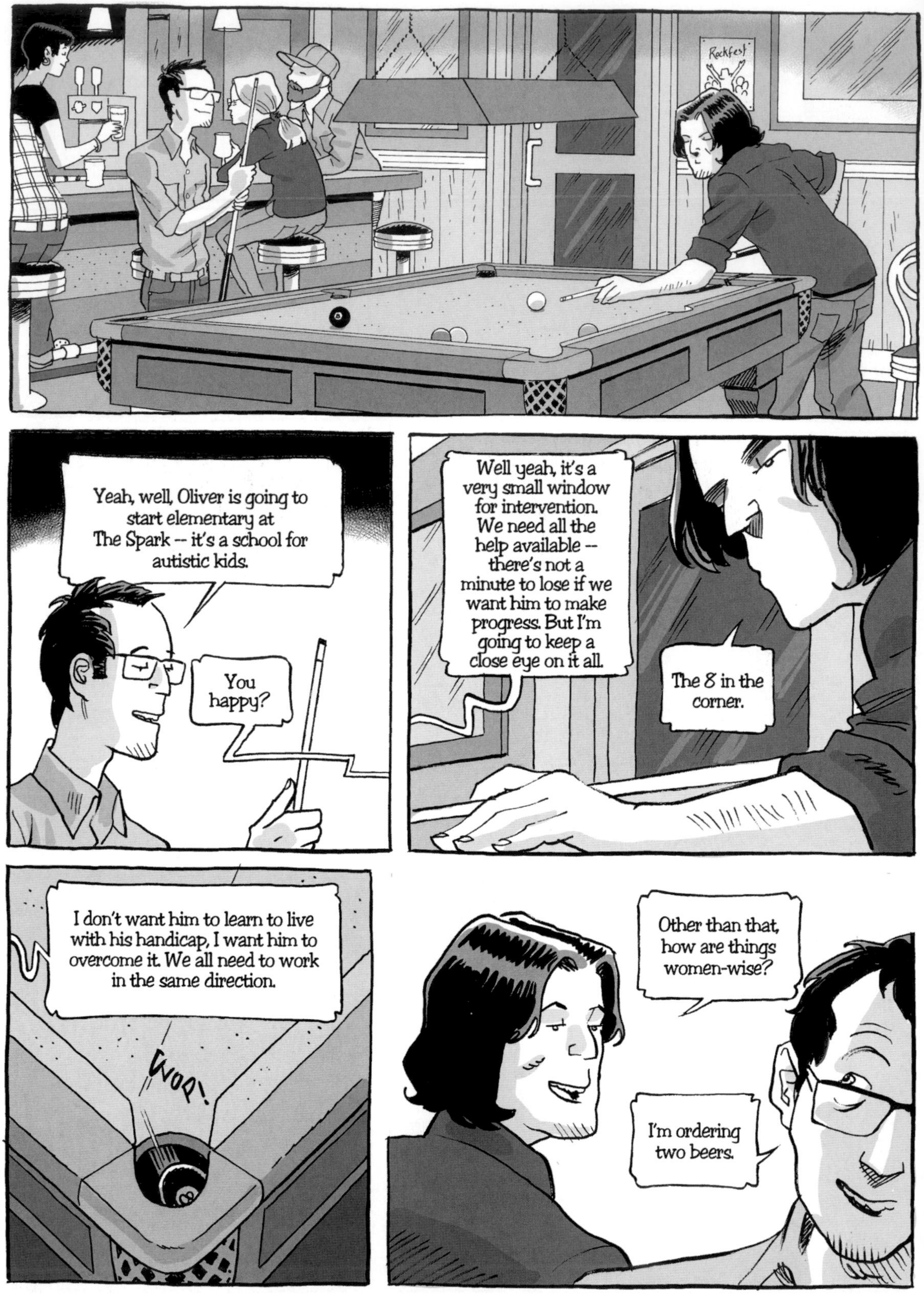
Rockfest
Yeah, well, Oliver is going to start elementary at The Spark -- it's a school for autistic kids.
You happy?
Well yeah, it's a very small window for intervention. We need all the help available -- there's not a minute to lose if we want him to make progress. But I'm going to keep a close eye on it all.
The 8 in the corner.
I don't want him to learn to live with his handicap, I want him to overcome it. We all need to work in the same direction.
WOP!
Other than that, how are things women-wise?
I'm ordering two beers.

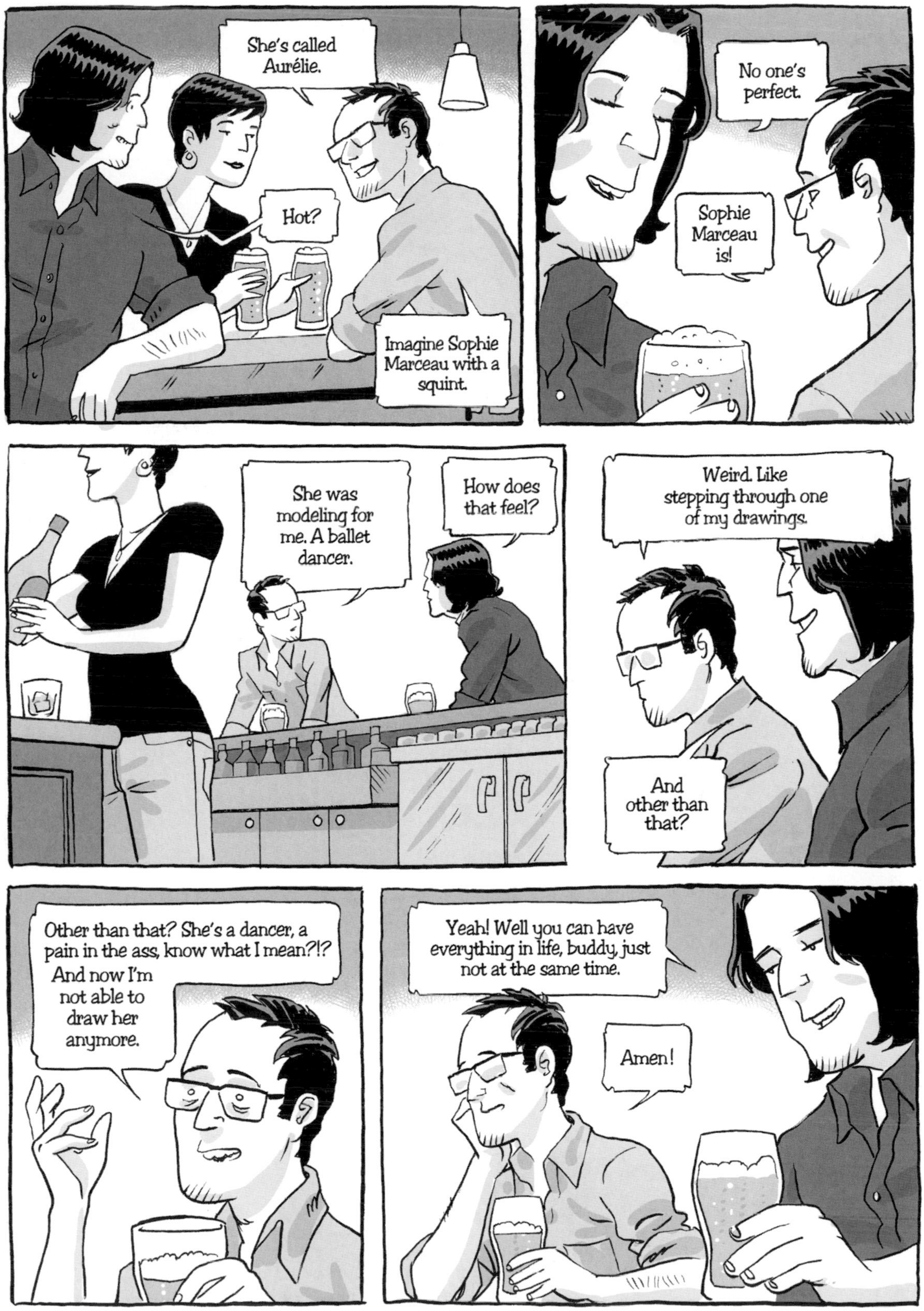
She's called Aurélie.
Hot?
Imagine Sophie Marceau with a squint.
No one's perfect.
Sophie Marceau is!
She was modeling for me. A ballet dancer.
How does that feel?
Weird. Like stepping through one of my drawings.
And other than that?
Other than that? She's a dancer, a pain in the ass, know what I mean?!?
And now I'm not able to draw her anymore.
Yeah! Well you can have everything in life, buddy, just not at the same time.
Amen!

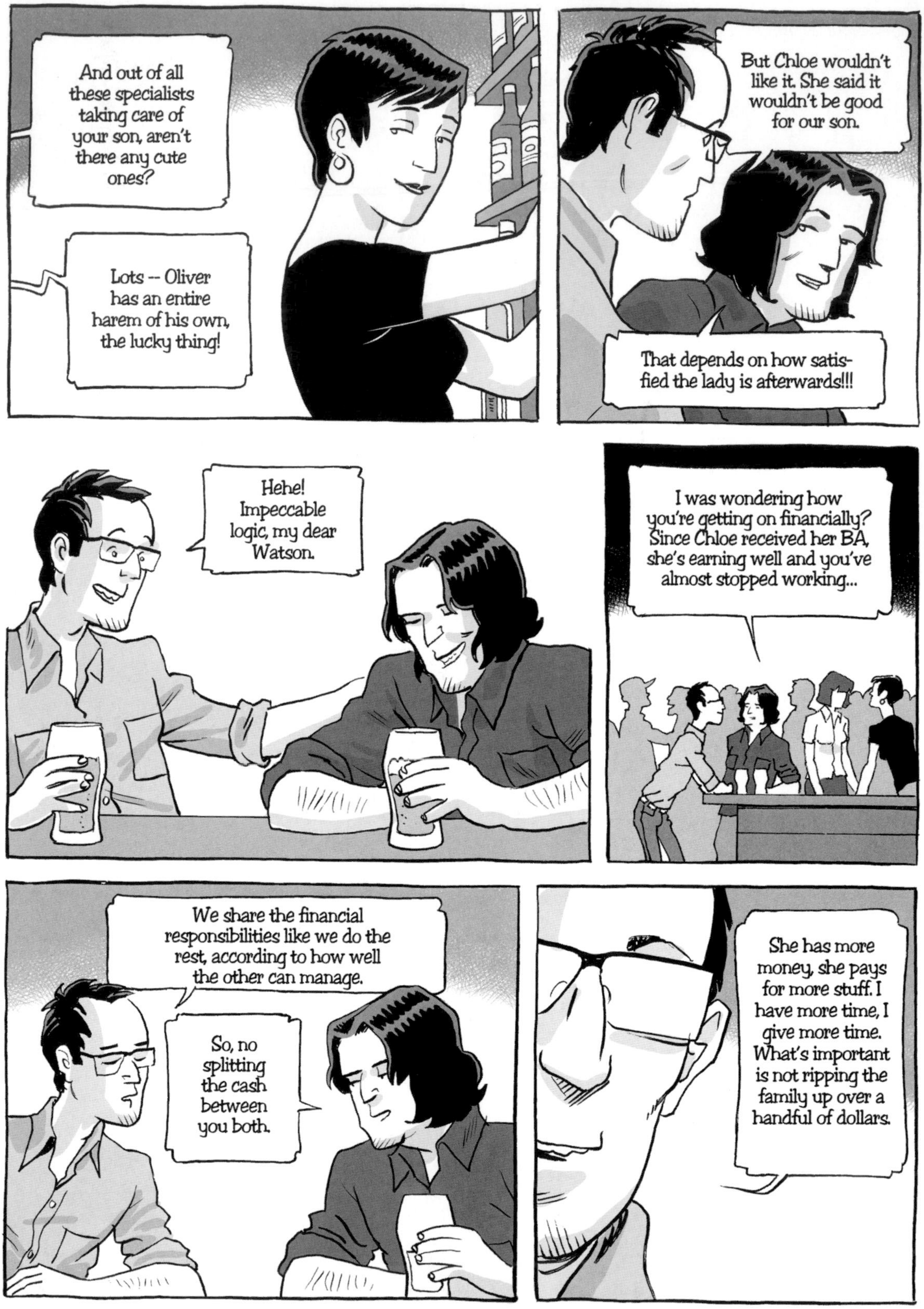
And out of all these specialists taking care of your son, aren't there any cute ones?
Lots -- Oliver has an entire harem of his own, the lucky thing!
But Chloe wouldn't like it. She said it wouldn't be good for our son.
That depends on how satisfied the lady is afterwards!!!
Hehe! Impeccable logic, my dear Watson.
I was wondering how you're getting on financially? Since Chloe received her BA, she's earning well and you've almost stopped working...
We share the financial responsibilities like we do the rest, according to how well the other can manage.
So, no splitting the cash between you both.
She has more money, she pays for more stuff. I have more time, I give more time. What's important is not ripping the family up over a handful of dollars.

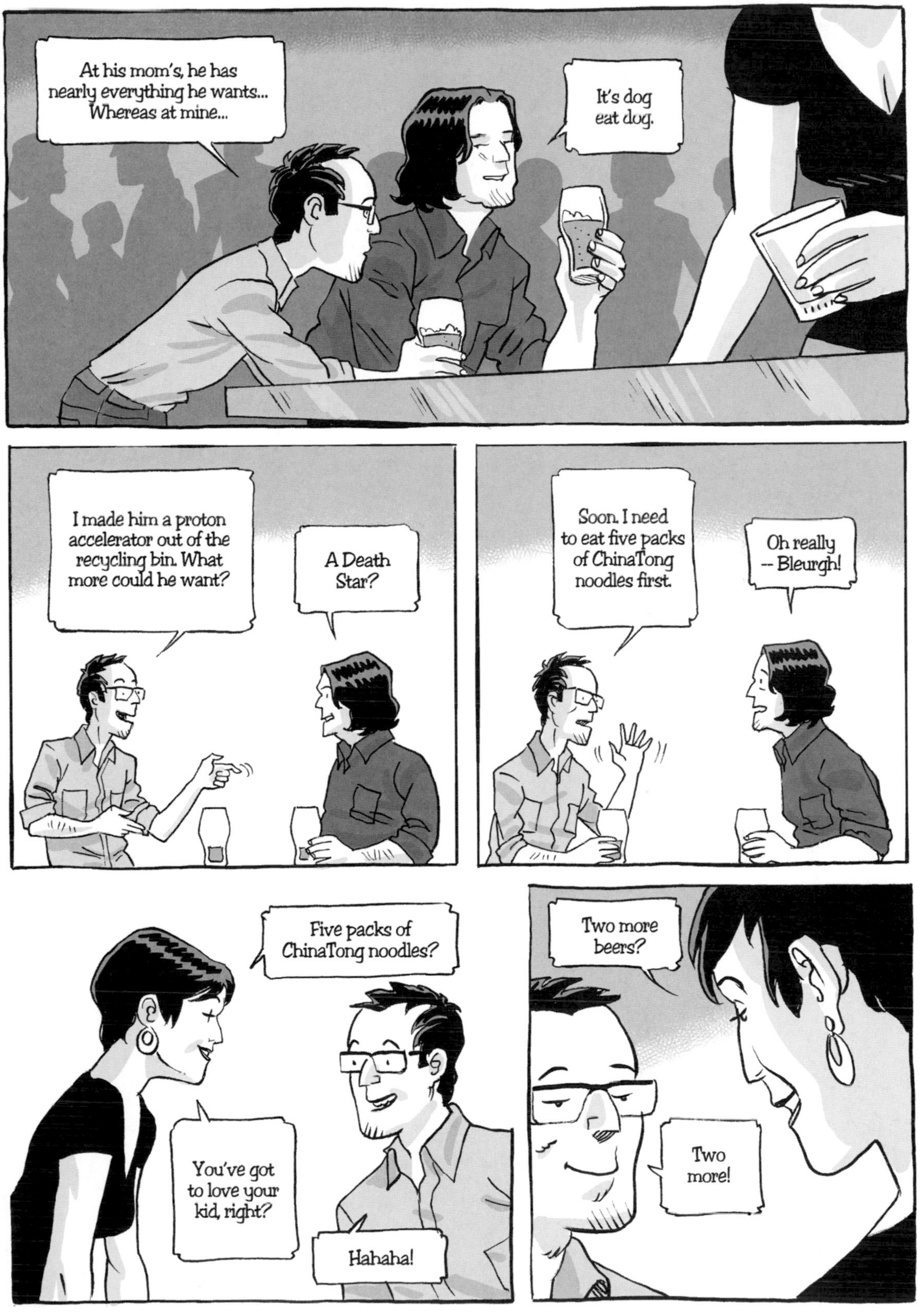
At his mom's, he has nearly everything he wants... Whereas at mine...
It's dog eat dog.
I made him a proton accelerator out of the recycling bin. What more could he want?
A Death Star?
Soon. I need to eat five packs of ChinaTong noodles first.
Oh really -- Bleurgh!
Five packs of ChinaTong noodles?
You've got to love your kid, right?
Hahaha!
Two more beers?
Two more!

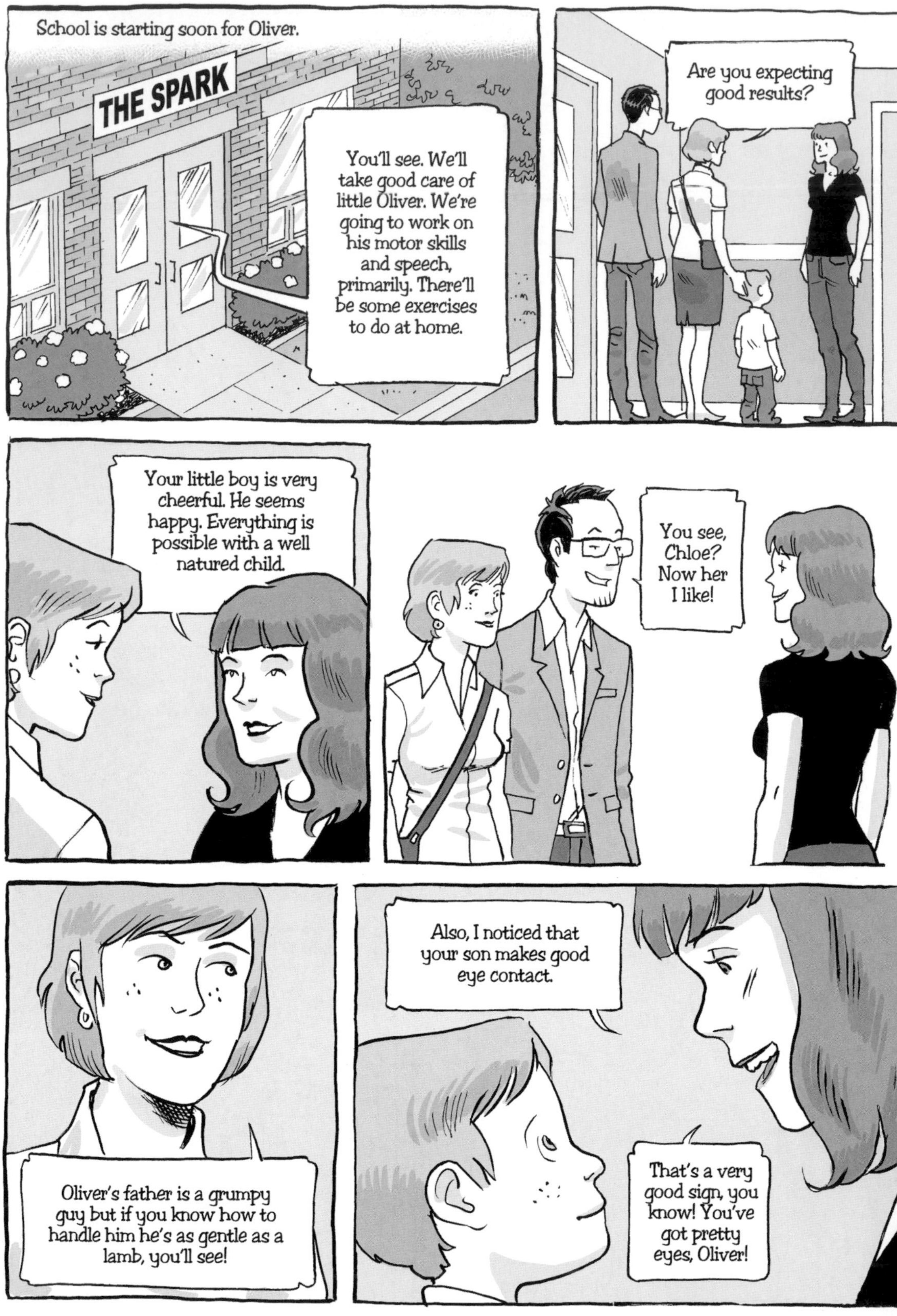
School is starting soon for Oliver.
THE SPARK
You'll see. We'll take good care of little Oliver. We're going to work on his motor skills and speech, primarily. There'll be some exercises to do at home.
Are you expecting good results?
Your little boy is very cheerful. He seems happy. Everything is possible with a well natured child.
You see, Chloe? Now her I like!
Oliver's father is a grumpy guy but if you know how to handle him he's as gentle as a lamb, you'll see!
Also, I noticed that your son makes good eye contact.
That's a very good sign, you know! You've got pretty eyes, Oliver!

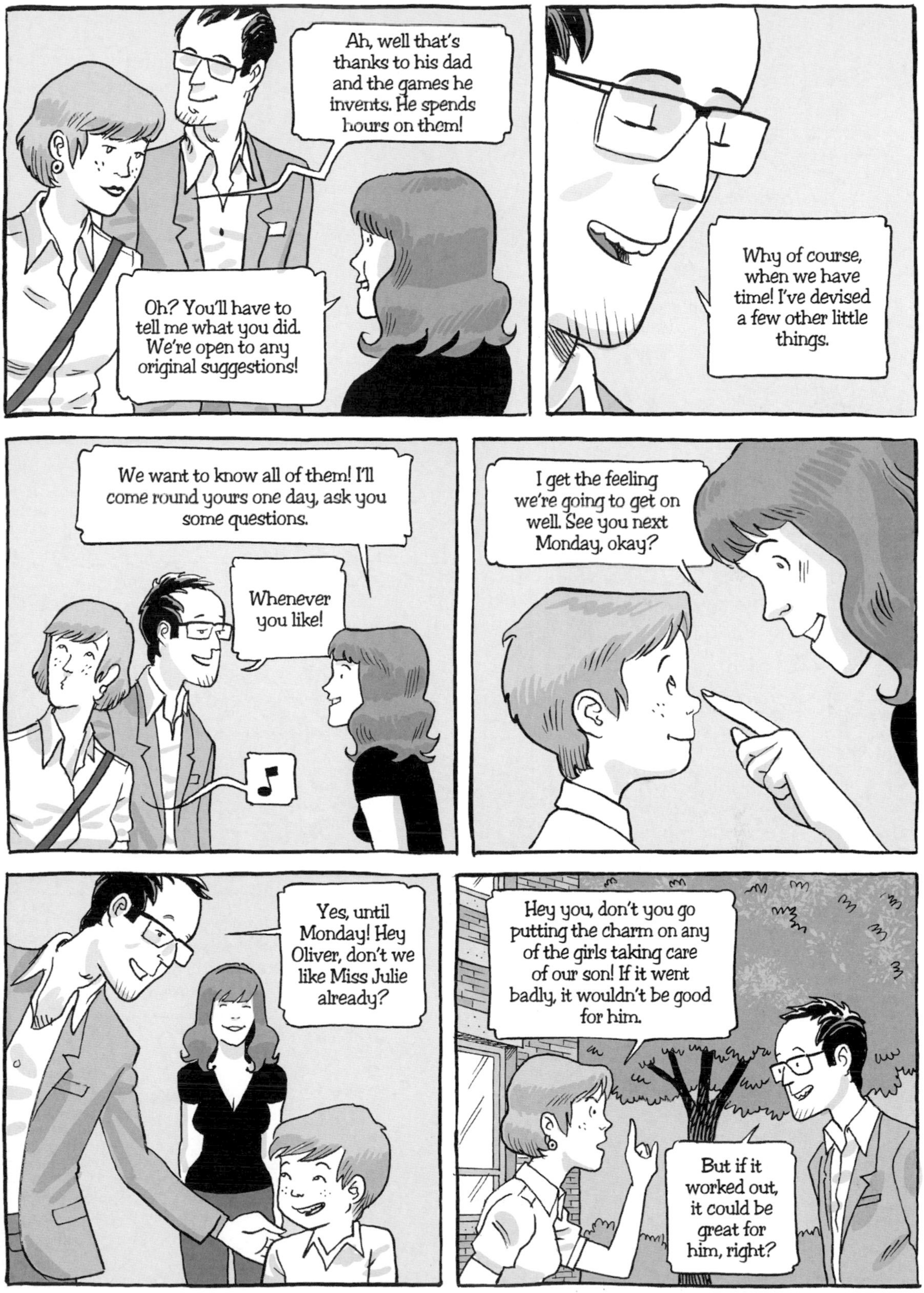
Ah, well that's thanks to his dad and the games he invents. He spends hours on them!
Oh? You'll have to tell me what you did. We're open to any original suggestions!
Why of course, when we have time! I've devised a few other little things.
We want to know all of them! I'll come round yours one day, ask you some questions.
Whenever you like!
I get the feeling we're going to get on well. See you next Monday, okay?
Yes, until Monday! Hey Oliver, don't we like Miss Julie already?
Hey you, don't you go putting the charm on any of the girls taking care of our son! If it went badly, it wouldn't be good for him.
But if it worked out, it could be great for him, right?

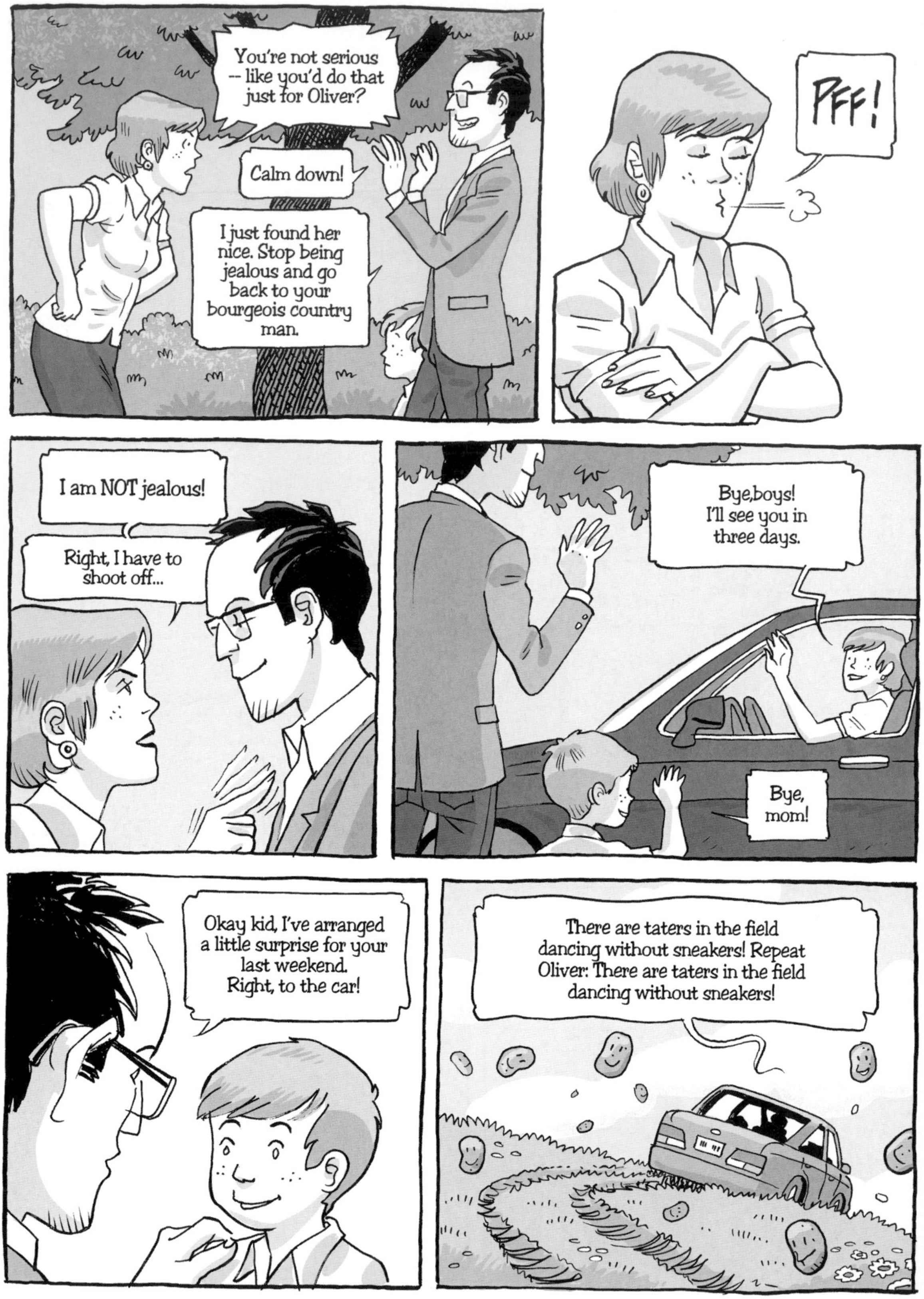
You're not serious -- like you'd do that just for Oliver?
Calm down!
I just found her nice. Stop being jealous and go back to your bourgeois country man.
PFF!
I am NOT jealous!
Right, I have to shoot off...
Bye,boys! I'll see you in three days.
Bye, mom!
Okay kid, I've arranged a little surprise for your last weekend. Right, to the car!
There are taters in the field dancing without sneakers! Repeat Oliver: There are taters in the field dancing without sneakers!

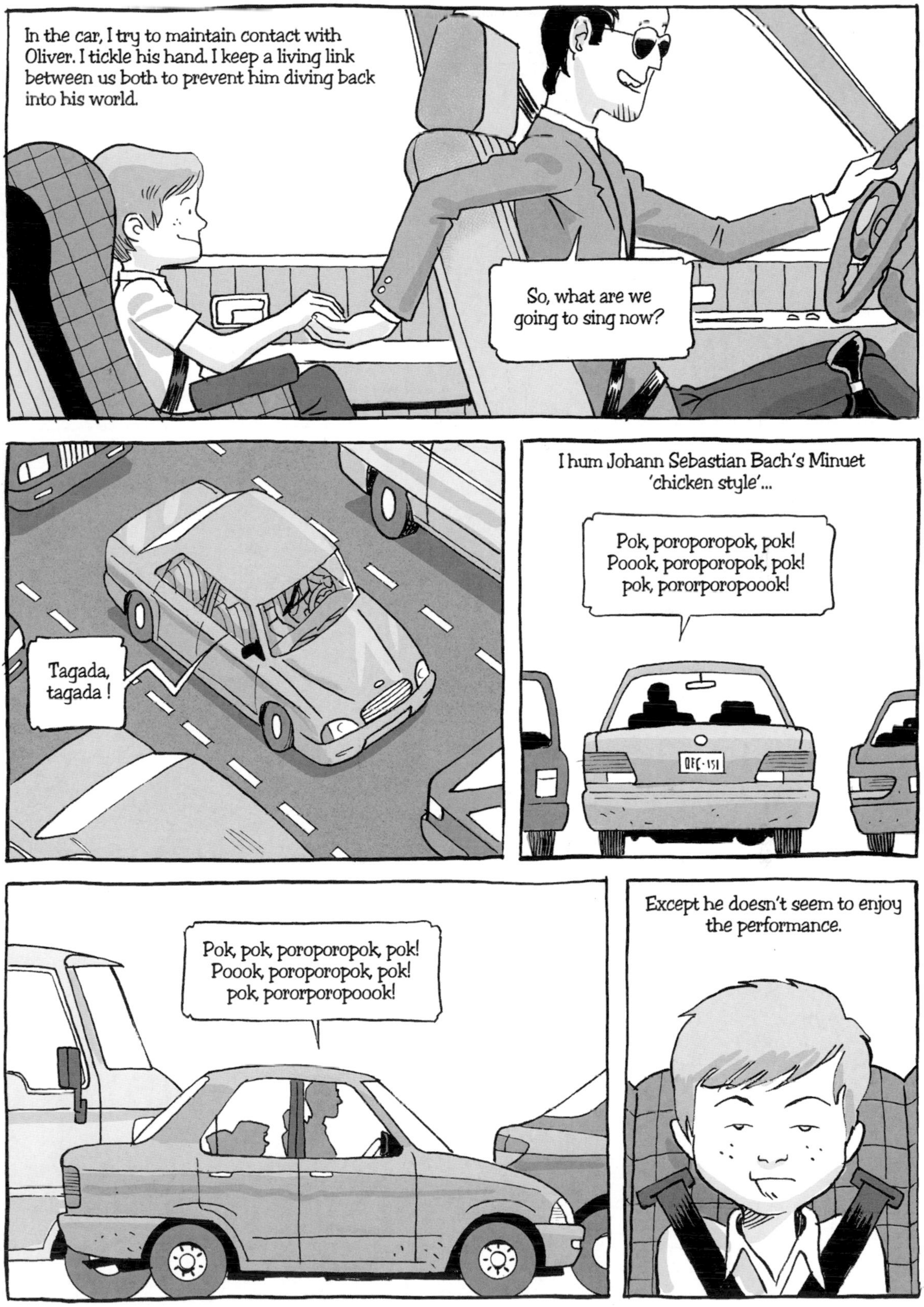
In the car, I try to maintain contact with Oliver. I tickle his hand. I keep a living link between us both to prevent him diving back into his world.
So, what are we going to sing now?
Tagada, tagada !
I hum Johann Sebastian Bach's Minuet 'chicken style'...
Pok, poroporopok, pok! Poook, poroporopok, pok! pok, pororporopoook!
Pok, pok, poroporopok, pok! Poook, poroporopok, pok! pok, pororporopoook!
Except he doesn't seem to enjoy the performance.

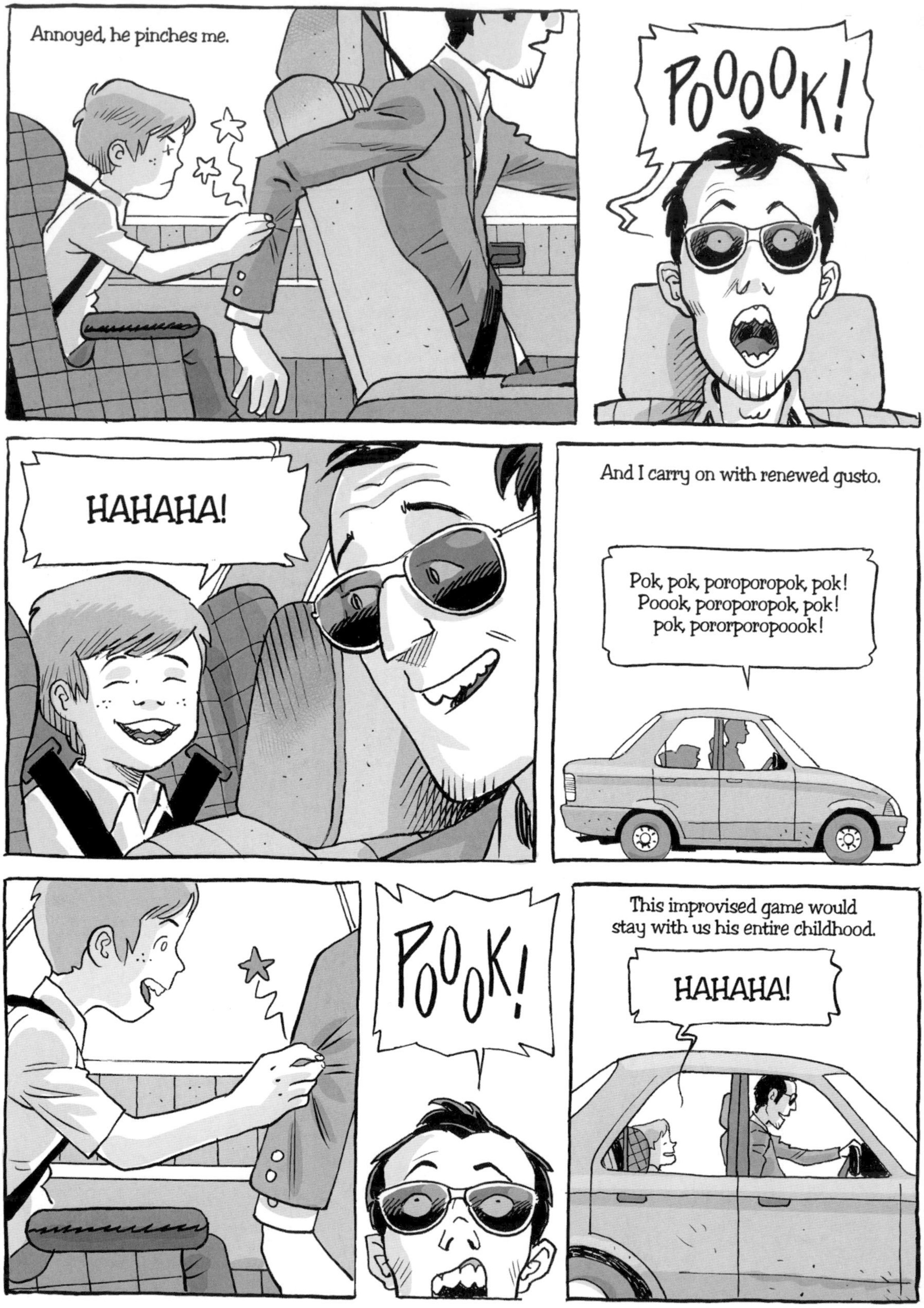
Annoyed, he pinches me.
POOOOK!
HAHAHA!
And I carry on with renewed gusto.
Pok, pok, poroporopok, pok! Poook, poroporopok, pok! pok, pororporopoook!
POOOK!
This improvised game would stay with us his entire childhood.
HAHAHA!

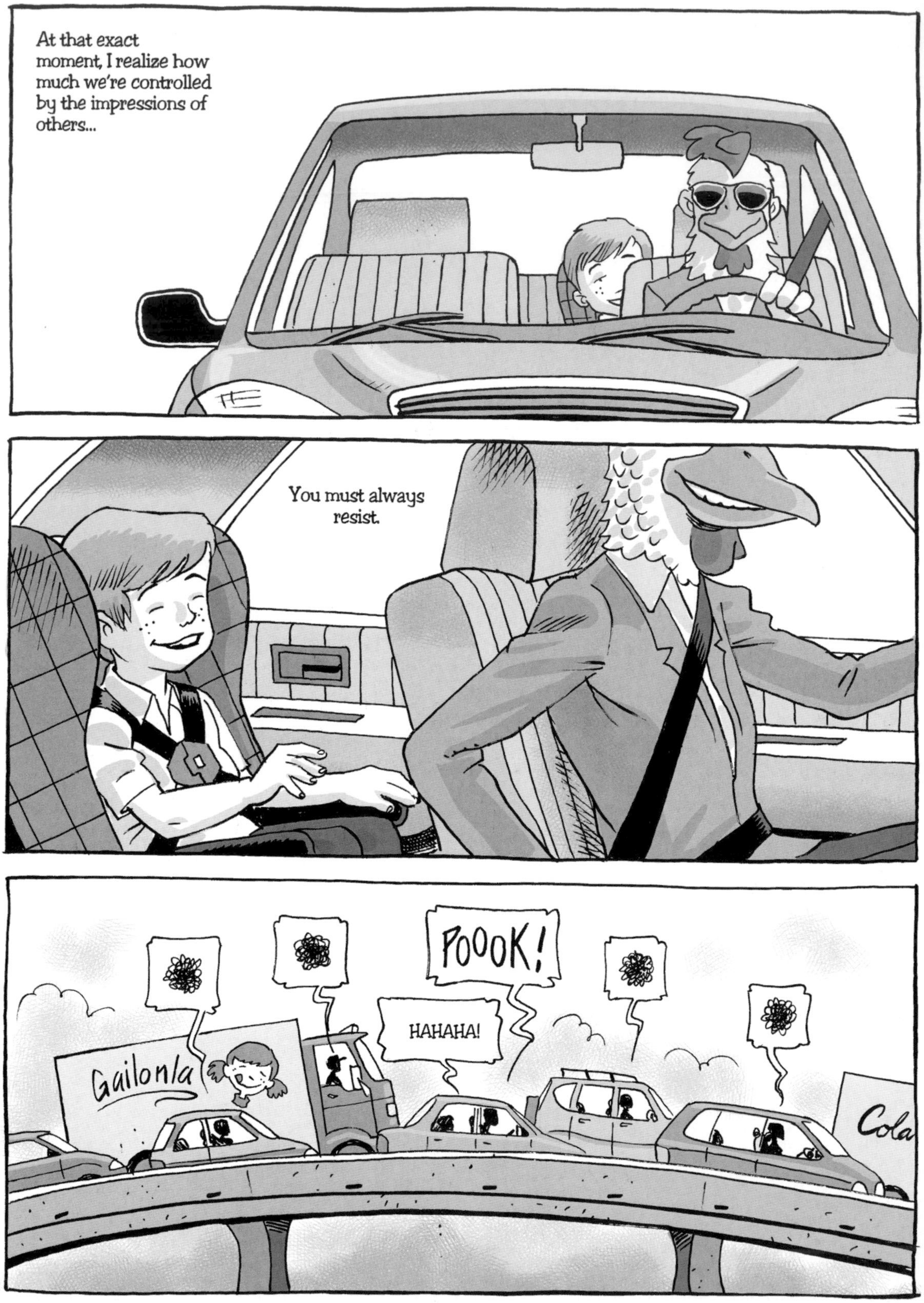
At that exact moment, I realize how much we're controlled by the impressions of others...
You must always resist.
Gailonla
POOOK!
HAHAHA!
Cola

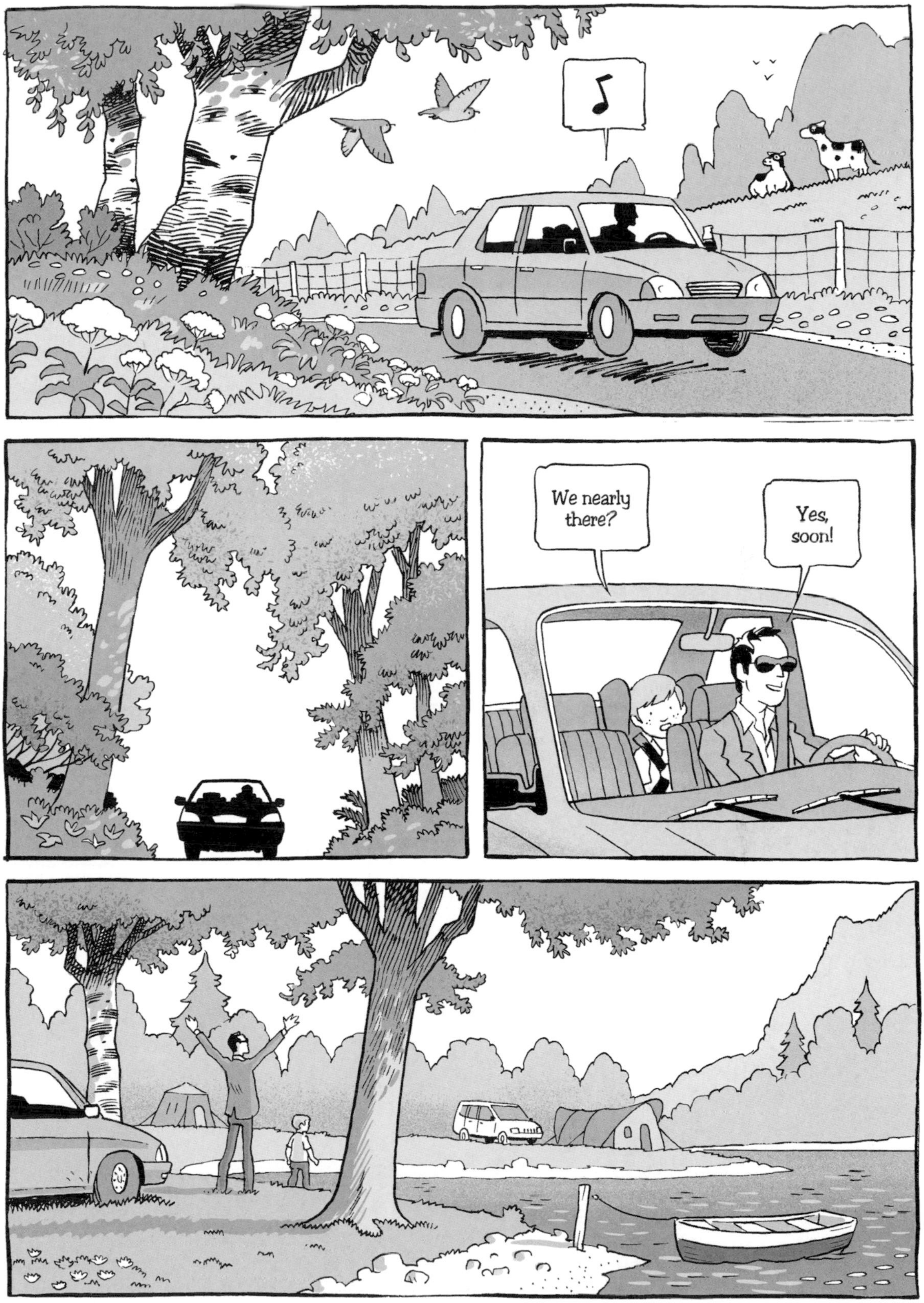
We nearly there?
Yes, soon!

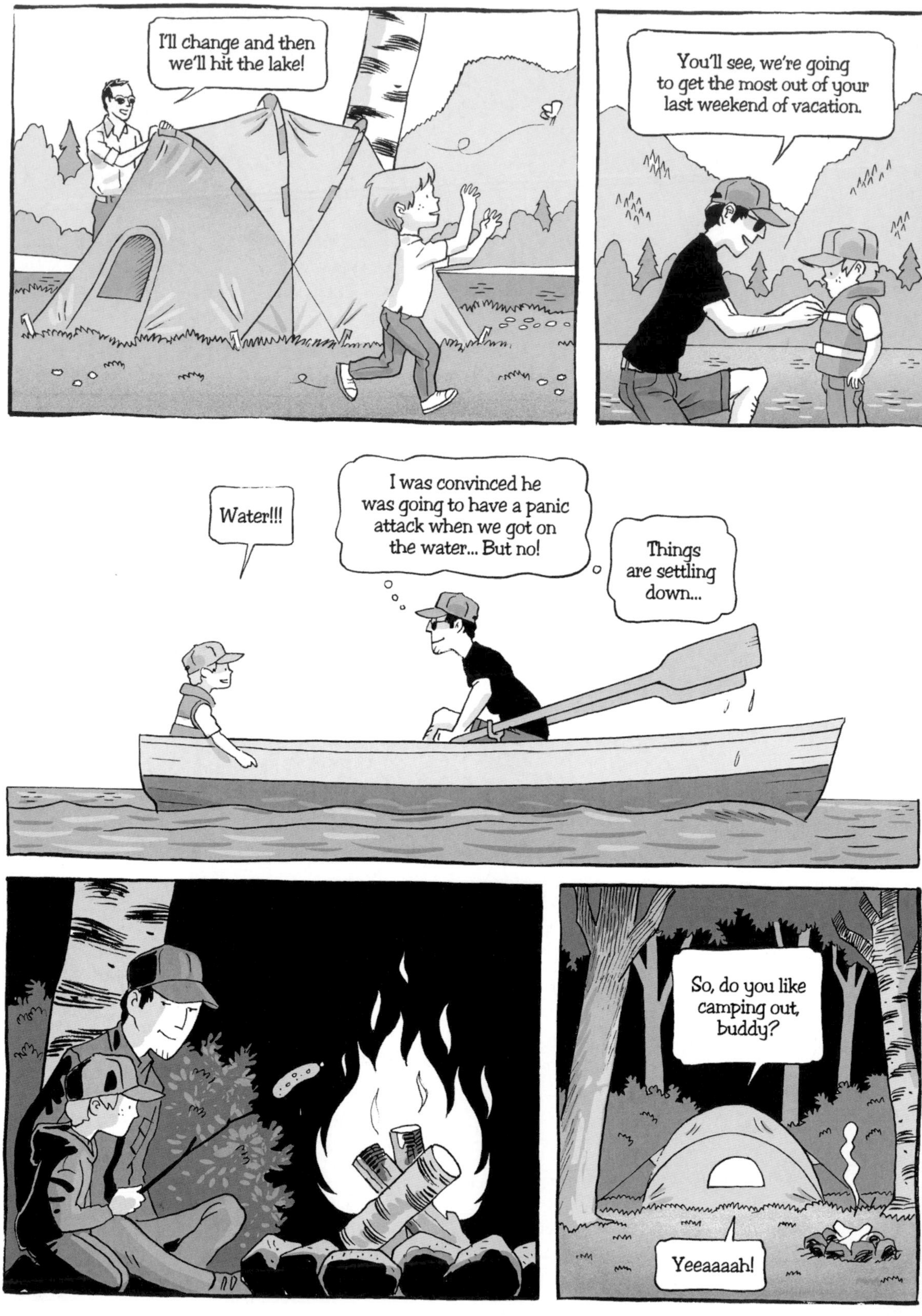
I'll change and then we'll hit the lake!
You'll see, we're going to get the most out of your last weekend of vacation.
Water!!!
I was convinced he was going to have a panic attack when we got on the water... But no!
Things are settling down...
So, do you like camping out, buddy?
Yeeaaaah!

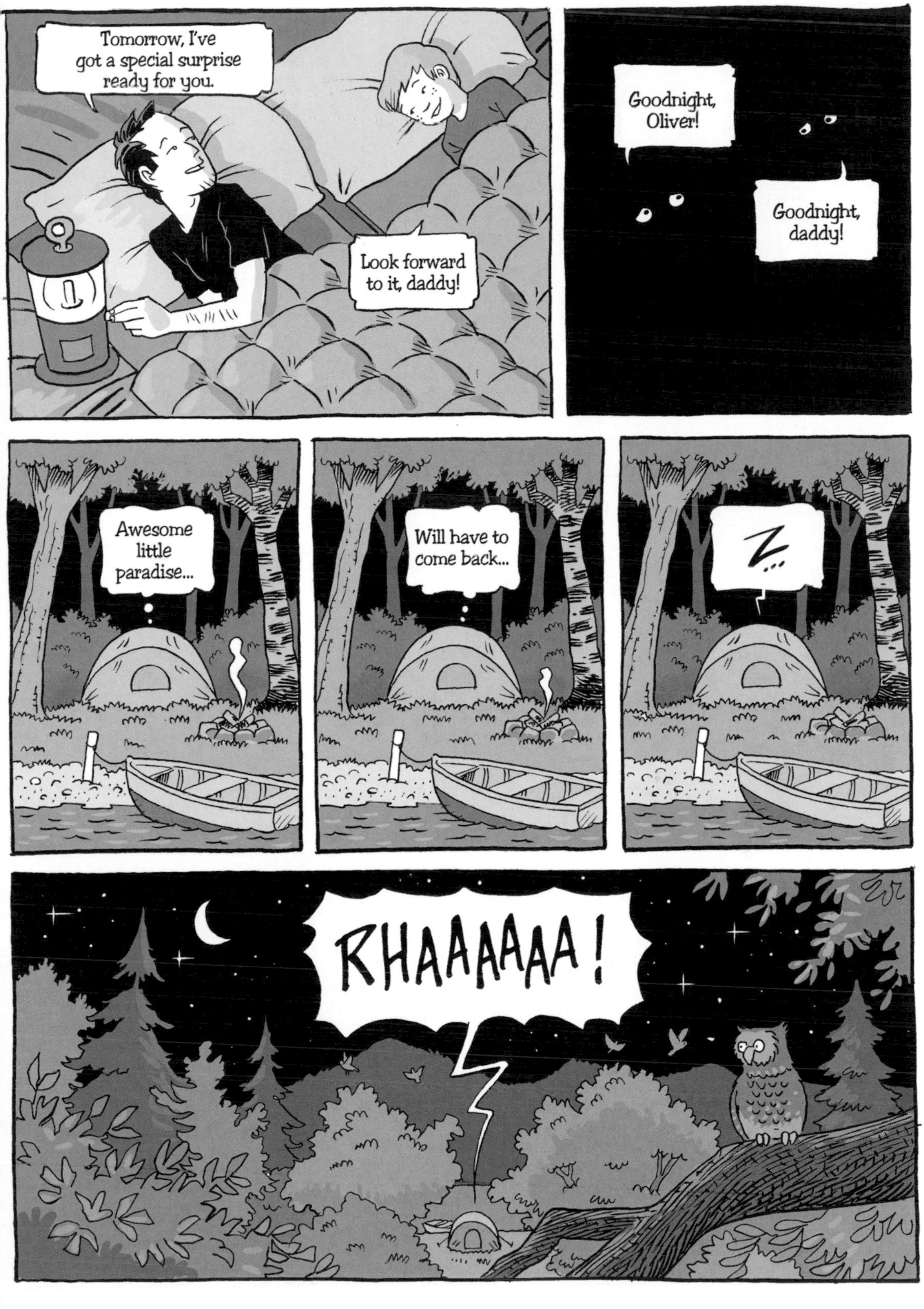
Tomorrow, I've got a special surprise ready for you.
Look forward to it, daddy!
Goodnight, Oliver!
Goodnight, daddy!
Awesome little paradise...
Will have to come back...
Z...
RHAAAAAA!

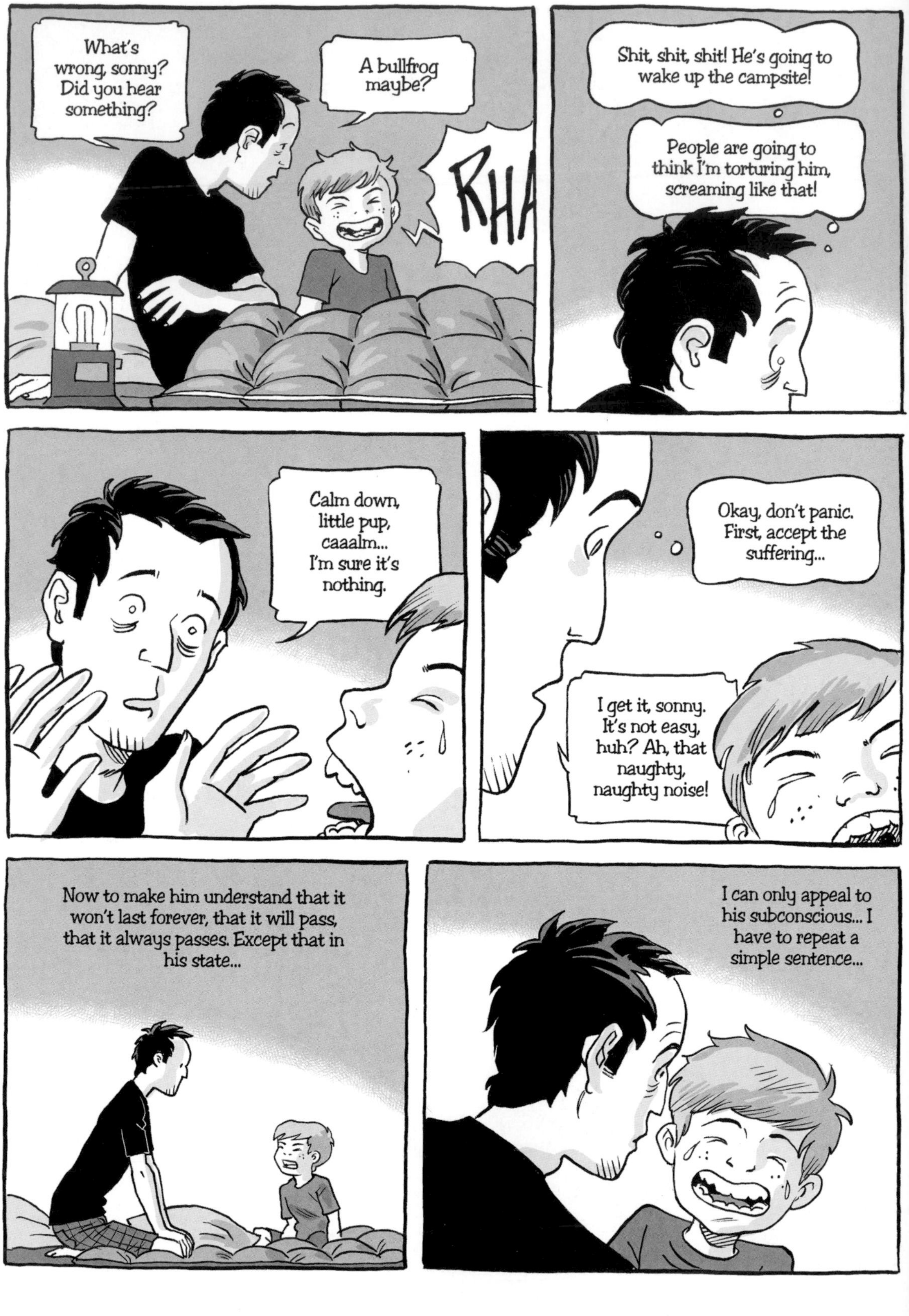
What's wrong, sonny? Did you hear something?
A bullfrog maybe?
RHA
Shit, shit, shit! He's going to wake up the campsite!
People are going to think I'm torturing him, screaming like that!
Calm down, little pup, caaalm... I'm sure it's nothing.
Okay, don't panic. First, accept the suffering...
I get it, sonny. It's not easy, huh? Ah, that naughty, naughty noise!
Now to make him understand that it won't last forever, that it will pass, that it always passes. Except that in his state...
I can only appeal to his subconscious... I have to repeat a simple sentence...

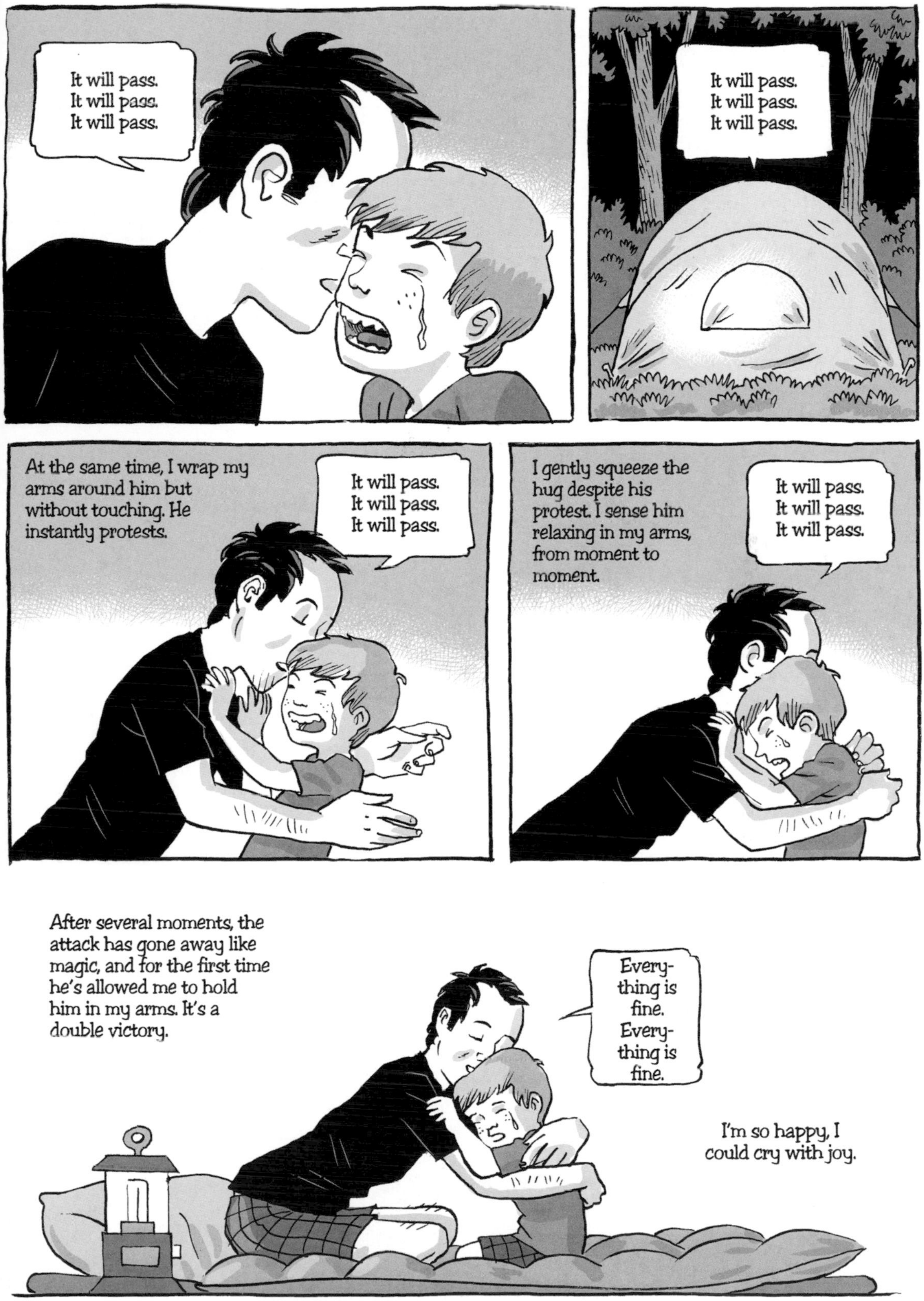
It will pass.
It will pass.
It will pass.
It will pass.
It will pass.
It will pass.
At the same time, I wrap my arms around him but without touching. He instantly protests.
It will pass.
It will pass.
It will pass.
I gently squeeze the hug despite his protest. I sense him relaxing in my arms, from moment to moment.
It will pass.
It will pass.
It will pass.
After several moments, the attack has gone away like magic, and for the first time he's allowed me to hold him in my arms. It's a double victory.
Every-thing is fine. Every-thing is fine.
I'm so happy, I could cry with joy.

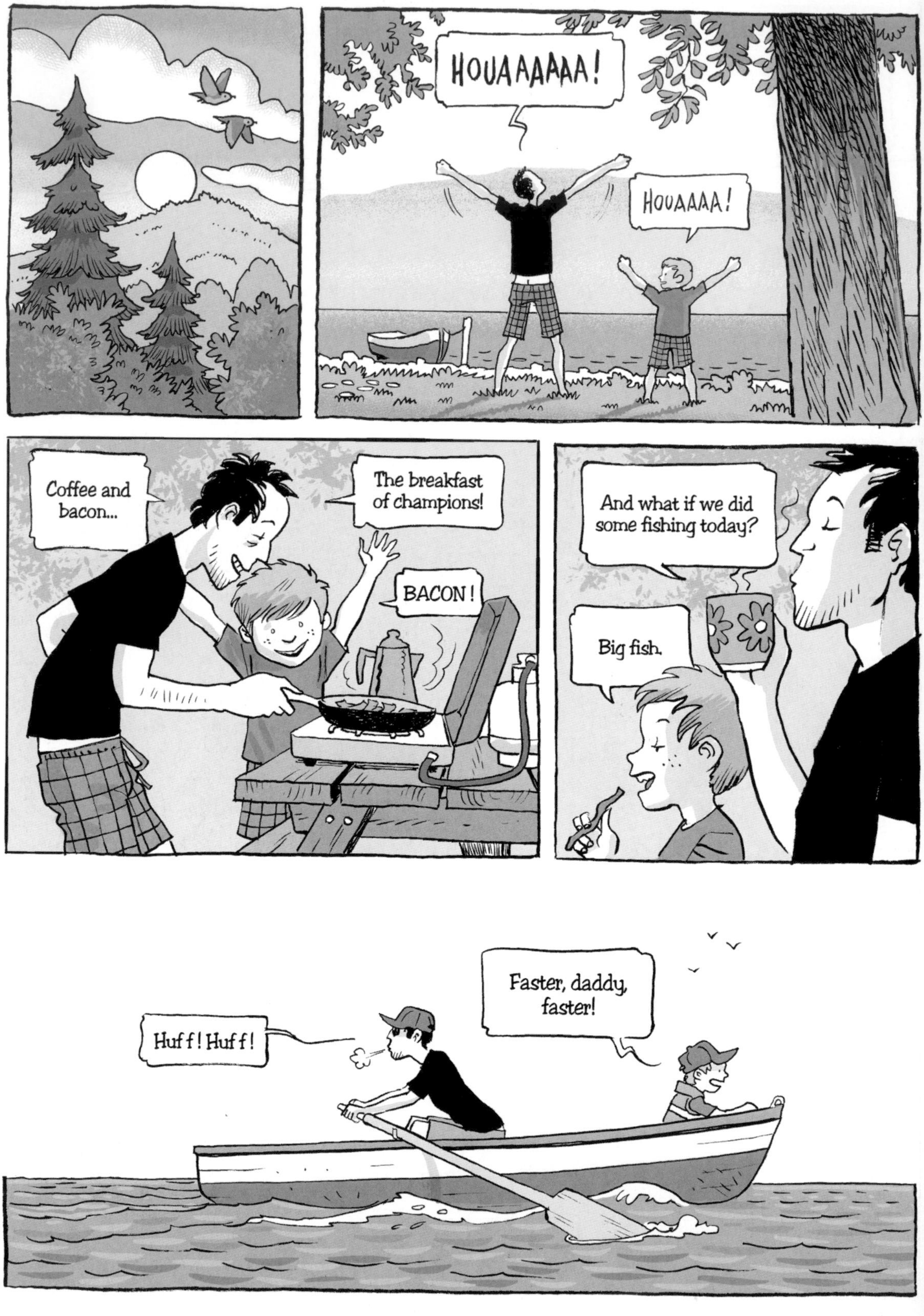
HOUAAAAAA!
HOUAAAA!
Coffee and bacon...
The breakfast of champions!
BACON!
And what if we did some fishing today?
Big fish.
Huff! Huff!
Faster, daddy, faster!

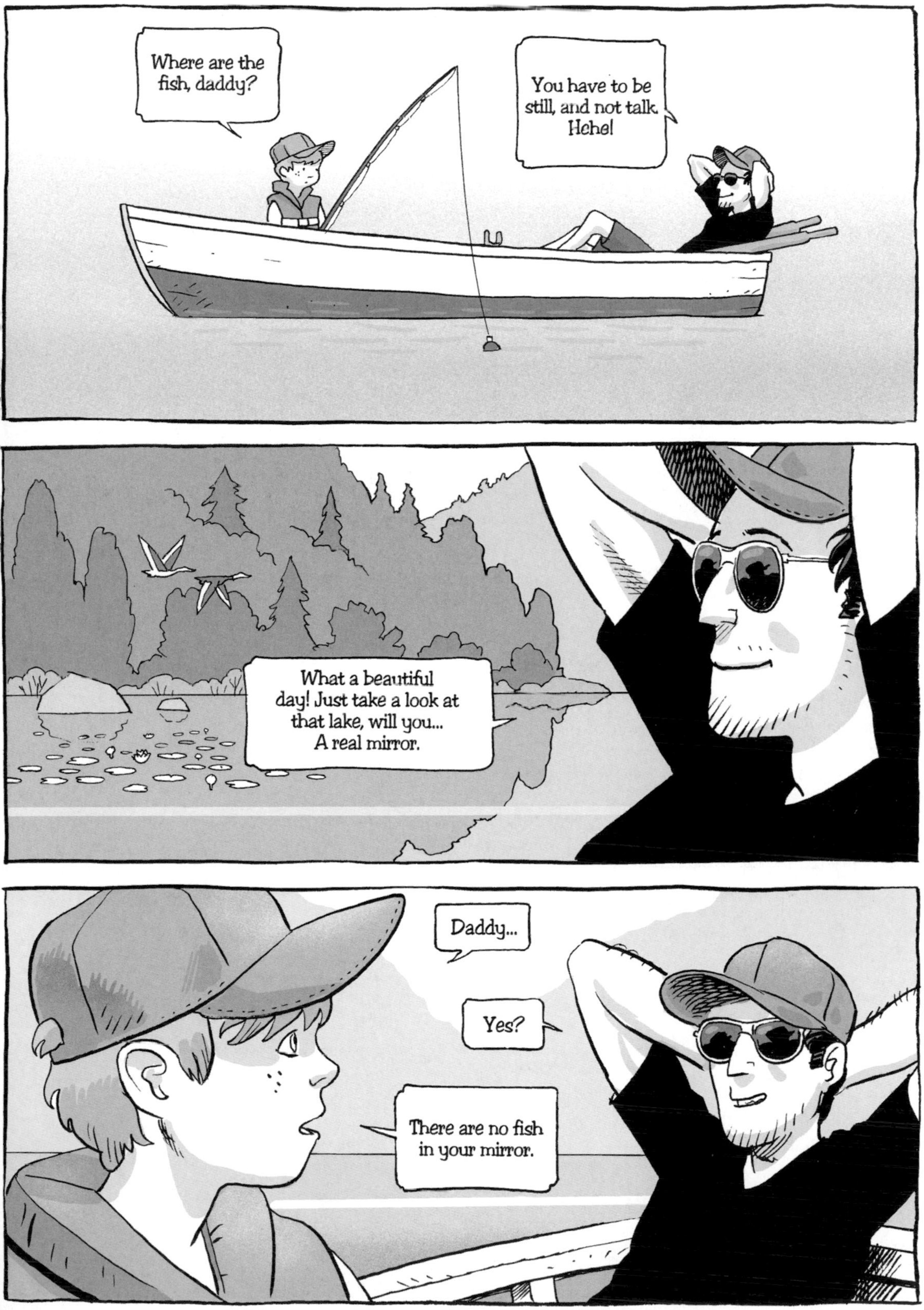
Where are the fish, daddy?
You have to be still, and not talk. Hehe!
What a beautiful day! Just take a look at that lake, will you... A real mirror.
Daddy...
Yes?
There are no fish in your mirror.

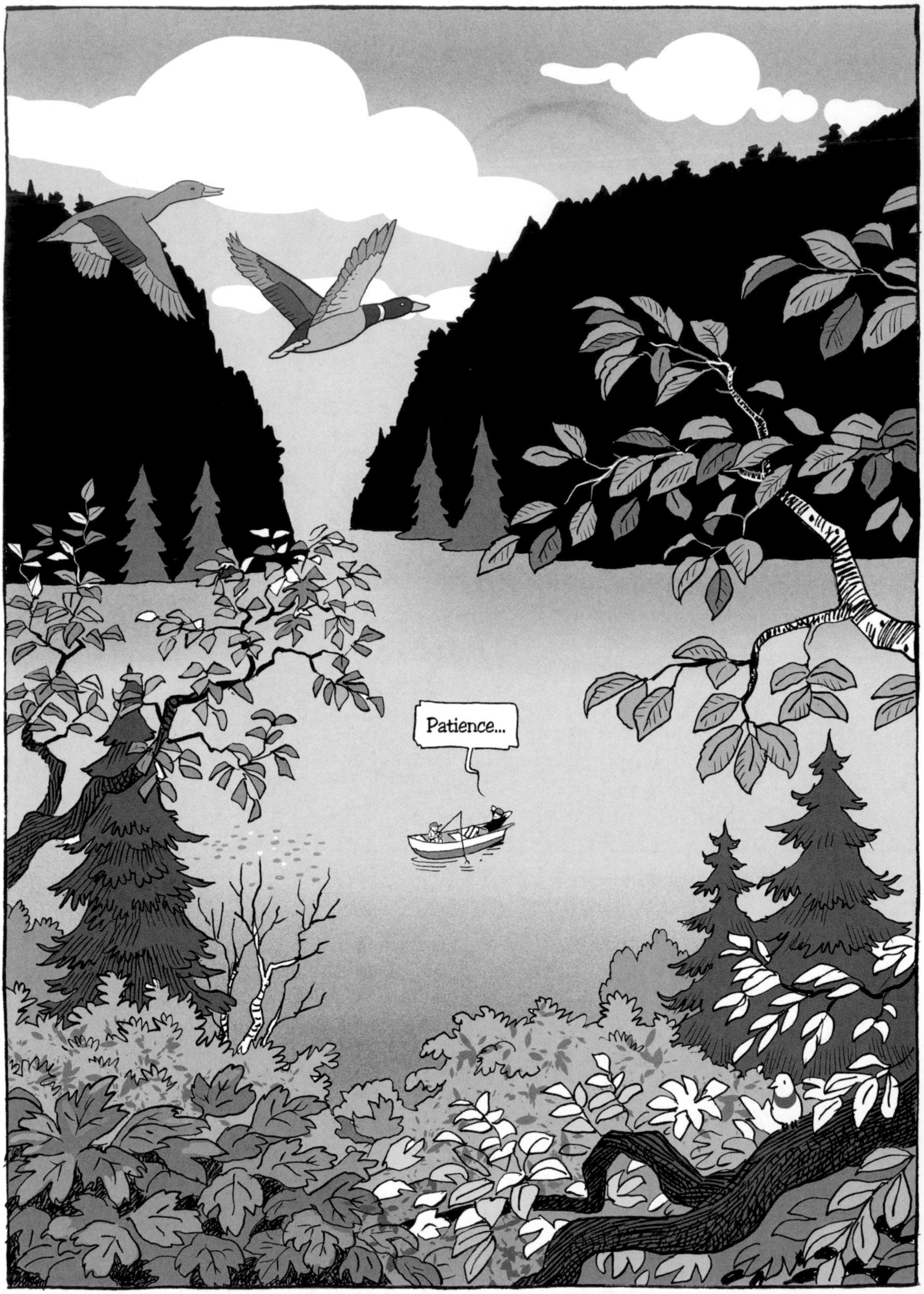
Patience...

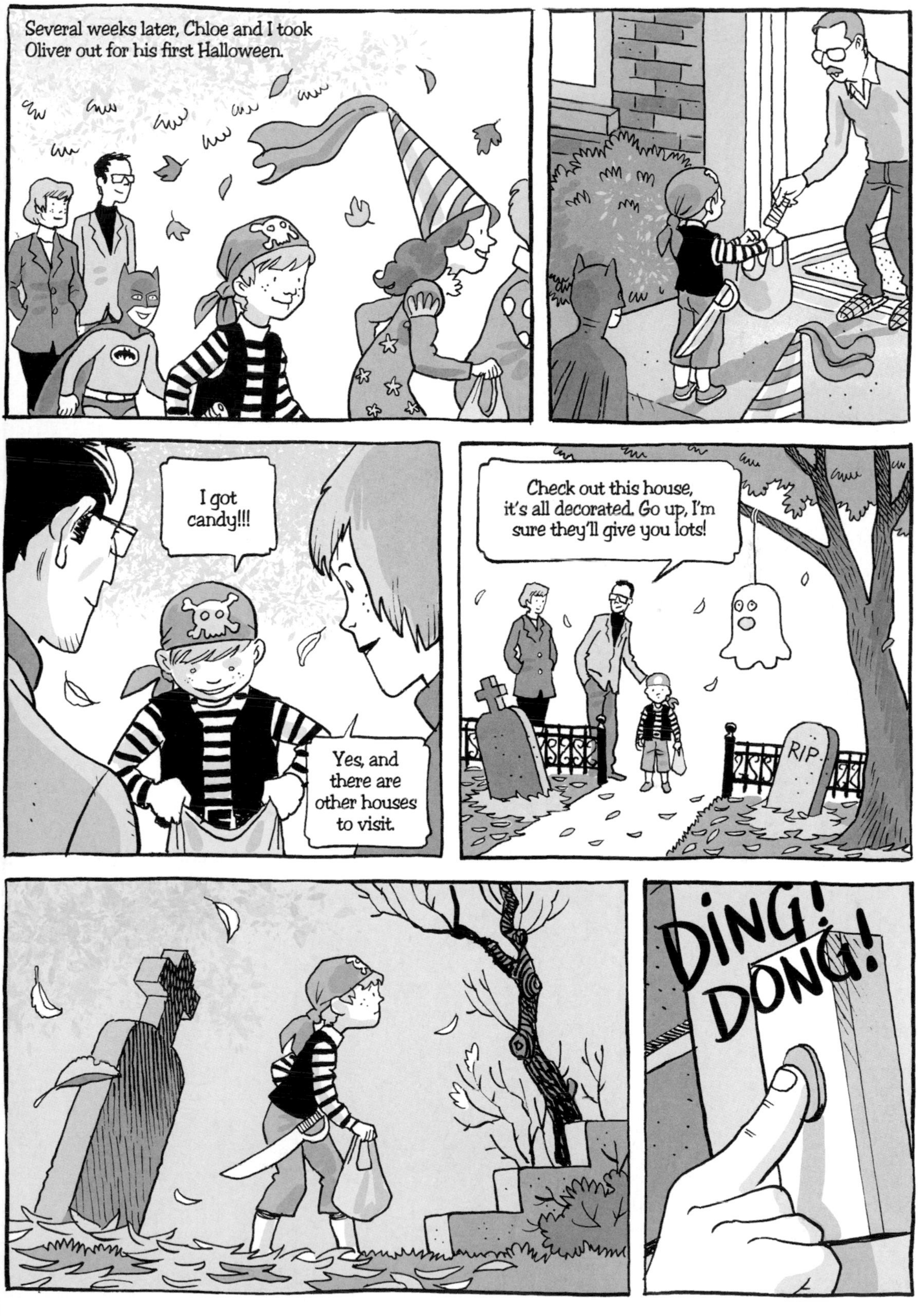
Several weeks later, Chloe and I took Oliver out for his first Halloween.
I got candy!!!
Yes, and there are other houses to visit.
Check out this house, it's all decorated. Go up, I'm sure they'll give you lots!
RIP
DING! DONG!

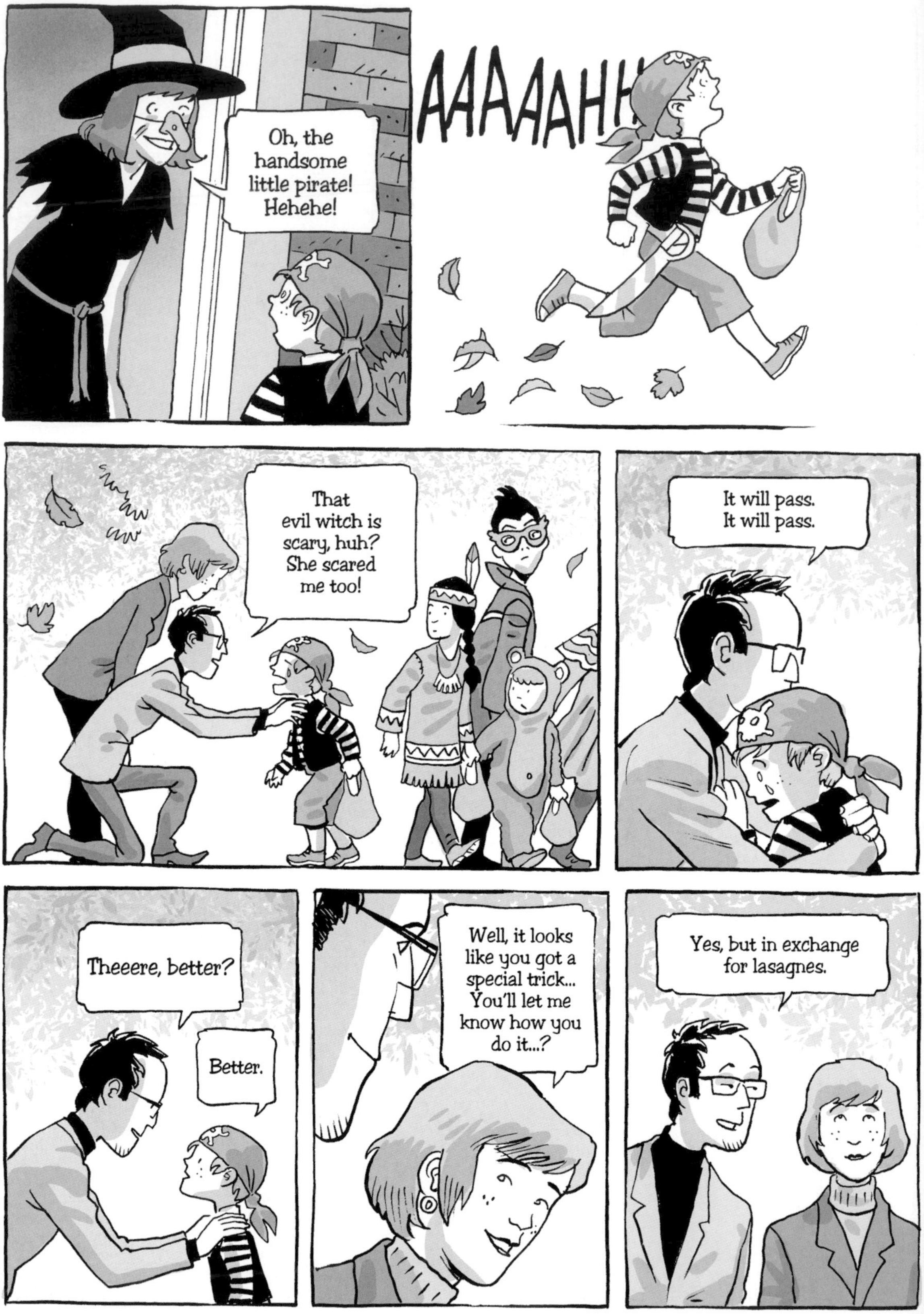
Oh, the handsome little pirate! Hehehe!
AAAAAHH
That evil witch is scary, huh? She scared me too!
It will pass. It will pass.
Theeere, better?
Better.
Well, it looks like you got a special trick... You'll let me know how you do it...?
Yes, but in exchange for lasagnes.

Time passes. Oliver's schooling at The Spark changes things a lot. He's making good progress.

We're all working in the same direction, if not with the same methods.

I carry on doing things my way. I feel the combination of both approaches could make some gains.

There is so much to learn about autism.

One thing is certain: the more Oliver is able to make eye contact with me...

...The more those other interventions work. It's like a release.

The eyes.
The eyes.
The eyes.

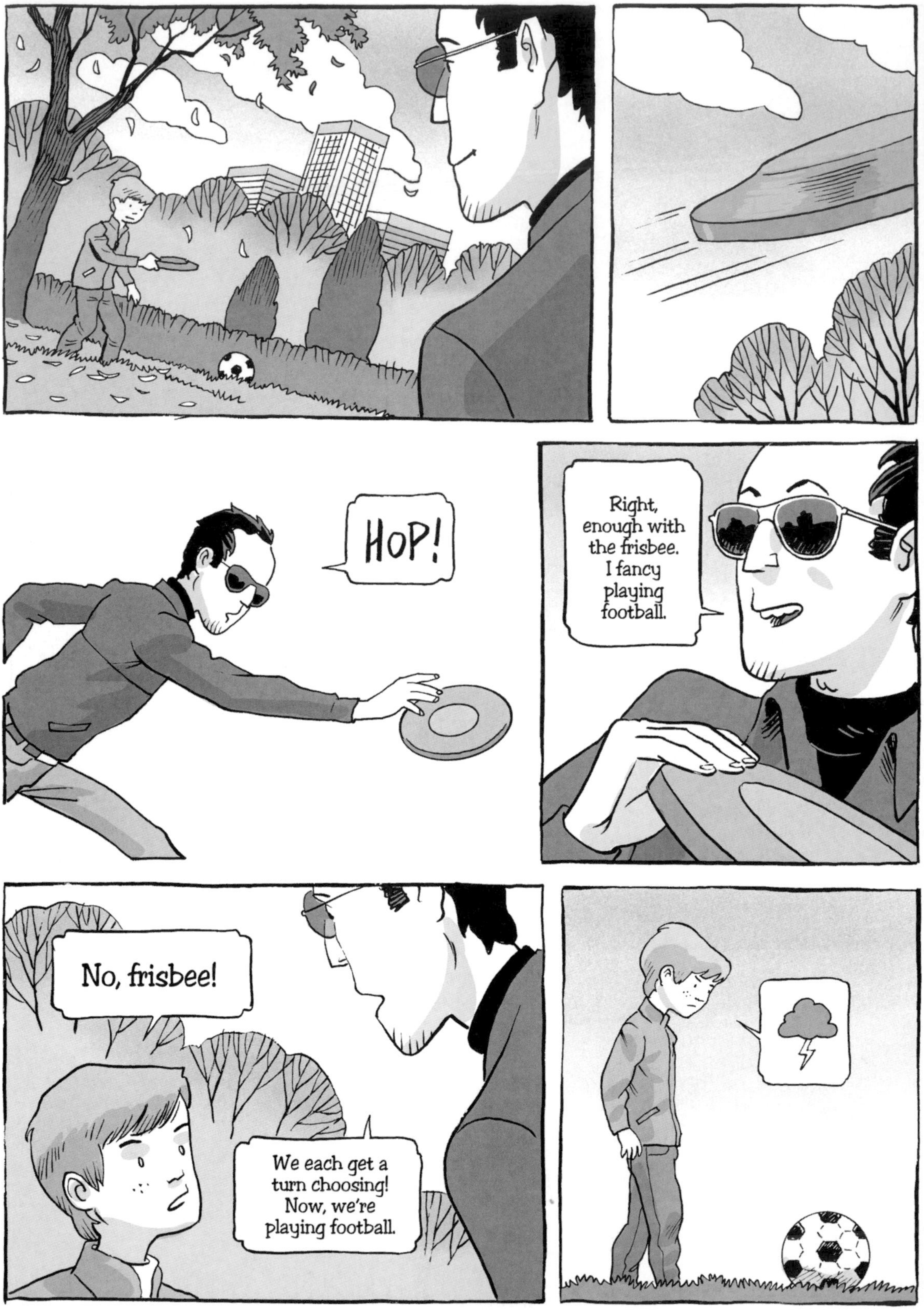
HOP!
Right, enough with the frisbee. I fancy playing football.
No, frisbee!
We each get a turn choosing! Now, we're playing football.

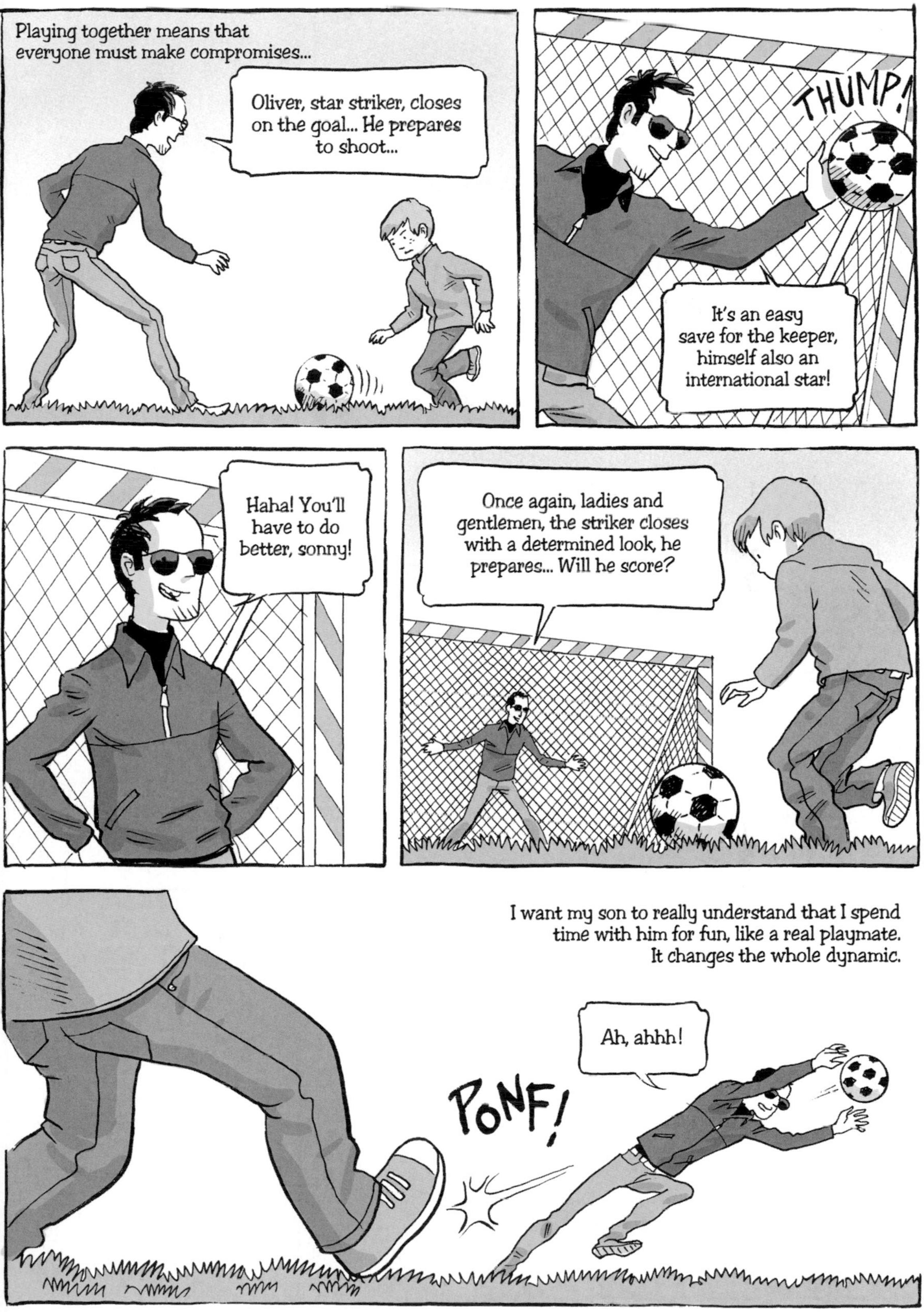
Playing together means that everyone must make compromises...
Oliver, star striker, closes on the goal... He prepares to shoot...
THUMP!
It's an easy save for the keeper, himself also an international star!
Haha! You'll have to do better, sonny!
Once again, ladies and gentlemen, the striker closes with a determined look, he prepares... Will he score?
I want my son to really understand that I spend time with him for fun, like a real playmate. It changes the whole dynamic.
Ah, ahhh!
PONF!

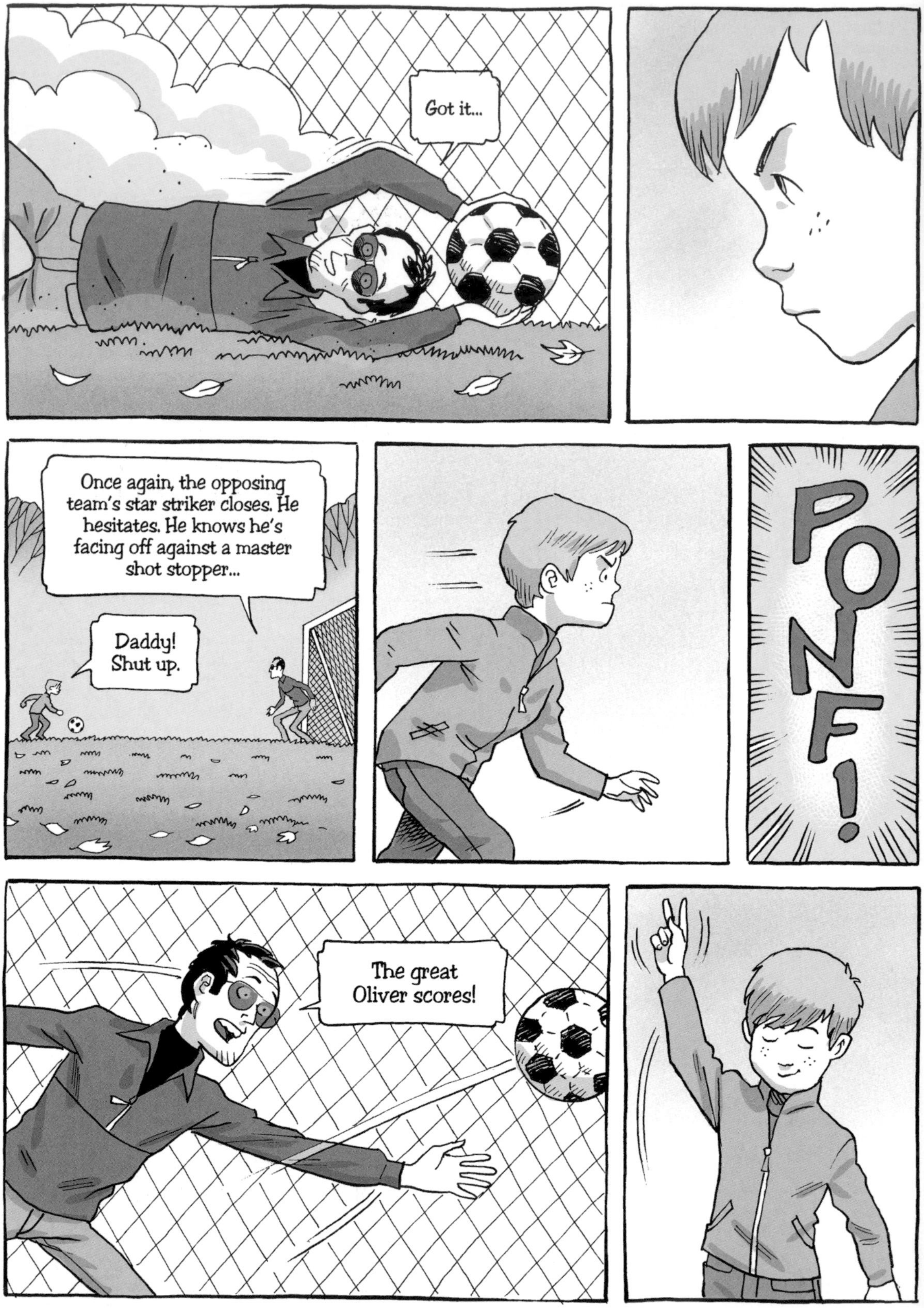
Got it...
Once again, the opposing team's star striker closes. He hesitates. He knows he's facing off against a master shot stopper...
Daddy! Shut up.
PONF!
The great Oliver scores!

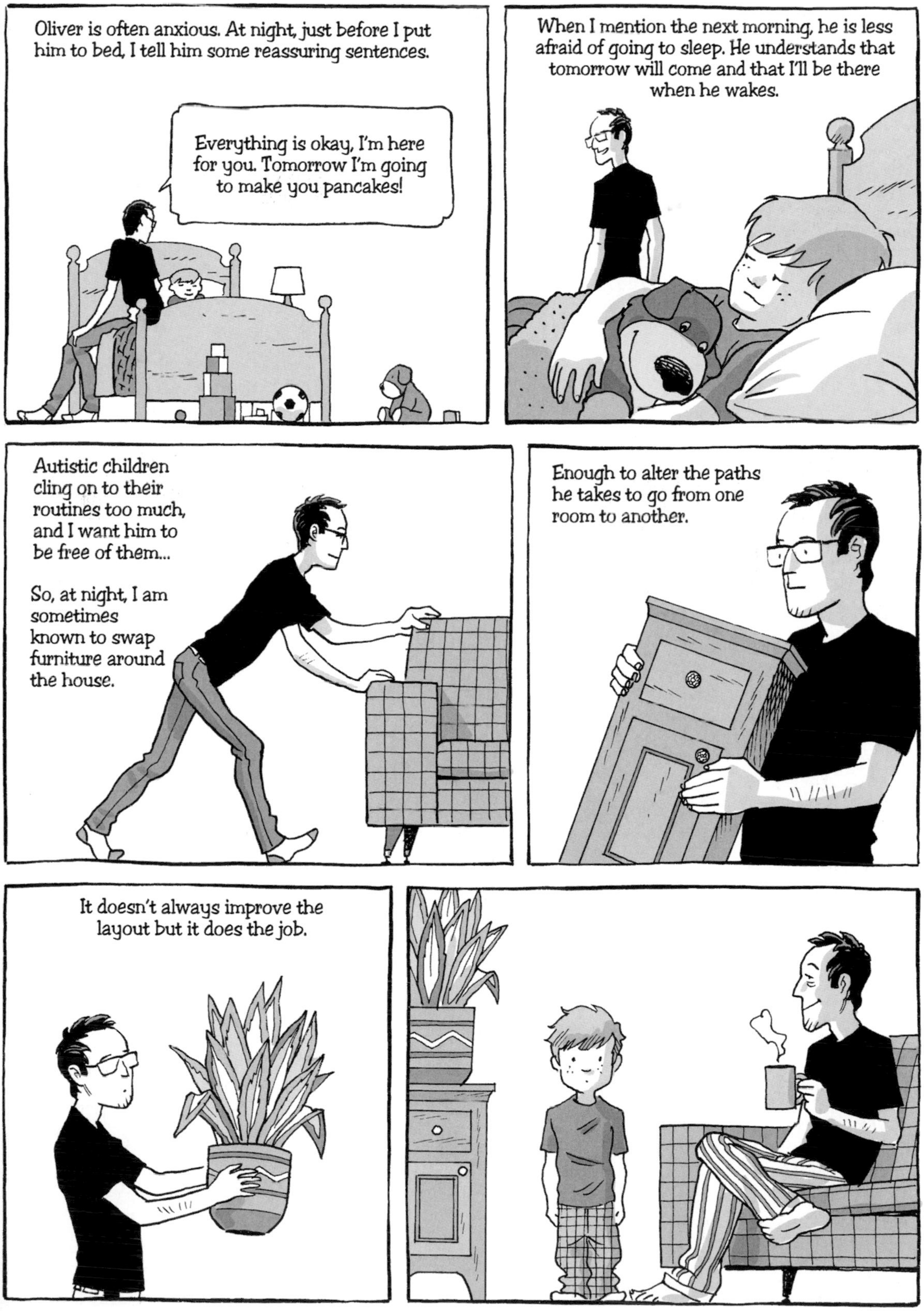

Oliver is often anxious. At night, just before I put him to bed, I tell him some reassuring sentences.
Everything is okay, I'm here for you. Tomorrow I'm going to make you pancakes!
When I mention the next morning, he is less afraid of going to sleep. He understands that tomorrow will come and that I'll be there when he wakes.
Autistic children cling on to their routines too much, and I want him to be free of them...
So, at night, I am sometimes known to swap furniture around the house.
Enough to alter the paths he takes to go from one room to another.
It doesn't always improve the layout but it does the job.

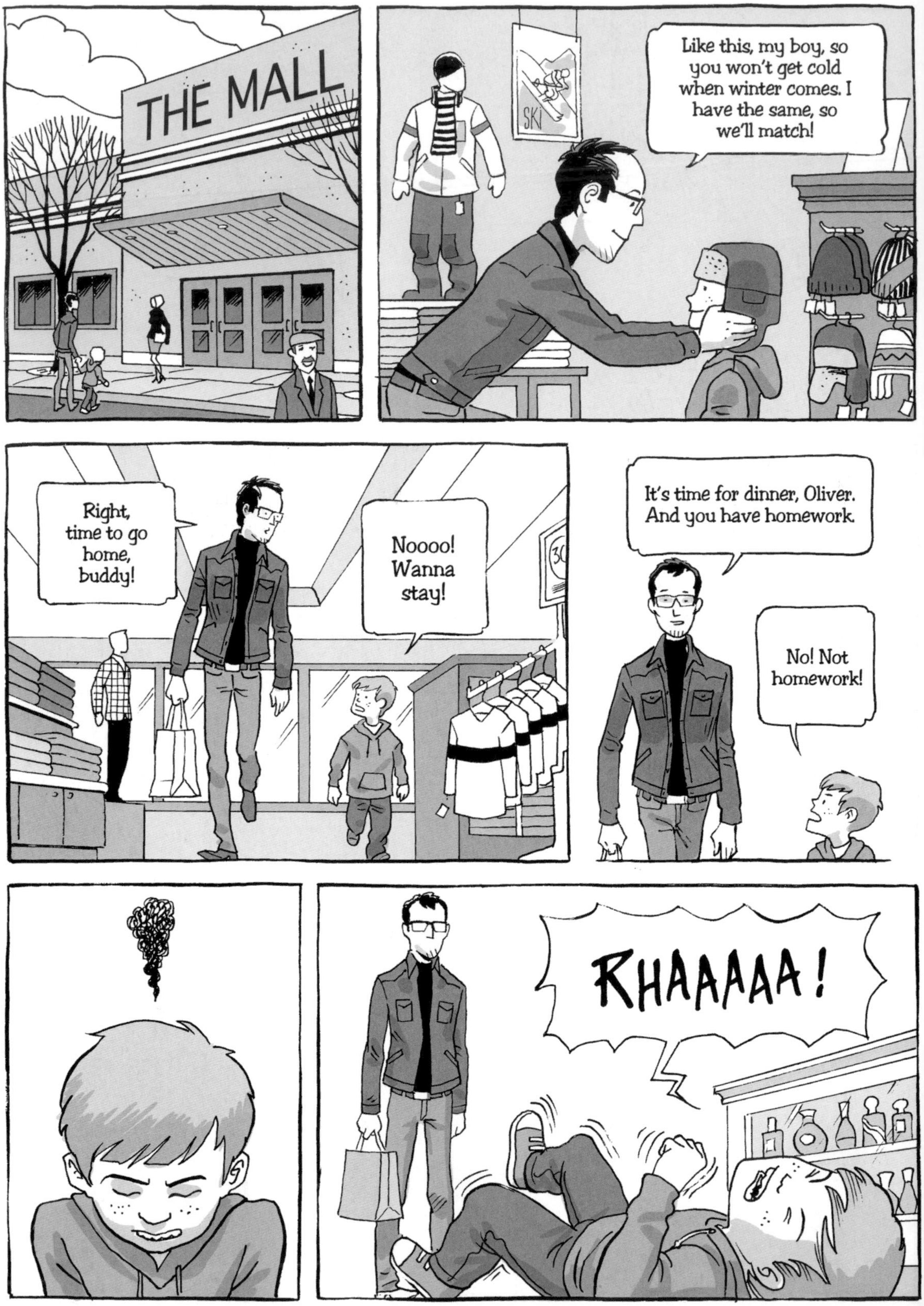
THE MALL
SKI
Like this, my boy, so you won't get cold when winter comes. I have the same, so we'll match!
Right, time to go home, buddy!
Noooo! Wanna stay!
It's time for dinner, Oliver. And you have homework.
No! Not homework!
RHAAAAA!

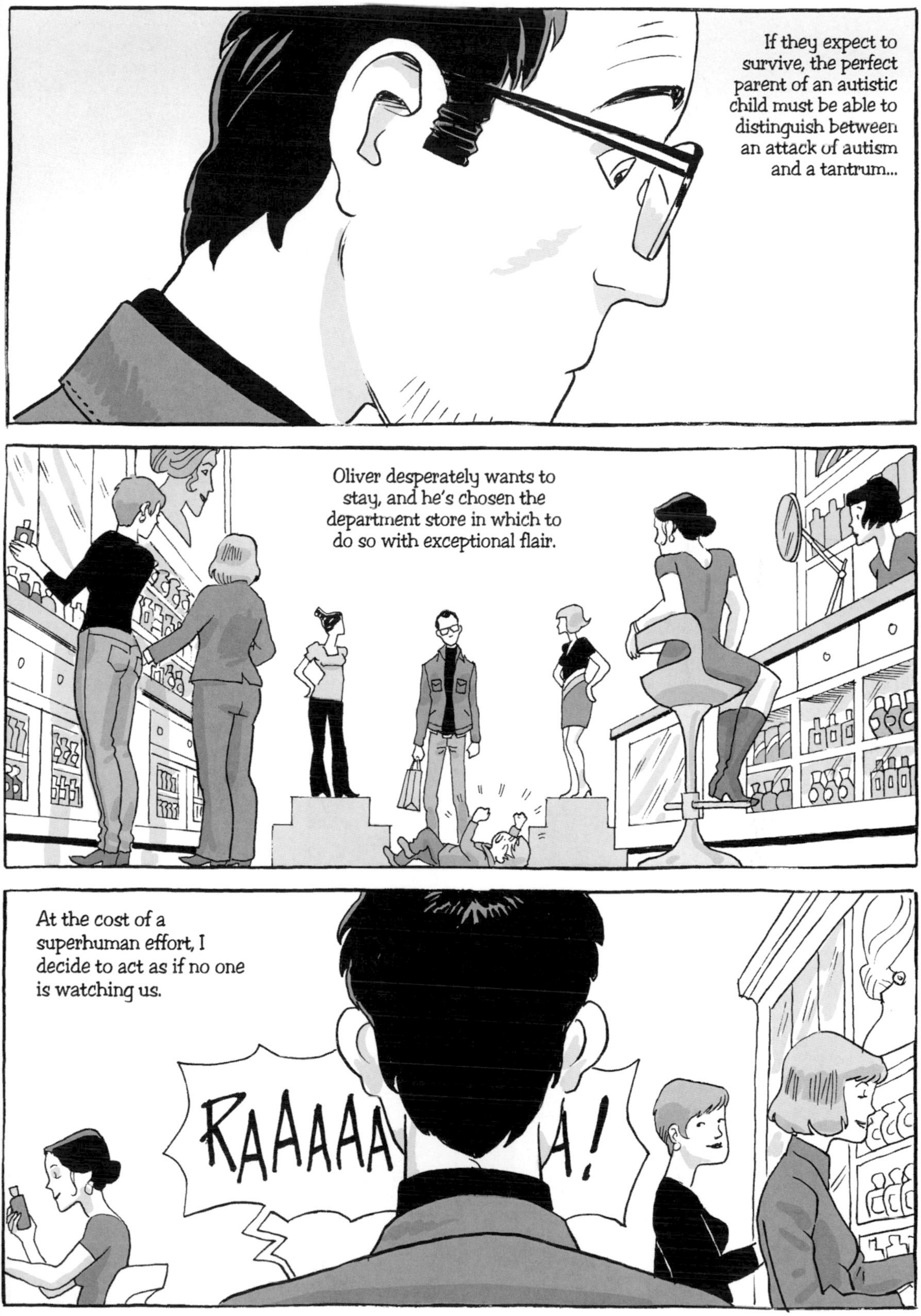
If they expect to survive, the perfect parent of an autistic child must be able to distinguish between an attack of autism and a tantrum...
Oliver desperately wants to stay, and he's chosen the department store in which to do so with exceptional flair.
At the cost of a superhuman effort, I decide to act as if no one is watching us.
RAAAAA
A!

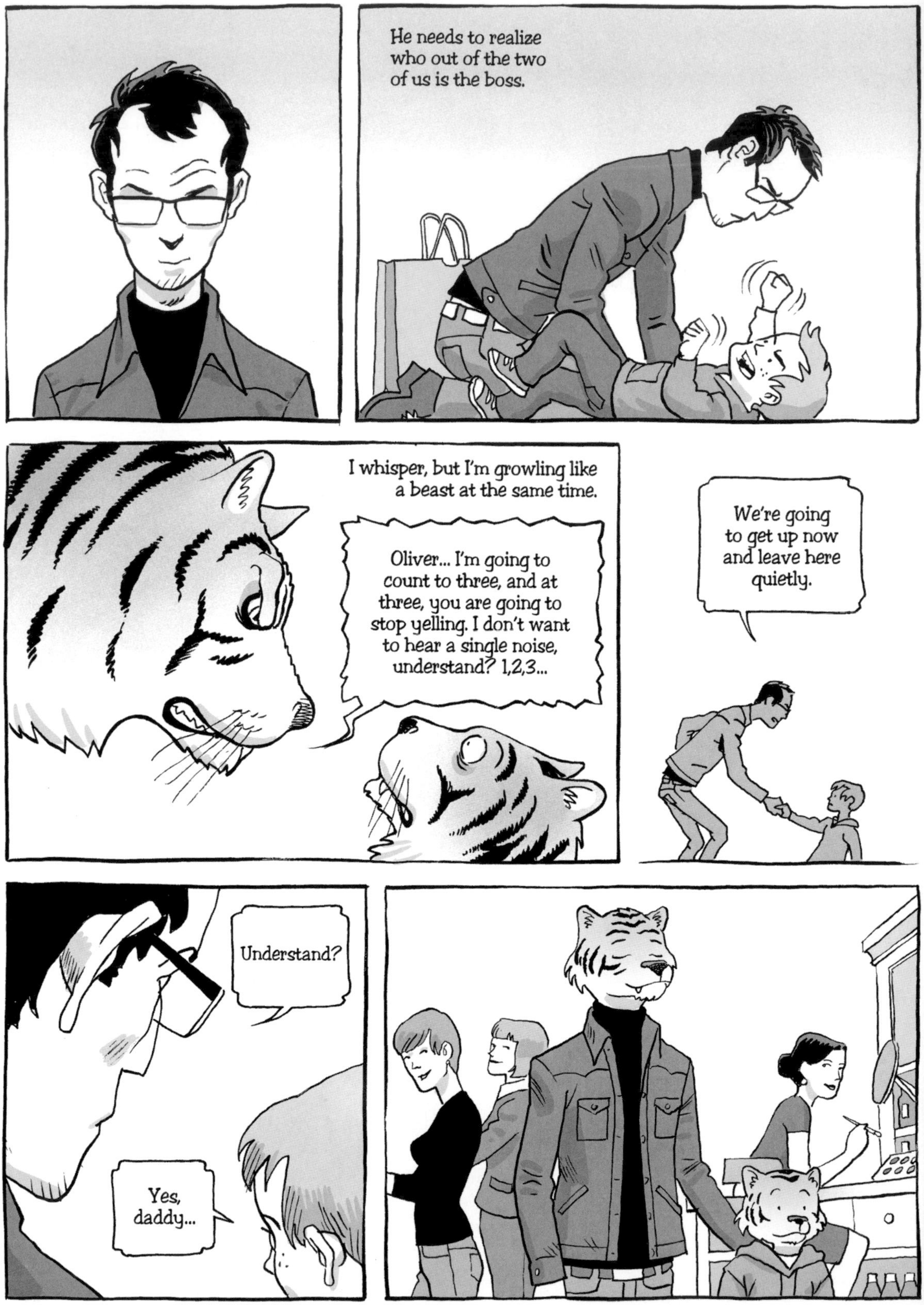
He needs to realize who out of the two of us is the boss.
I whisper, but I'm growling like a beast at the same time.
Oliver... I'm going to count to three, and at three, you are going to stop yelling. I don't want to hear a single noise, understand? 1,2,3...
We're going to get up now and leave here quietly.
Understand?
Yes, daddy...

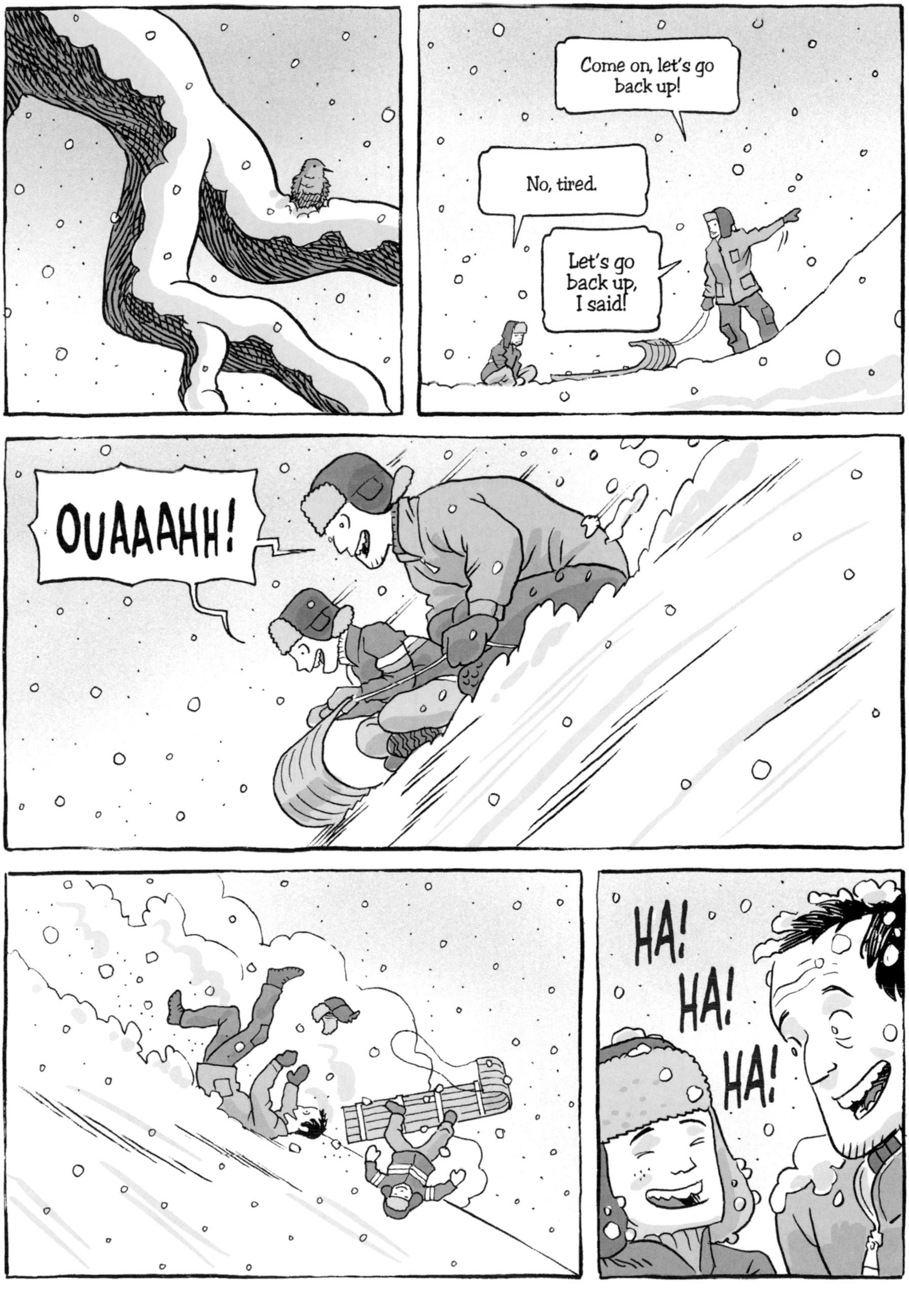
Come on, let's go back up!
No, tired.
Let's go back up, I said!
OUAAAHH!
HA! HA! HA!

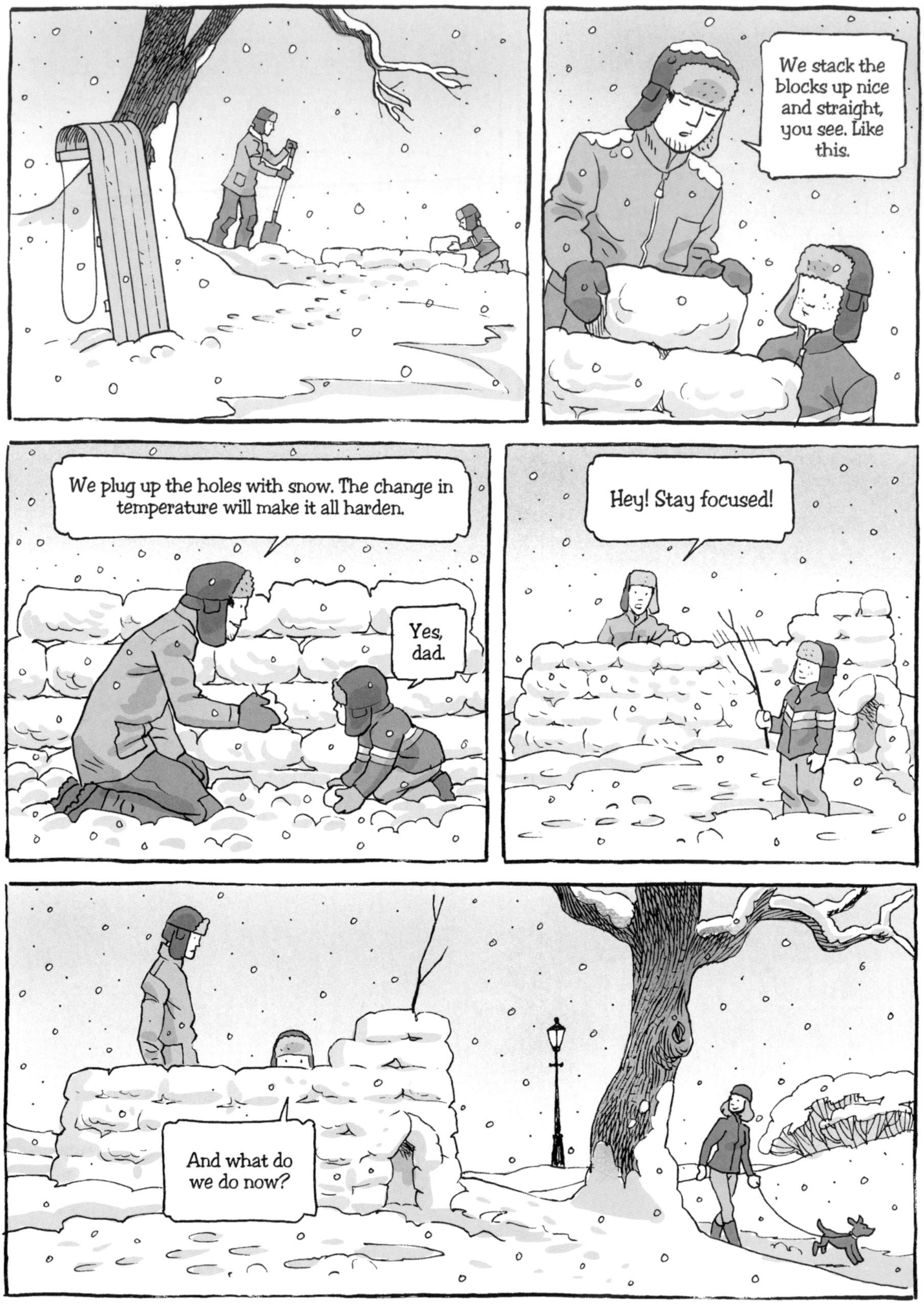
We stack the blocks up nice and straight, you see. Like this.
We plug up the holes with snow. The change in temperature will make it all harden.
Yes, dad.
Hey! Stay focused!
And what do we do now?

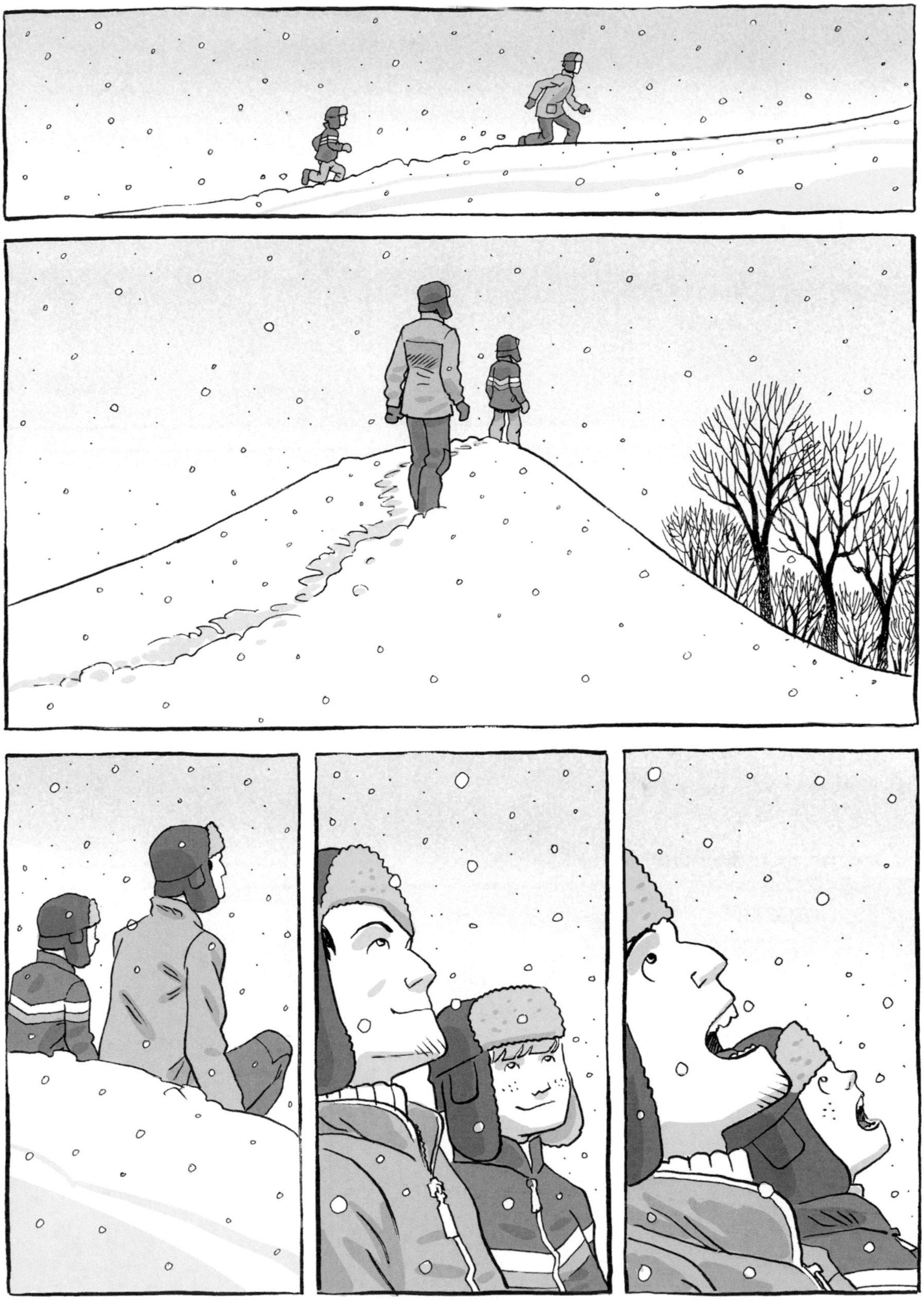

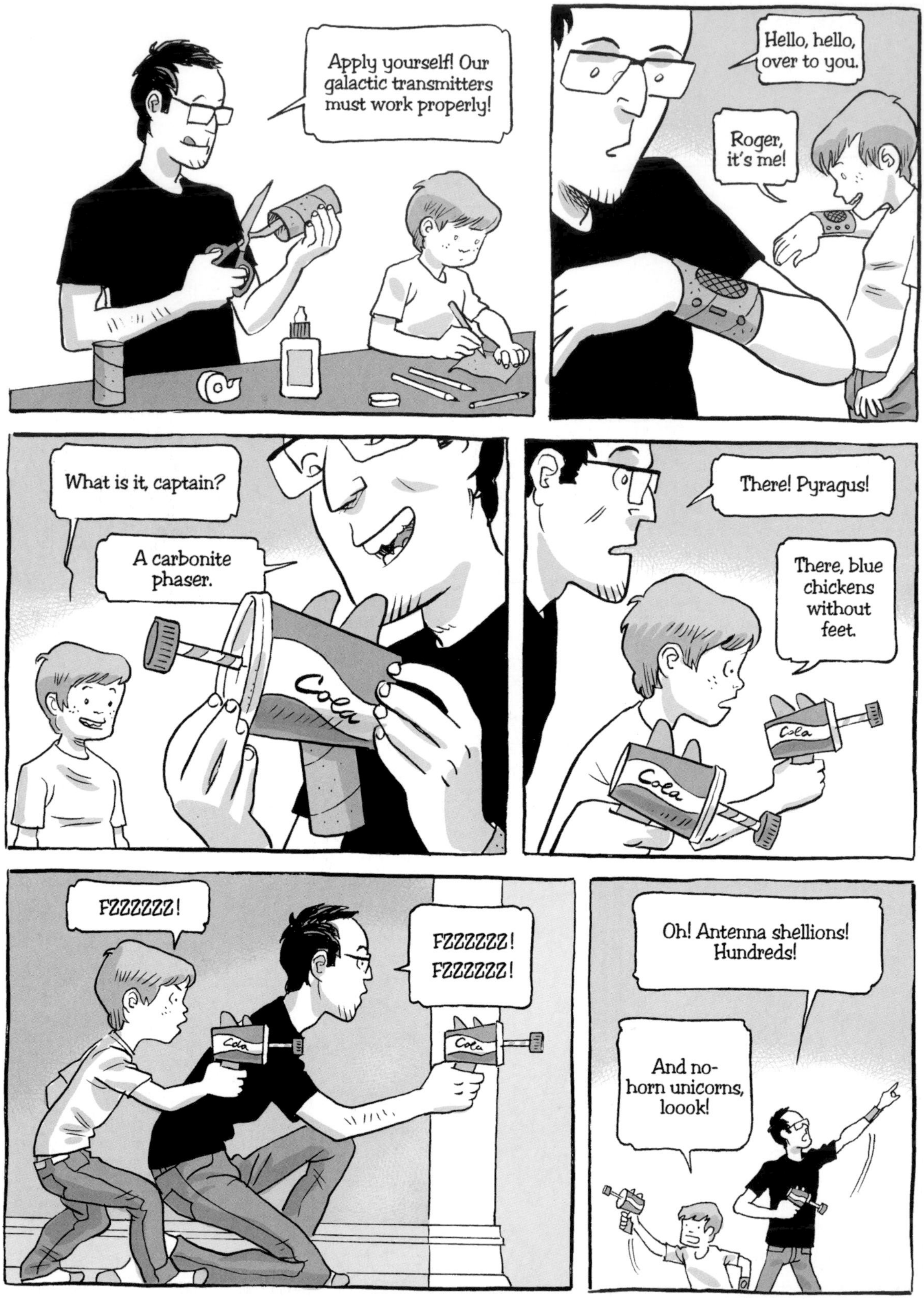
Apply yourself! Our galactic transmitters must work properly!
Hello, hello, over to you.
Roger, it's me!
What is it, captain?
A carbonite phaser.
Cola
There! Pyragus!
There, blue chickens without feet.
Cola
Cola
FZZZZZZ!
FZZZZZZ! FZZZZZZ!
Cola
Cola
Oh! Antenna shellions! Hundreds!
And no-horn unicorns, loook!

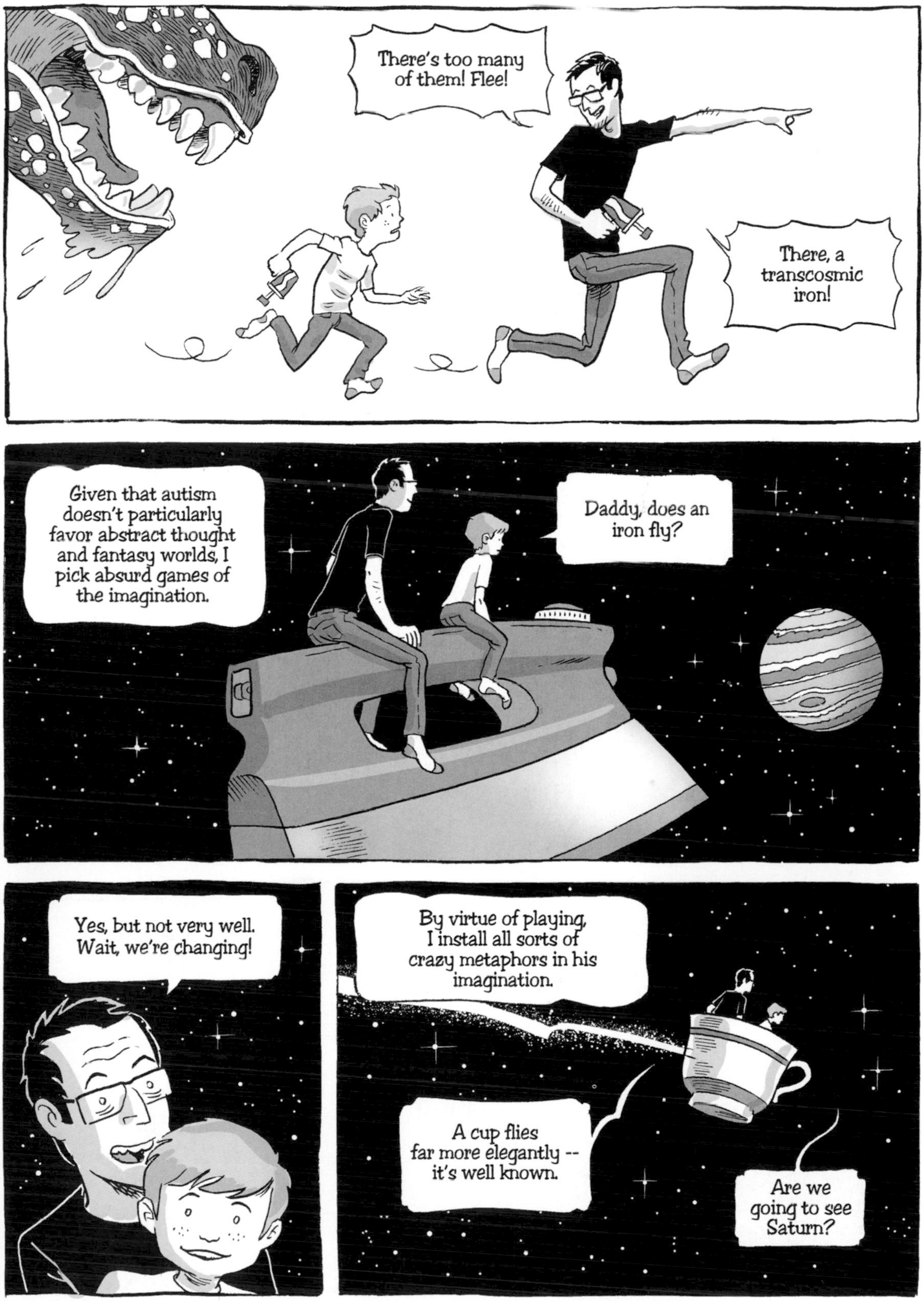
There's too many of them! Flee!
There, a transcosmic iron!
Given that autism doesn't particularly favor abstract thought and fantasy worlds, I pick absurd games of the imagination.
Daddy, does an iron fly?
Yes, but not very well. Wait, we're changing!
By virtue of playing, I install all sorts of crazy metaphors in his imagination.
A cup flies far more elegantly -- it's well known.
Are we going to see Saturn?

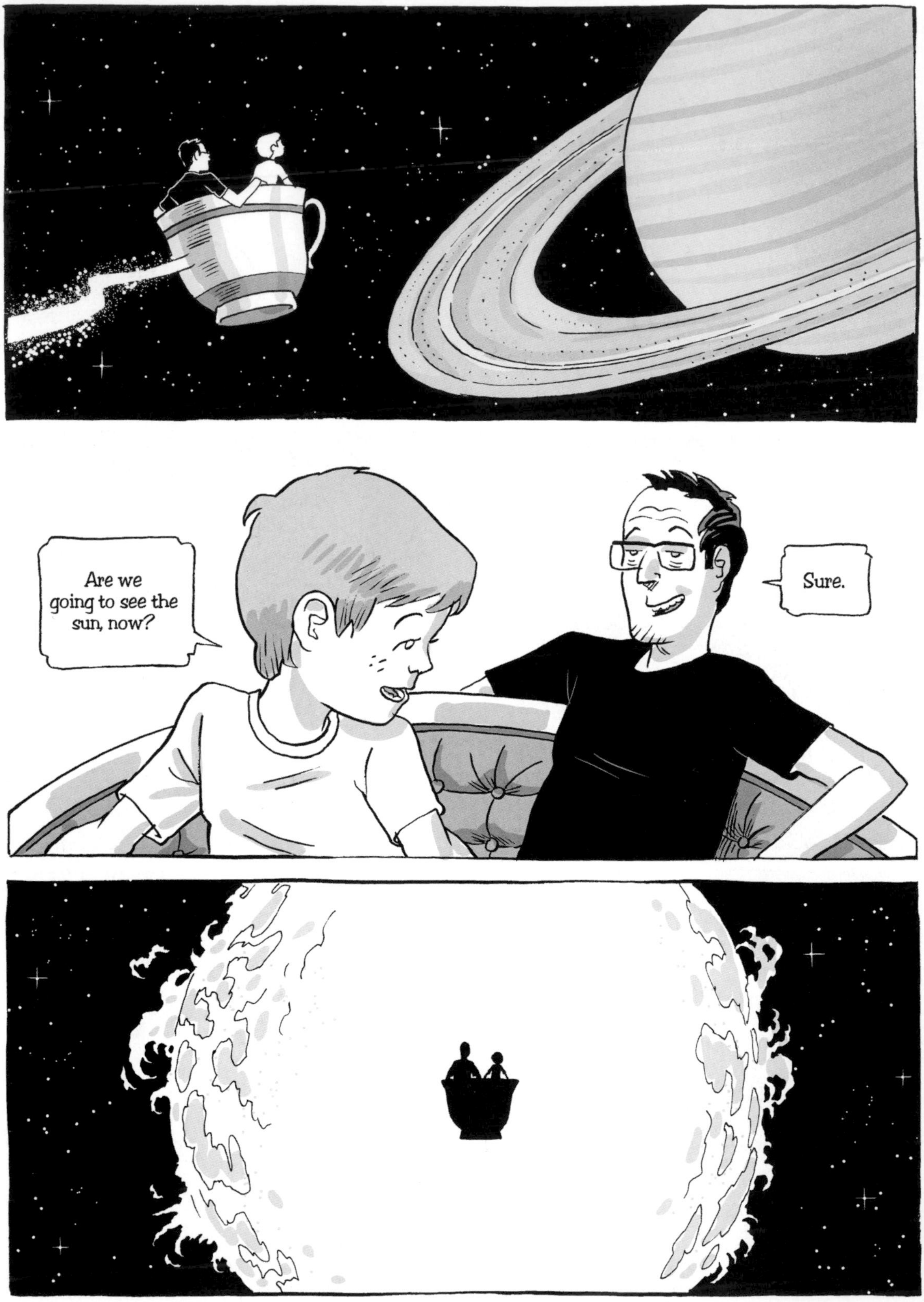
Are we going to see the sun, now?
Sure.

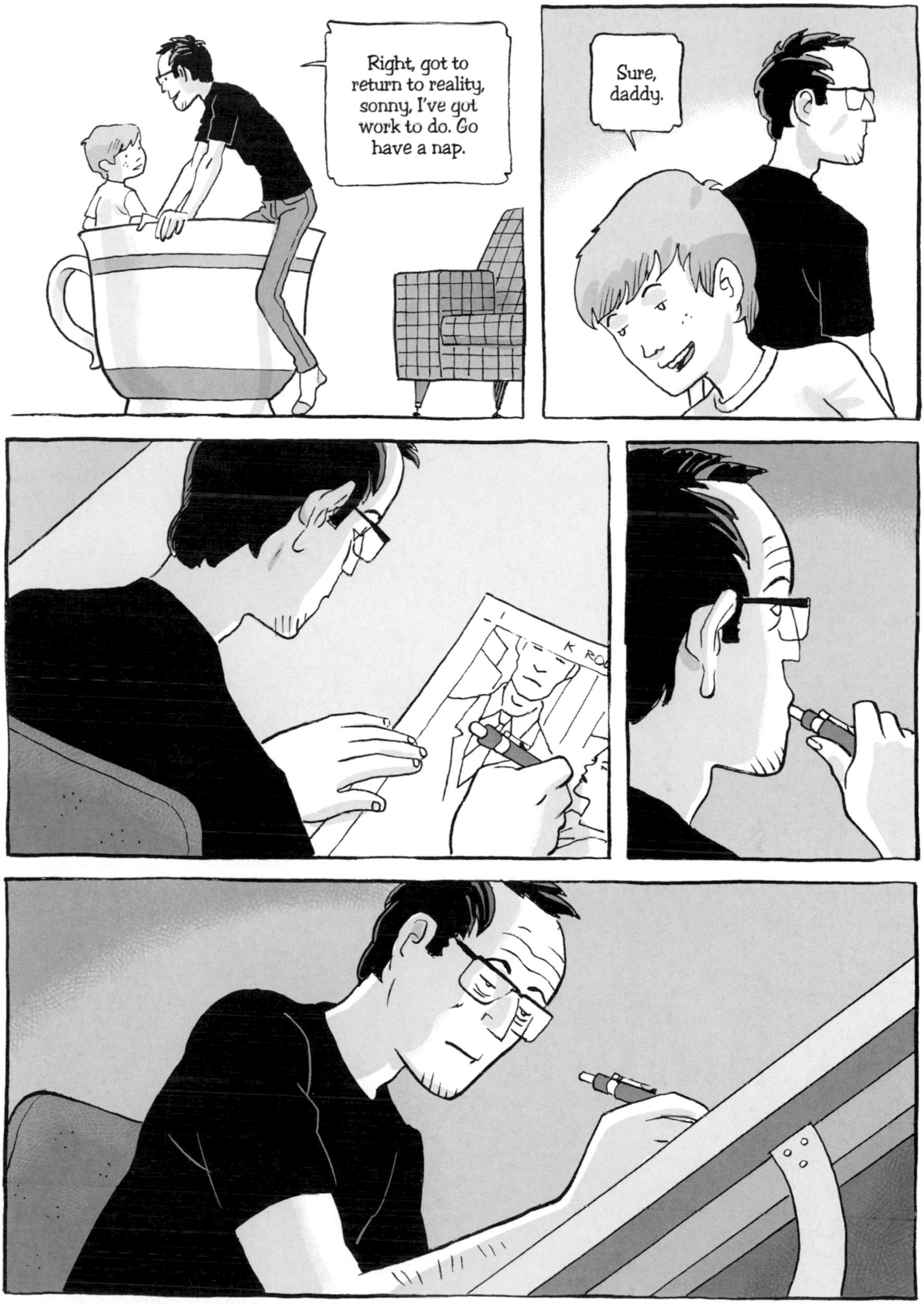
Right, got to return to reality, sonny, I've got work to do. Go have a nap.
Sure, daddy.

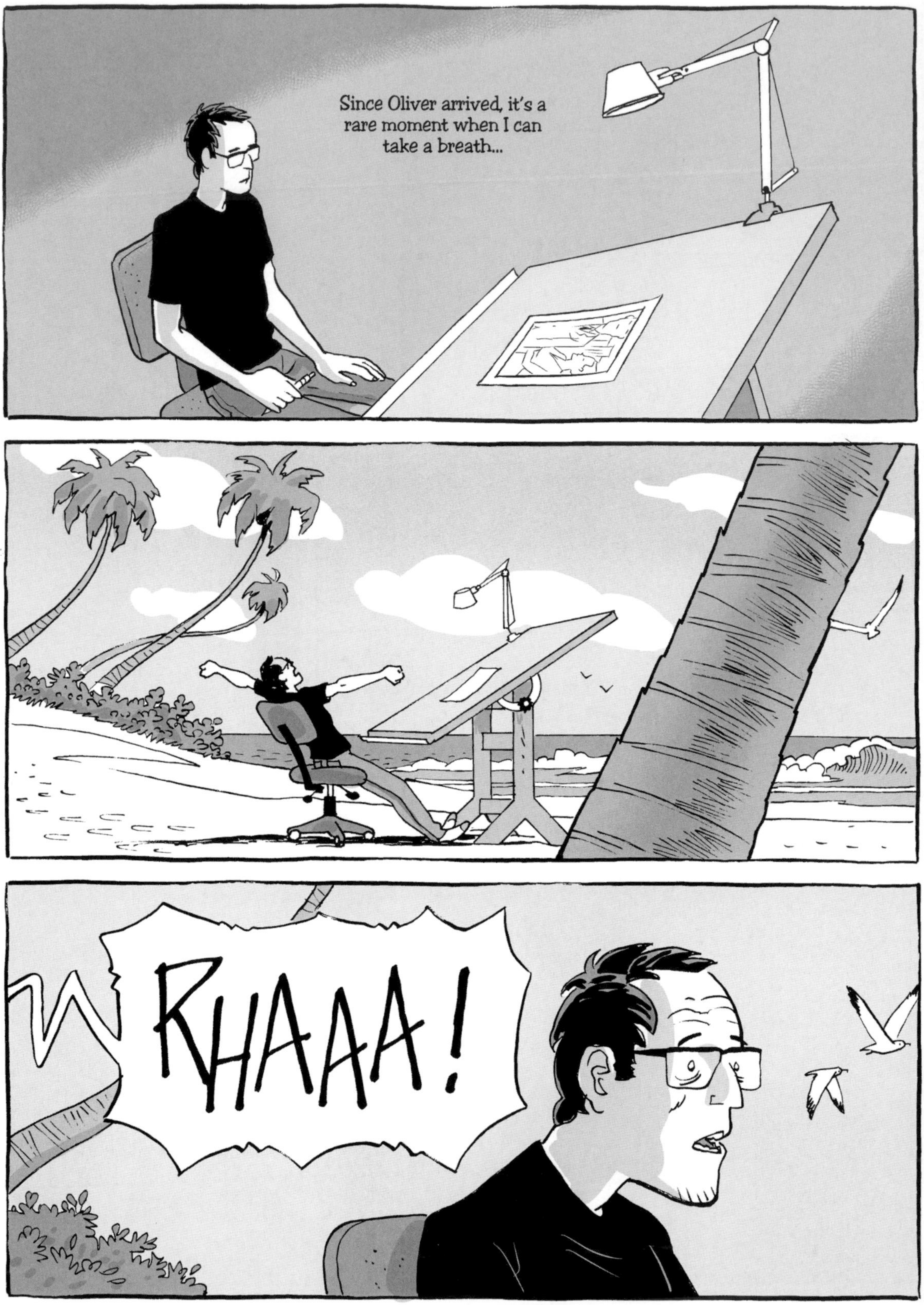

Since Oliver arrived, it's a rare moment when I can take a breath...
RHAAA!

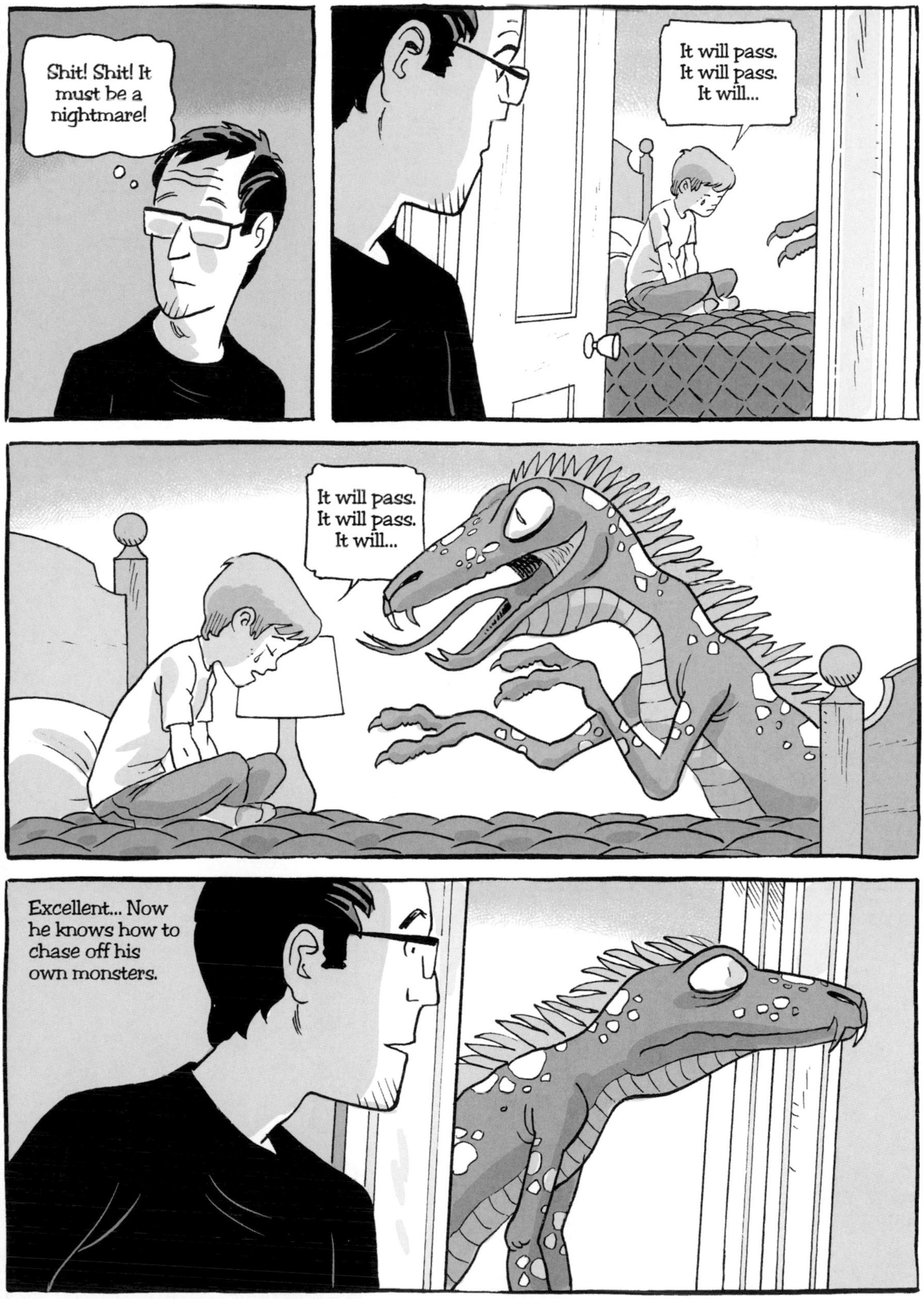
Shit! Shit! It must be a nightmare!
It will pass. It will pass. It will...
It will pass. It will pass. It will...
Excellent... Now he knows how to chase off his own monsters.

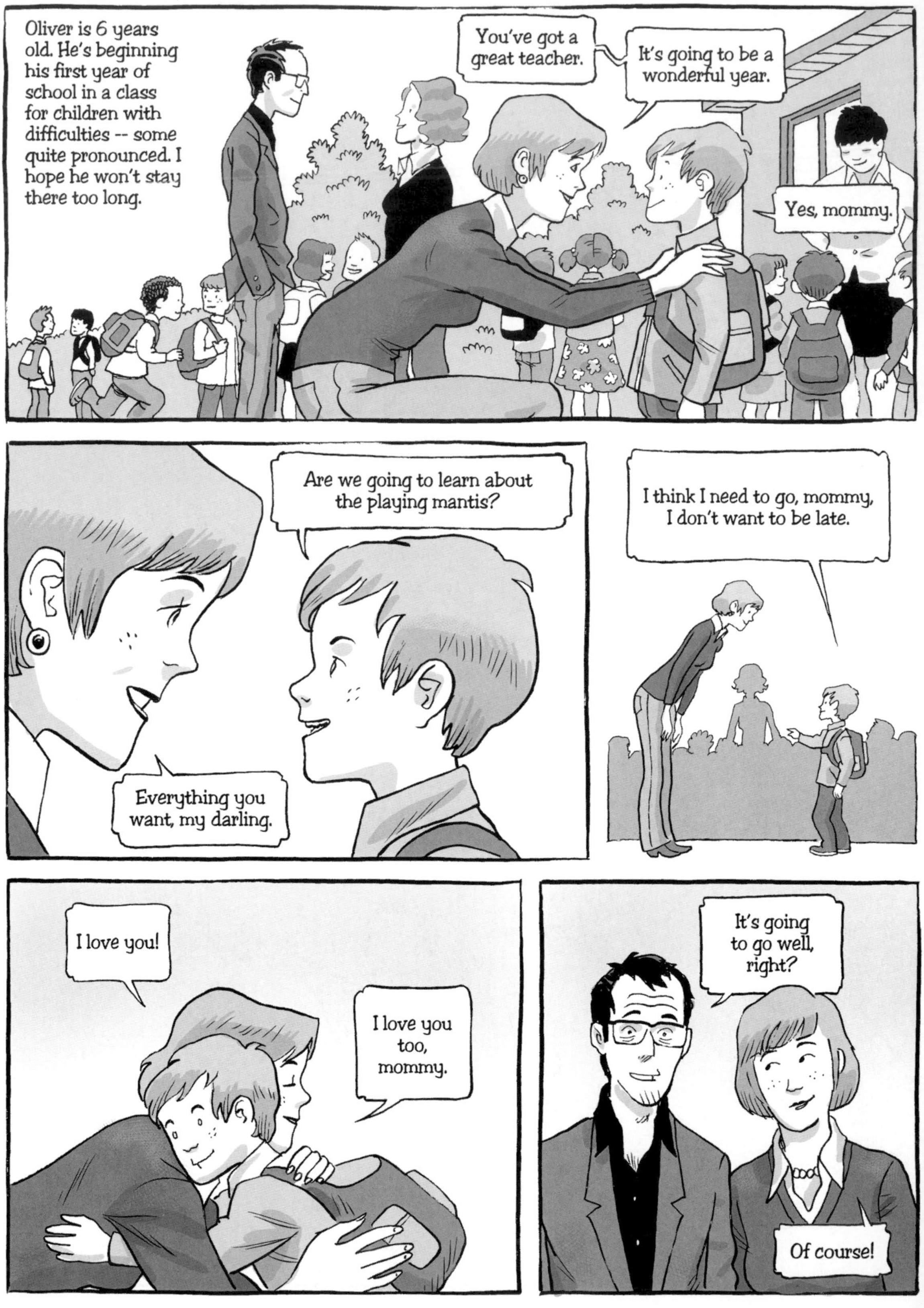
Oliver is 6 years old. He's beginning his first year of school in a class for children with difficulties -- some quite pronounced. I hope he won't stay there too long.
You've got a great teacher.
It's going to be a wonderful year.
Yes, mommy.
Are we going to learn about the playing mantis?
Everything you want, my darling.
I think I need to go, mommy, I don't want to be late.
I love you!
I love you too, mommy.
It's going to go well, right?
Of course!

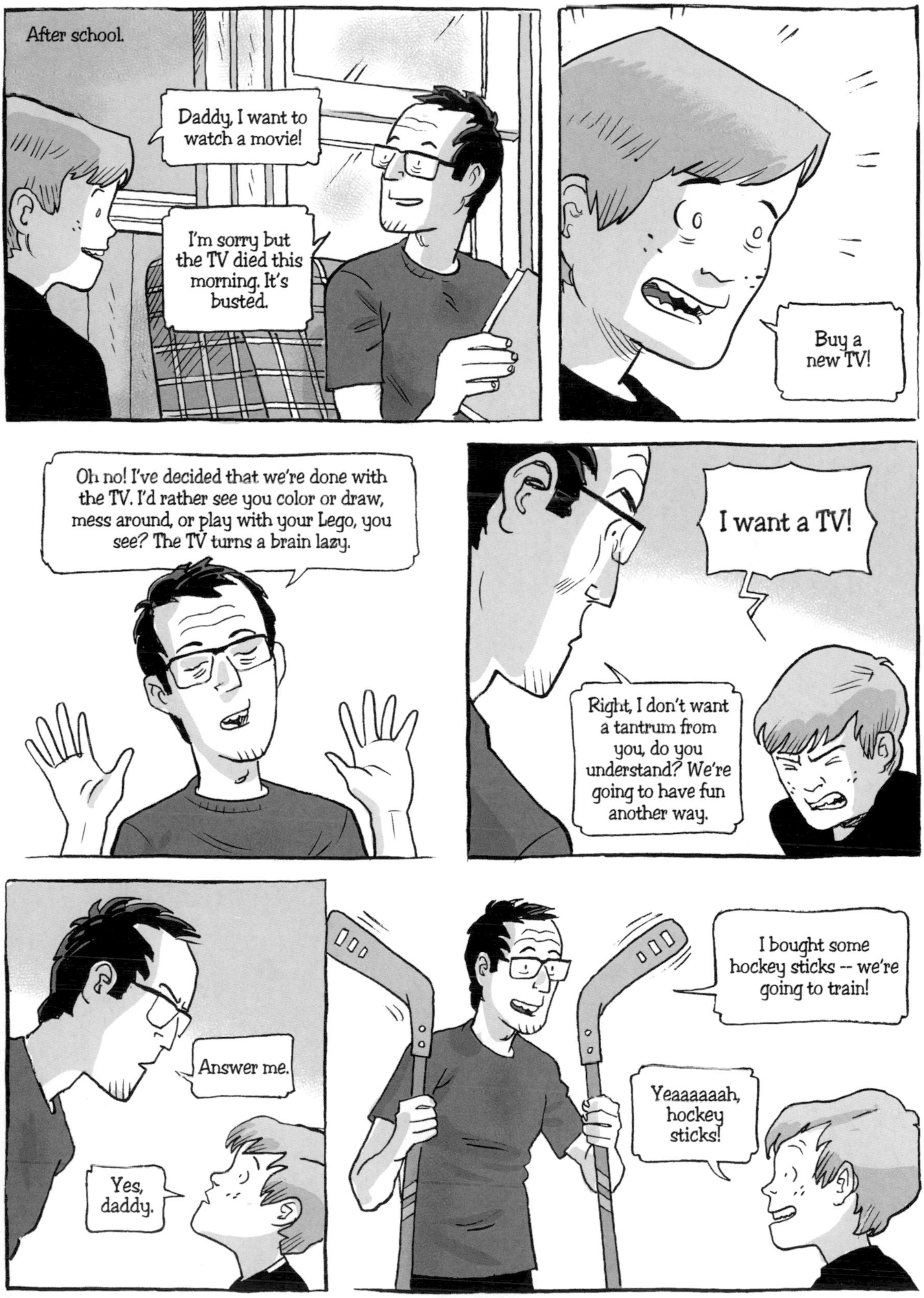
After school.
Daddy, I want to watch a movie!
I'm sorry but the TV died this morning. It's busted.
Buy a new TV!
Oh no! I've decided that we're done with the TV. I'd rather see you color or draw, mess around, or play with your Lego, you see? The TV turns a brain lazy.
I want a TV!
Right, I don't want a tantrum from you, do you understand? We're going to have fun another way.
Answer me.
Yes, daddy.
I bought some hockey sticks -- we're going to train!
Yeaaaaaah, hockey sticks!

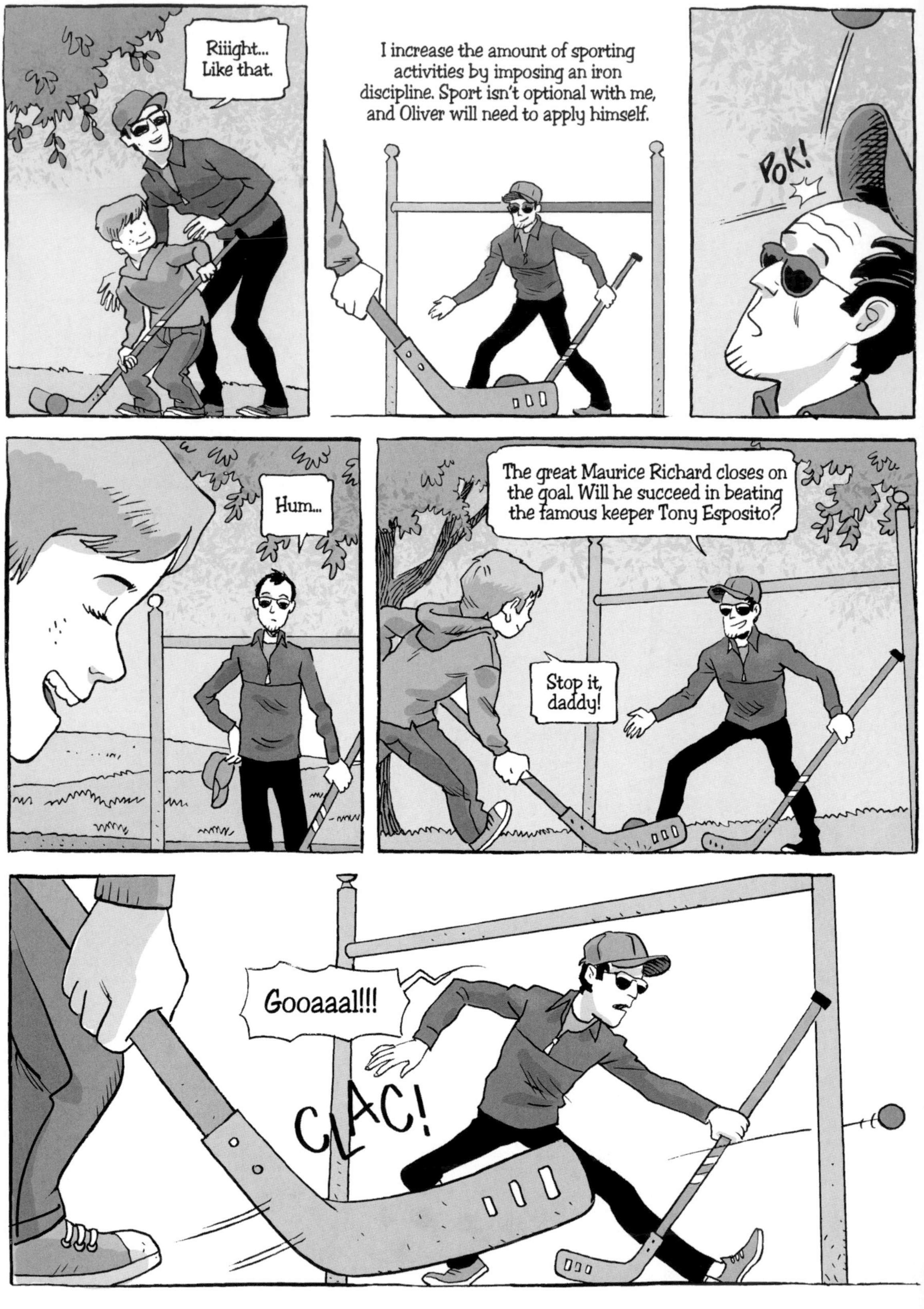
Riiight... Like that.
I increase the amount of sporting activities by imposing an iron discipline. Sport isn't optional with me, and Oliver will need to apply himself.
POK!
Hum...
The great Maurice Richard closes on the goal. Will he succeed in beating the famous keeper Tony Esposito?
Stop it, daddy!
Gooaaal!!!
CLAC!

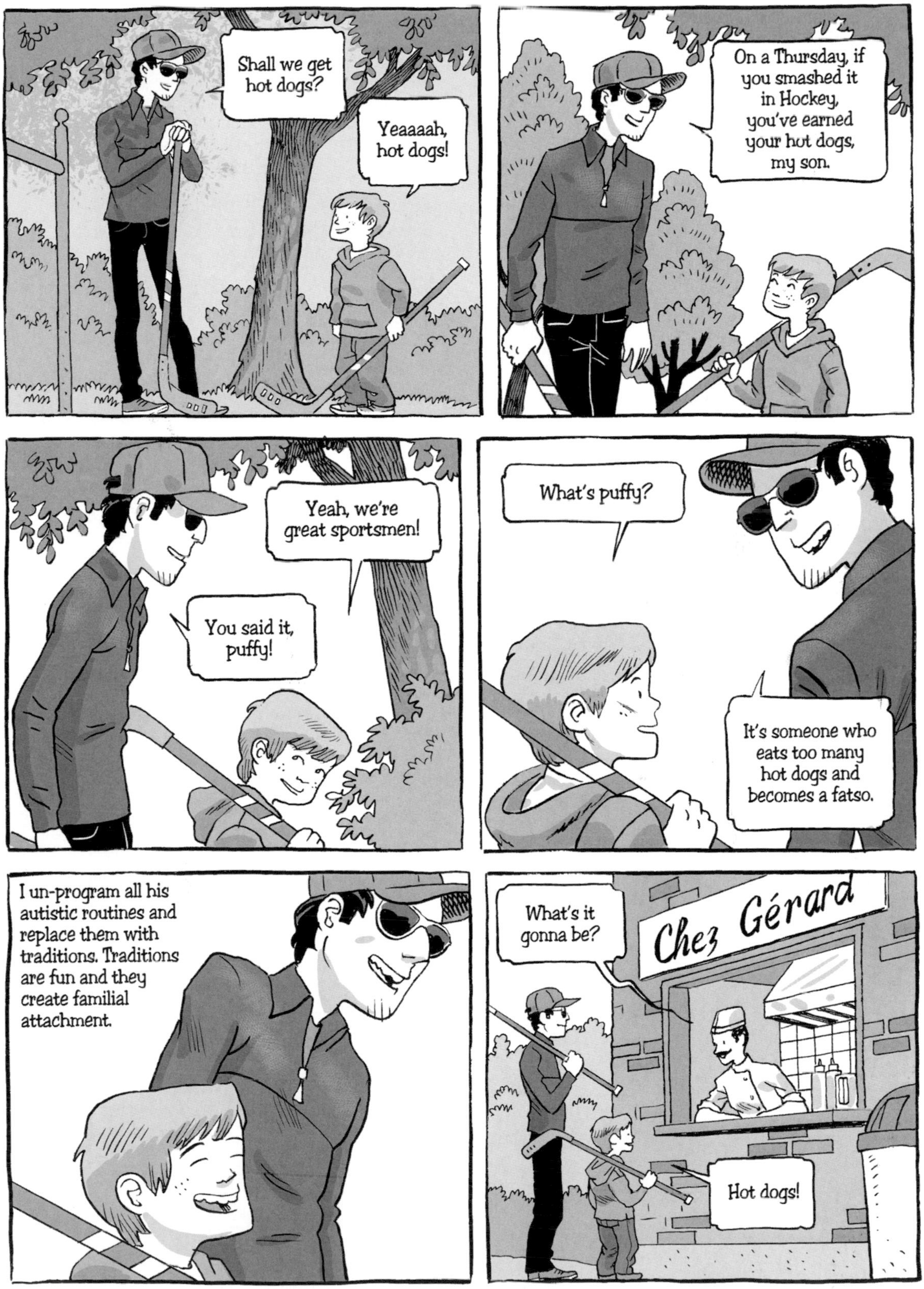
Shall we get hot dogs?
Yeaaaah, hot dogs!
On a Thursday, if you smashed it in Hockey, you've earned your hot dogs, my son.
Yeah, we're great sportsmen!
You said it, puffy!
What's puffy?
It's someone who eats too many hot dogs and becomes a fatso.
I un-program all his autistic routines and replace them with traditions. Traditions are fun and they create familial attachment.
What's it gonna be?
Chez Gérard
Hot dogs!

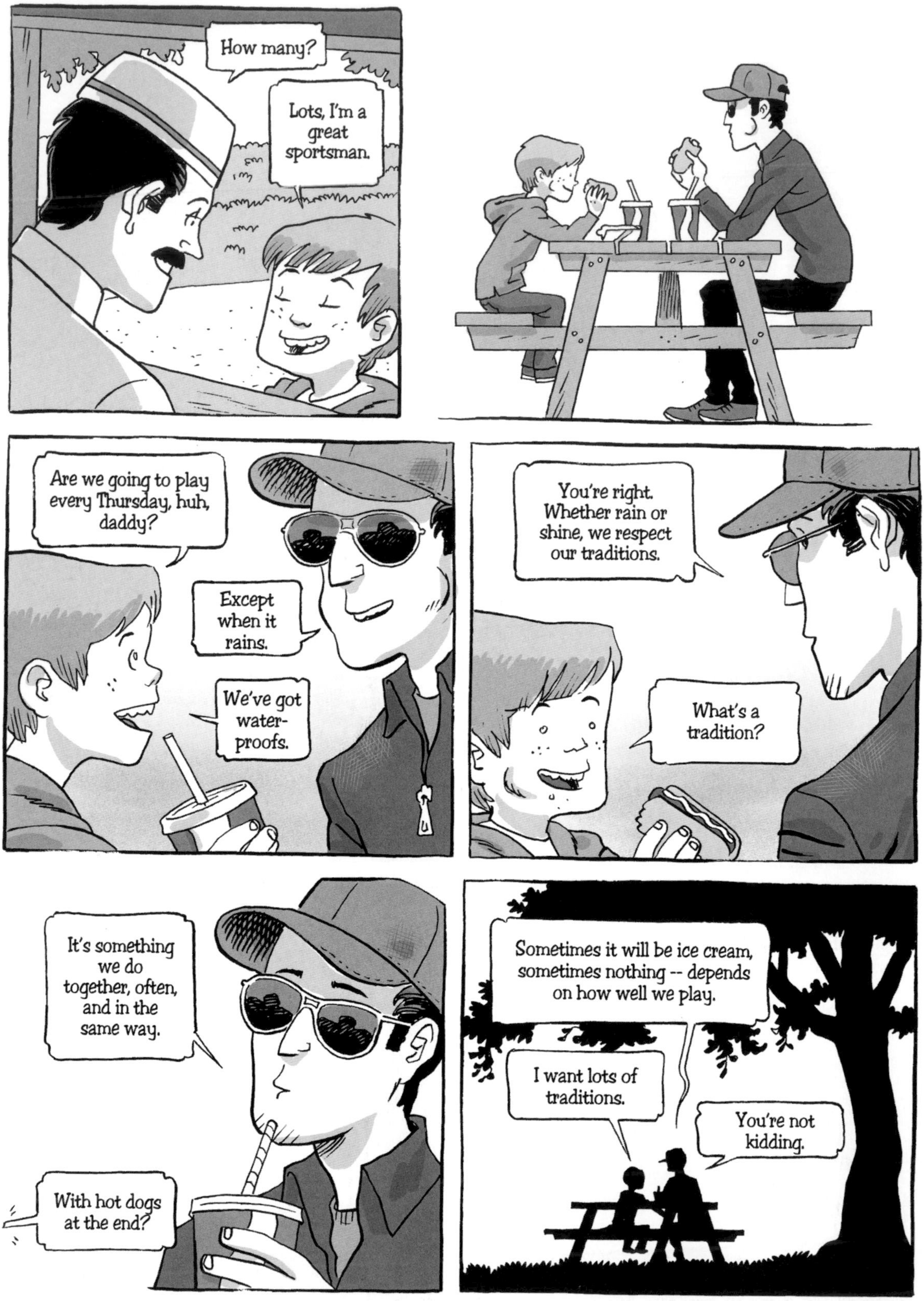
How many?
Lots, I'm a great sportsman.
Are we going to play every Thursday, huh, daddy?
Except when it rains.
We've got water-proofs.
You're right. Whether rain or shine, we respect our traditions.
What's a tradition?
It's something we do together, often, and in the same way.
With hot dogs at the end?
Sometimes it will be ice cream, sometimes nothing -- depends on how well we play.
I want lots of traditions.
You're not kidding.

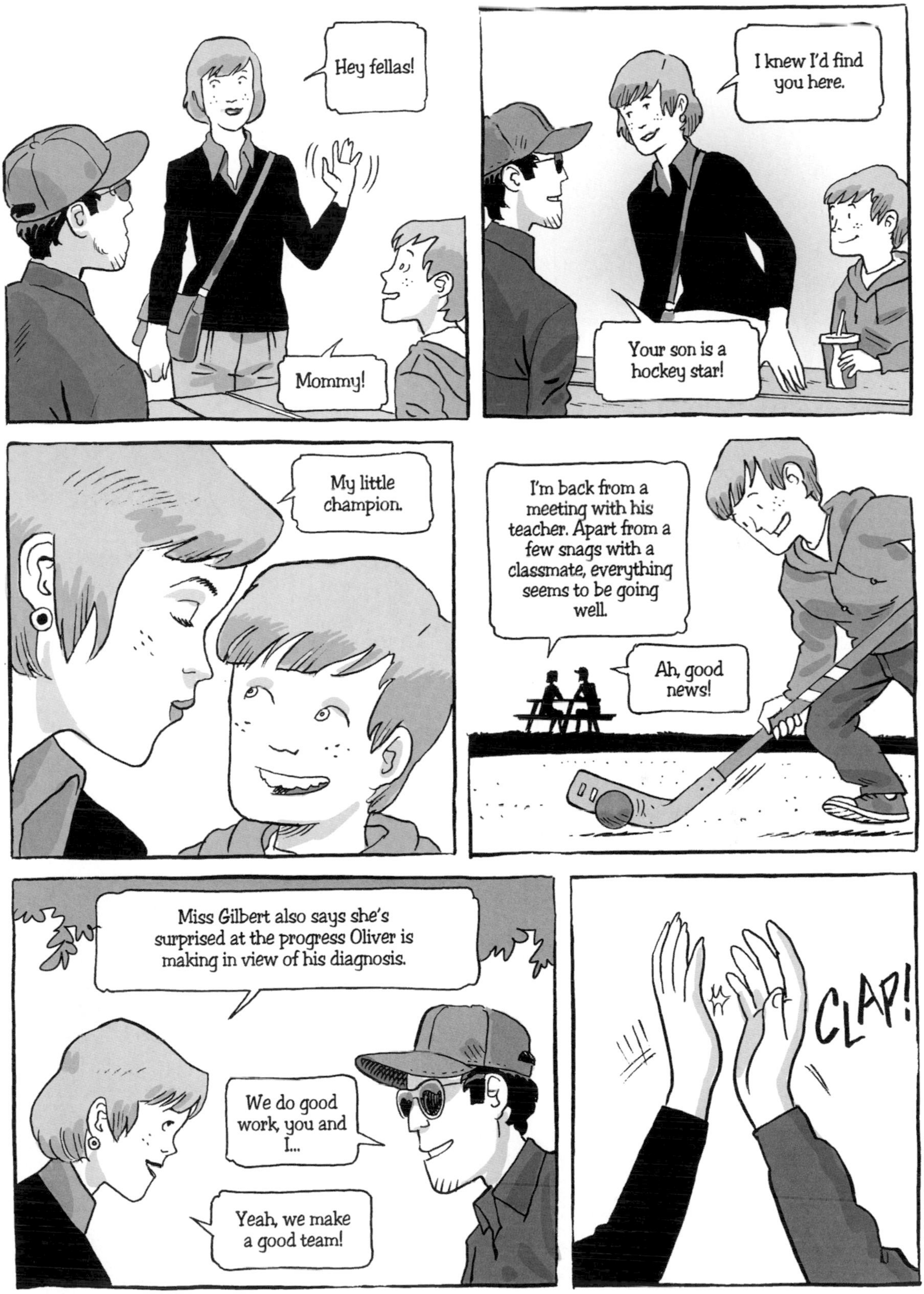
Hey fellas!
Mommy!
I knew I'd find you here.
Your son is a hockey star!
My little champion.
I'm back from a meeting with his teacher. Apart from a few snags with a classmate, everything seems to be going well.
Ah, good news!
Miss Gilbert also says she's surprised at the progress Oliver is making in view of his diagnosis.
We do good work, you and I...
Yeah, we make a good team!
CLAP!

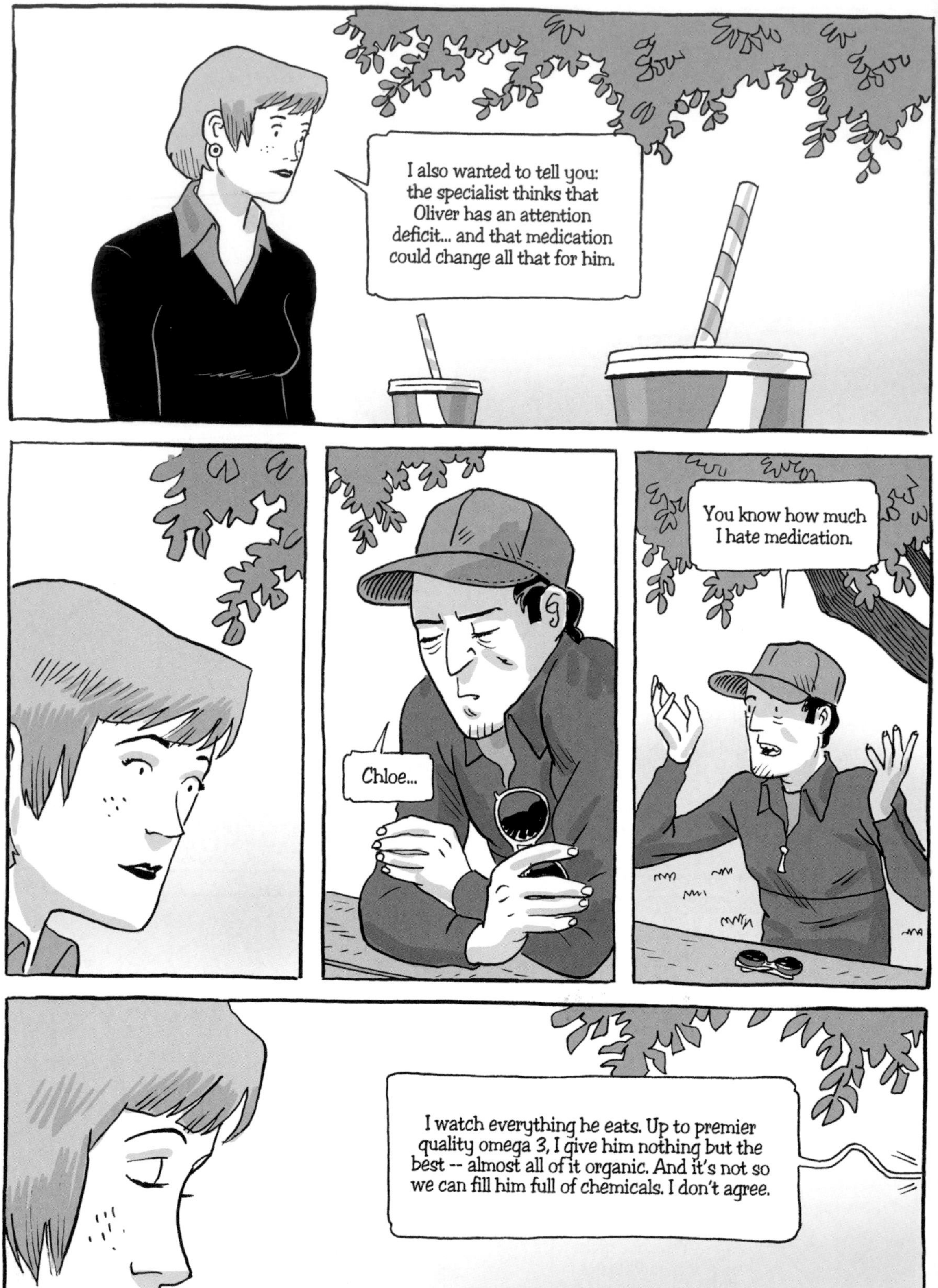
I also wanted to tell you: the specialist thinks that Oliver has an attention deficit... and that medication could change all that for him.
Chloe...
You know how much I hate medication.
I watch everything he eats. Up to premier quality omega 3, I give him nothing but the best -- almost all of it organic. And it's not so we can fill him full of chemicals. I don't agree.

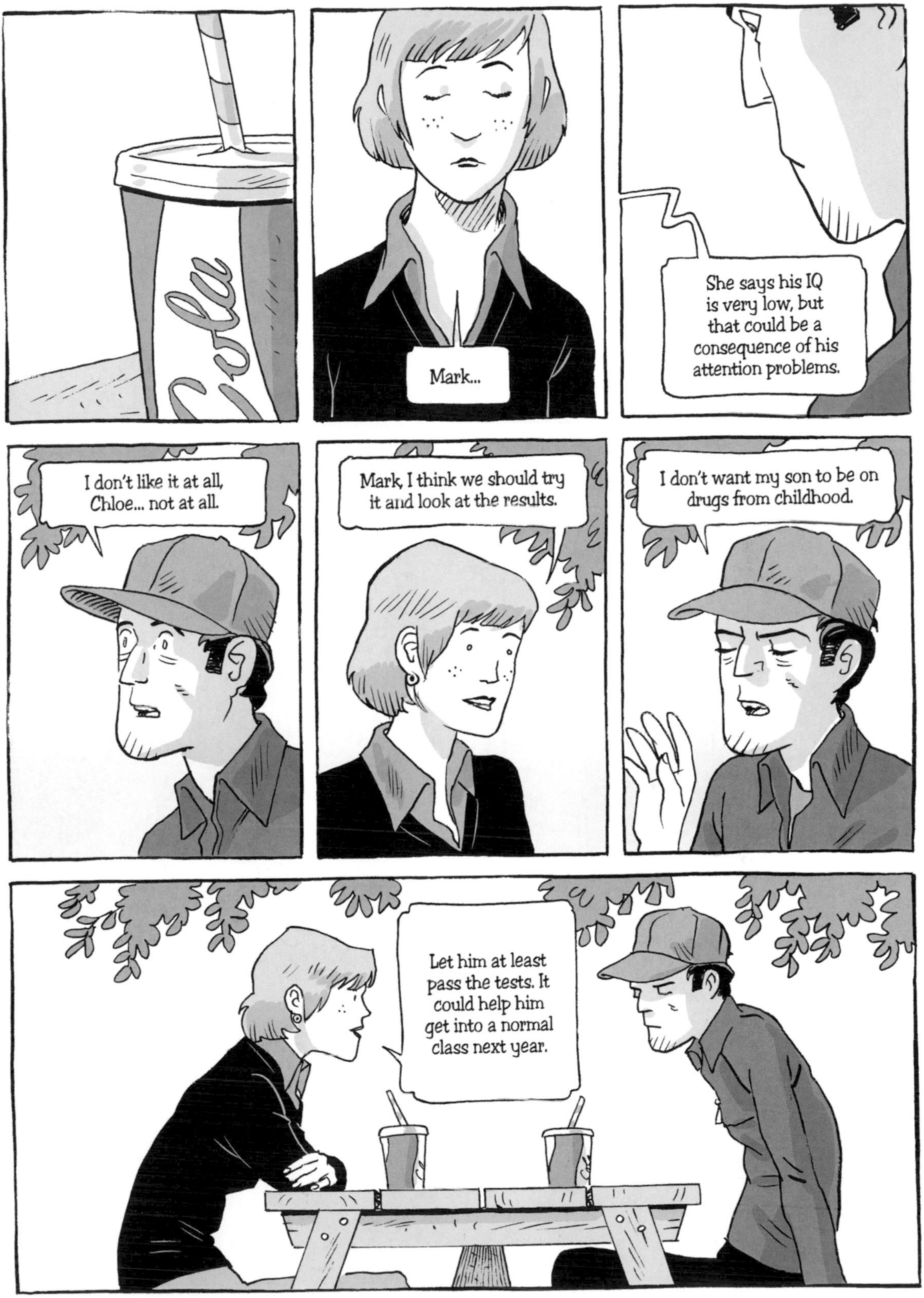
Mark...
She says his IQ is very low, but that could be a consequence of his attention problems.
I don't like it at all, Chloe... not at all.
Mark, I think we should try it and look at the results.
I don't want my son to be on drugs from childhood.
Let him at least pass the tests. It could help him get into a normal class next year.

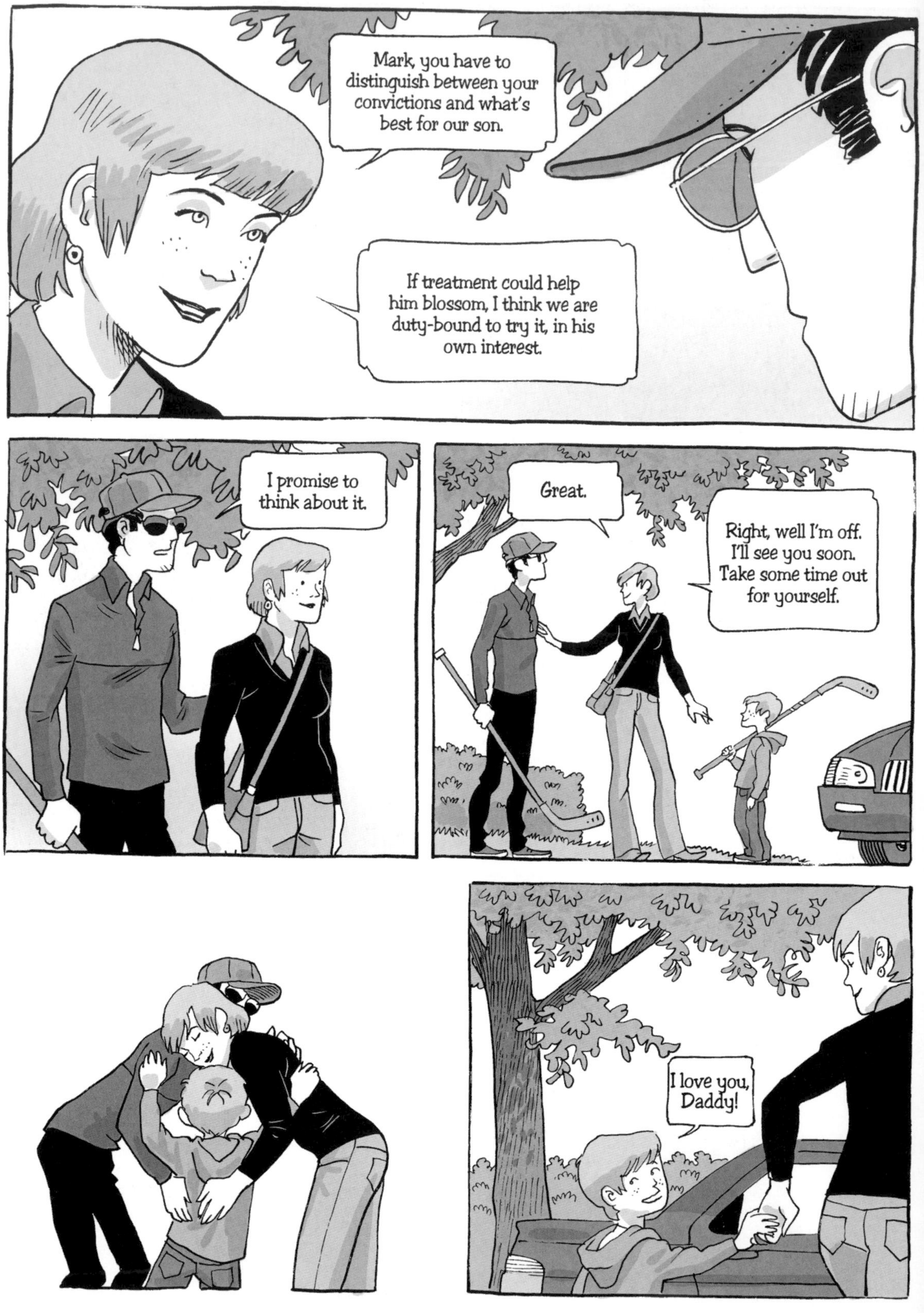
Mark, you have to distinguish between your convictions and what's best for our son.
If treatment could help him blossom, I think we are duty-bound to try it, in his own interest.
I promise to think about it.
Great.
Right, well I'm off. I'll see you soon. Take some time out for yourself.
I love you, Daddy!

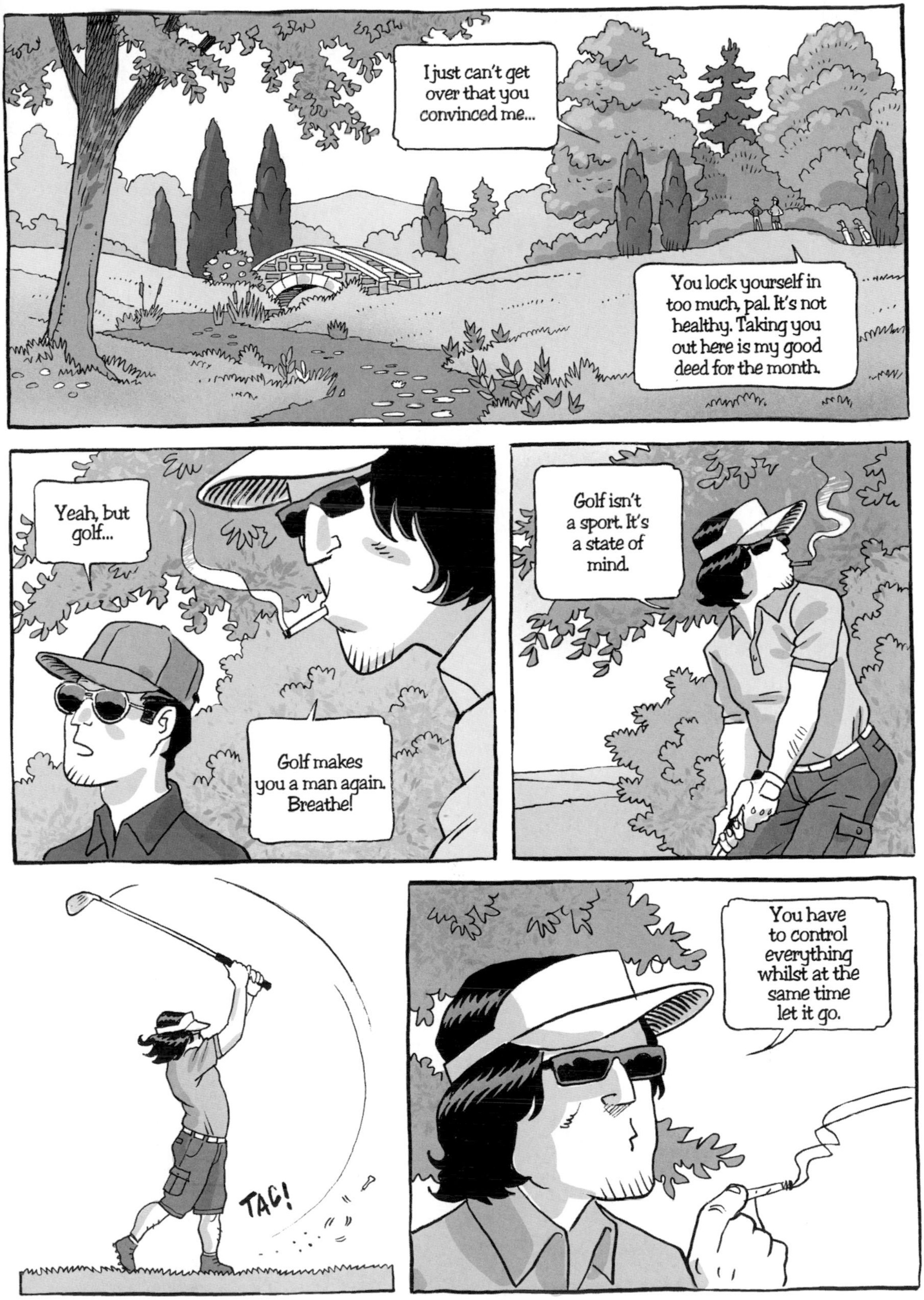
I just can't get over that you convinced me...
You lock yourself in too much, pal. It's not healthy. Taking you out here is my good deed for the month.
Yeah, but golf...
Golf makes you a man again. Breathe!
Golf isn't a sport. It's a state of mind.
TAC!
You have to control everything whilst at the same time let it go.

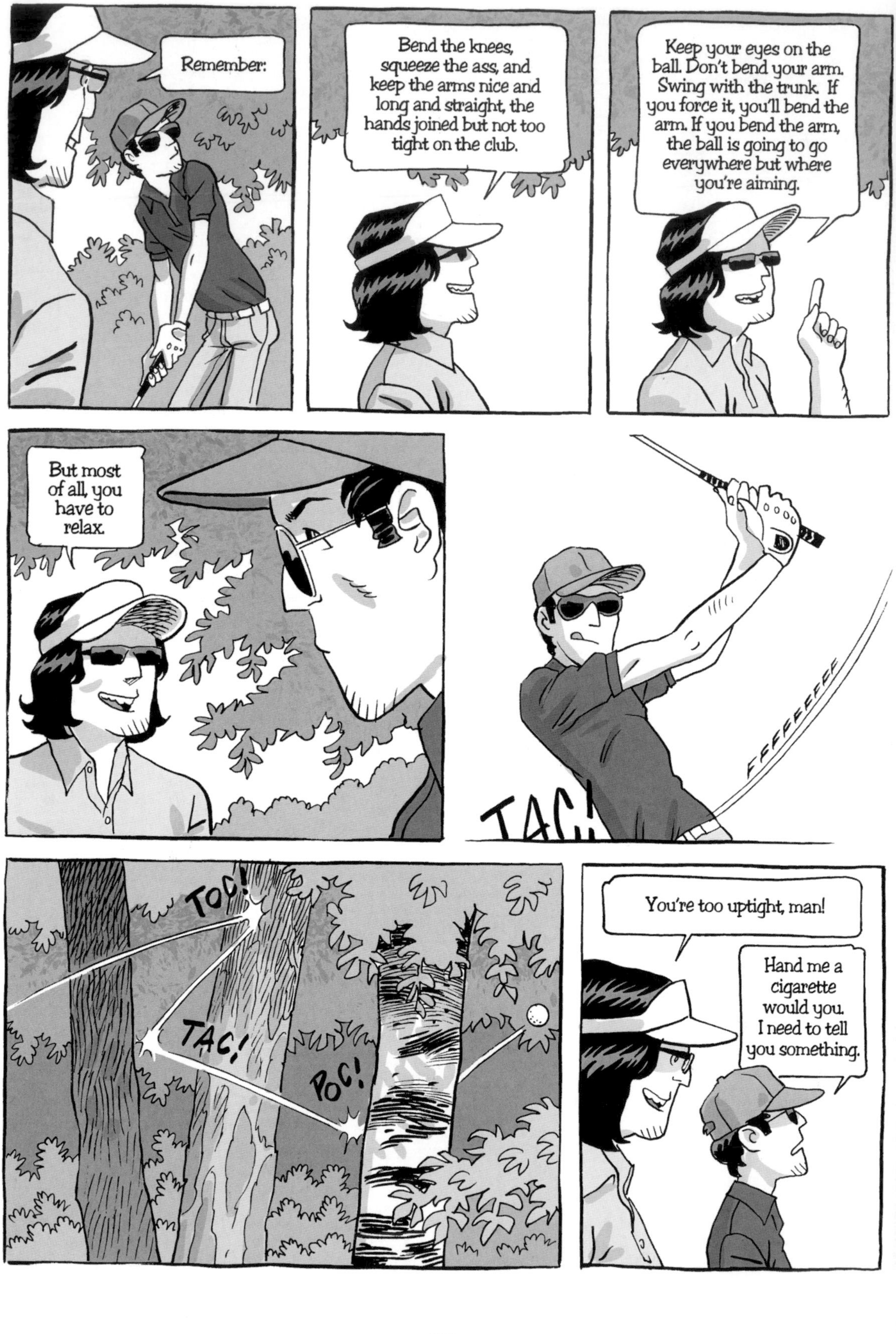
Remember:
Bend the knees, squeeze the ass, and keep the arms nice and long and straight, the hands joined but not too tight on the club.
Keep your eyes on the ball. Don't bend your arm. Swing with the trunk. If you force it, you'll bend the arm. If you bend the arm, the ball is going to go everywhere but where you're aiming.
But most of all, you have to relax.
FFFFFFFF
TAC!
TOC!
TAC!
POC!
You're too uptight, man!
Hand me a cigarette would you. I need to tell you something.

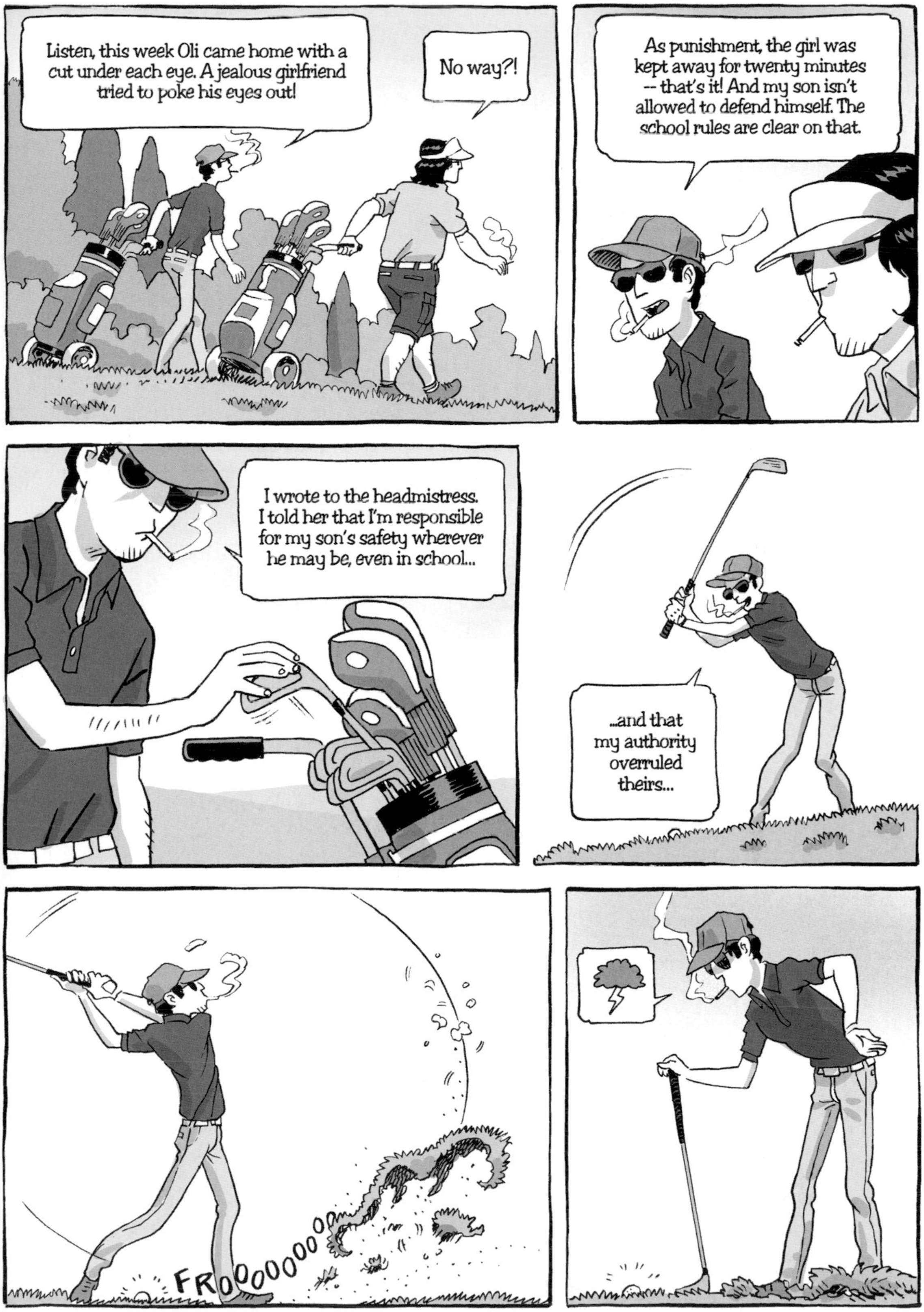
Listen, this week Oli came home with a cut under each eye. A jealous girlfriend tried to poke his eyes out!
No way?!
As punishment, the girl was kept away for twenty minutes -- that's it! And my son isn't allowed to defend himself. The school rules are clear on that.
I wrote to the headmistress. I told her that I'm responsible for my son's safety wherever he may be, even in school...
...and that my authority overruled theirs...
FROOOOOOOOO

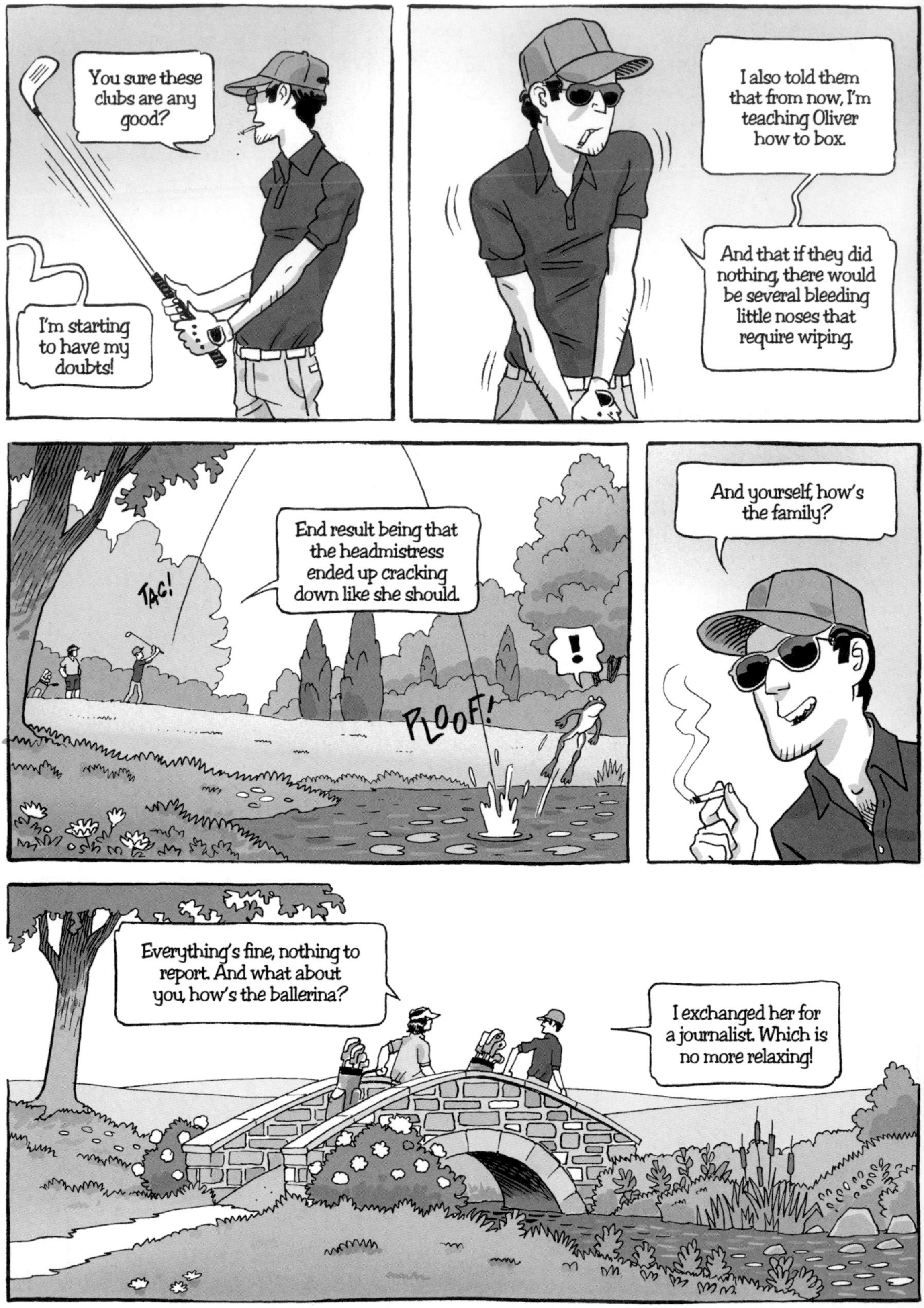

You sure these clubs are any good?
I'm starting to have my doubts!
I also told them that from now, I'm teaching Oliver how to box.
And that if they did nothing, there would be several bleeding little noses that require wiping.
TAC!
End result being that the headmistress ended up cracking down like she should.
!
PLOOF!
And yourself, how's the family?
Everything's fine, nothing to report. And what about you, how's the ballerina?
I exchanged her for a journalist. Which is no more relaxing!

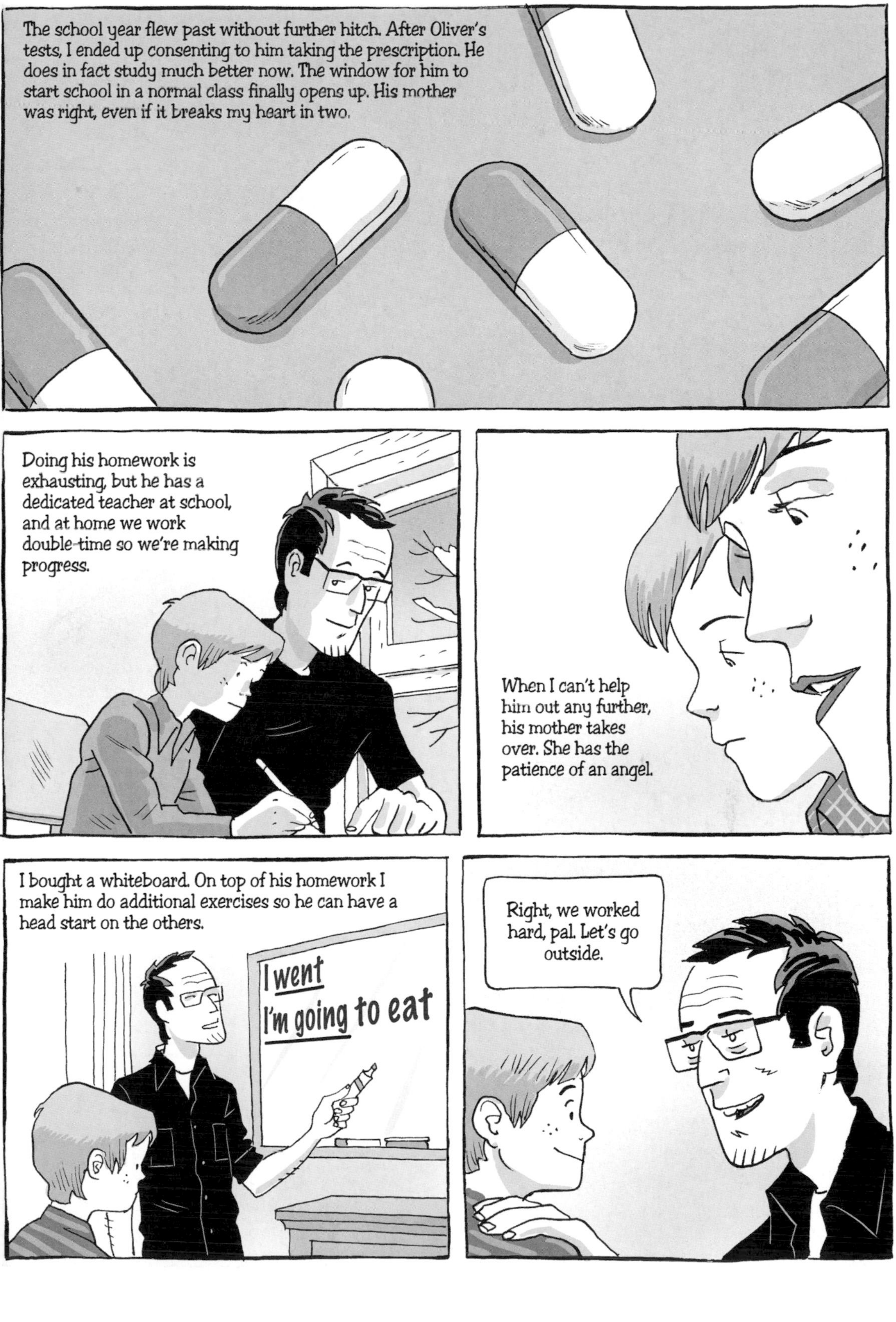

The school year flew past without further hitch. After Oliver's tests, I ended up consenting to him taking the prescription. He does in fact study much better now. The window for him to start school in a normal class finally opens up. His mother was right, even if it breaks my heart in two.
Doing his homework is exhausting, but he has a dedicated teacher at school, and at home we work double-time so we're making progress.
When I can't help him out any further, his mother takes over. She has the patience of an angel.
I bought a whiteboard. On top of his homework I make him do additional exercises so he can have a head start on the others.
I went
I'm going to eat
Right, we worked hard, pal. Let's go outside.

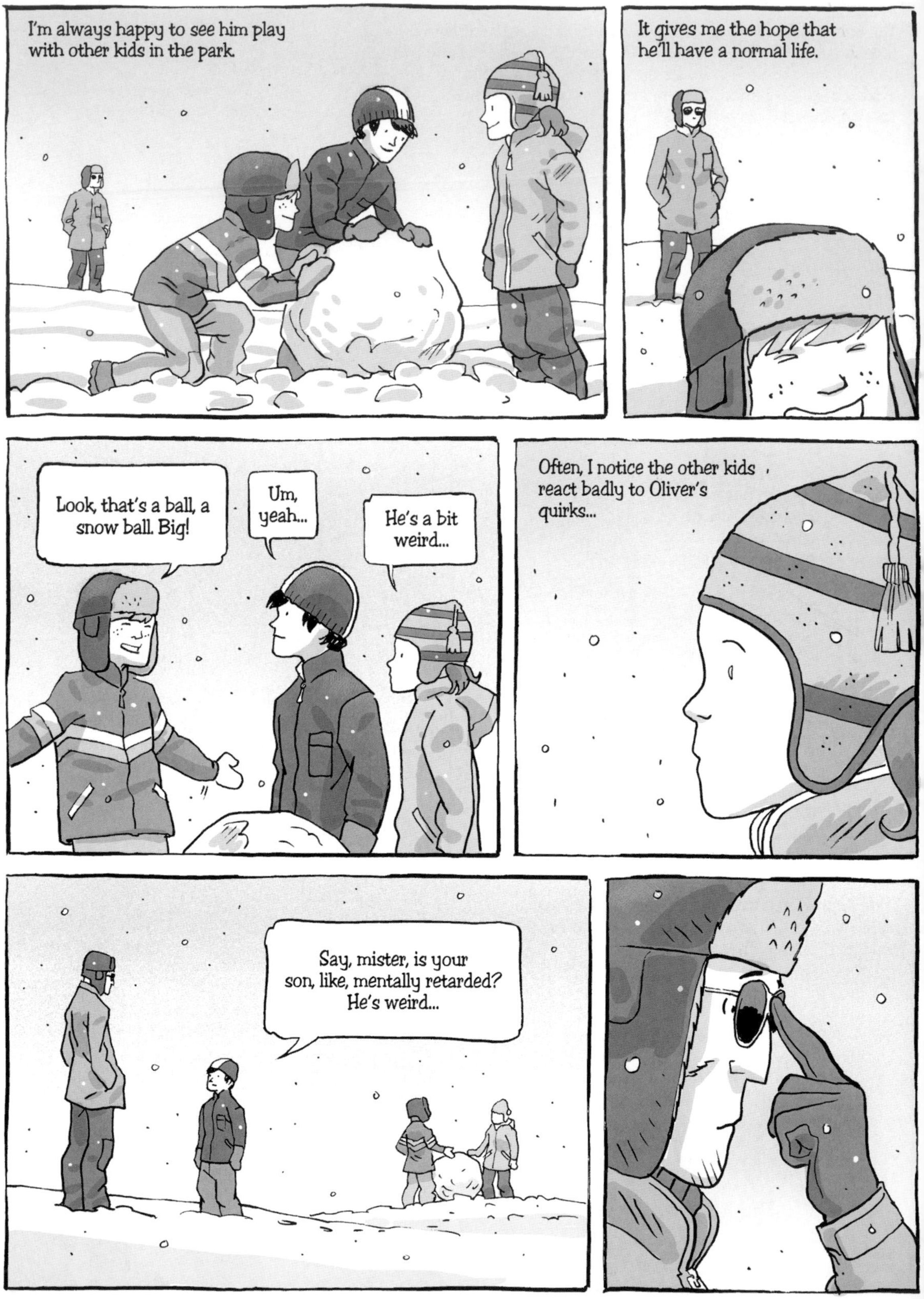
I'm always happy to see him play with other kids in the park.
It gives me the hope that he'll have a normal life.
Look, that's a ball, a snow ball. Big!
Um, yeah...
He's a bit weird...
Often, I notice the other kids react badly to Oliver's quirks...
Say, mister, is your son, like, mentally retarded? He's weird...

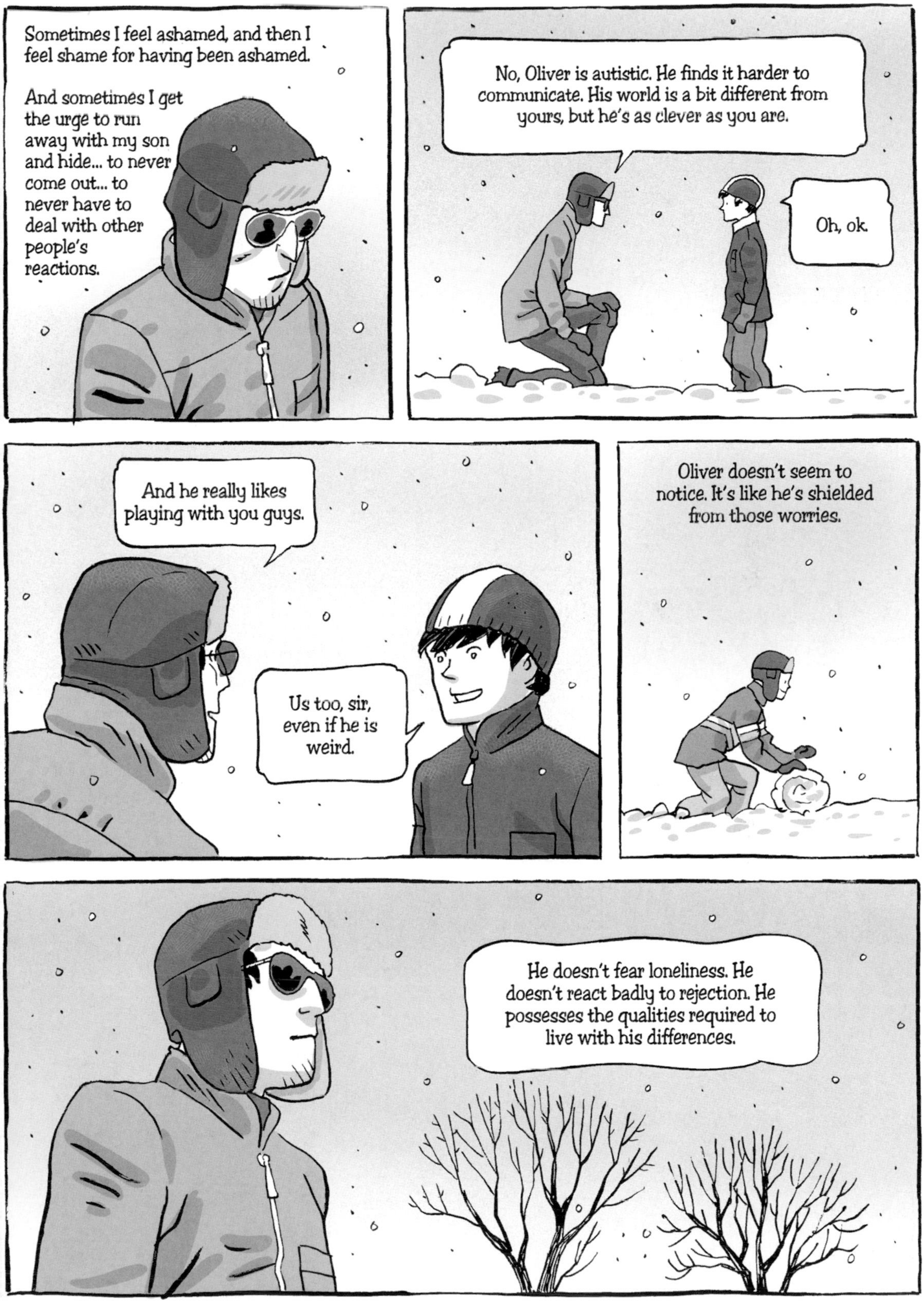
Sometimes I feel ashamed, and then I feel shame for having been ashamed.
And sometimes I get the urge to run away with my son and hide... to never come out... to never have to deal with other people's reactions.
No, Oliver is autistic. He finds it harder to communicate. His world is a bit different from yours, but he's as clever as you are.
Oh, ok.
And he really likes playing with you guys.
Us too, sir, even if he is weird.
Oliver doesn't seem to notice. It's like he's shielded from those worries.
He doesn't fear loneliness. He doesn't react badly to rejection. He possesses the qualities required to live with his differences.

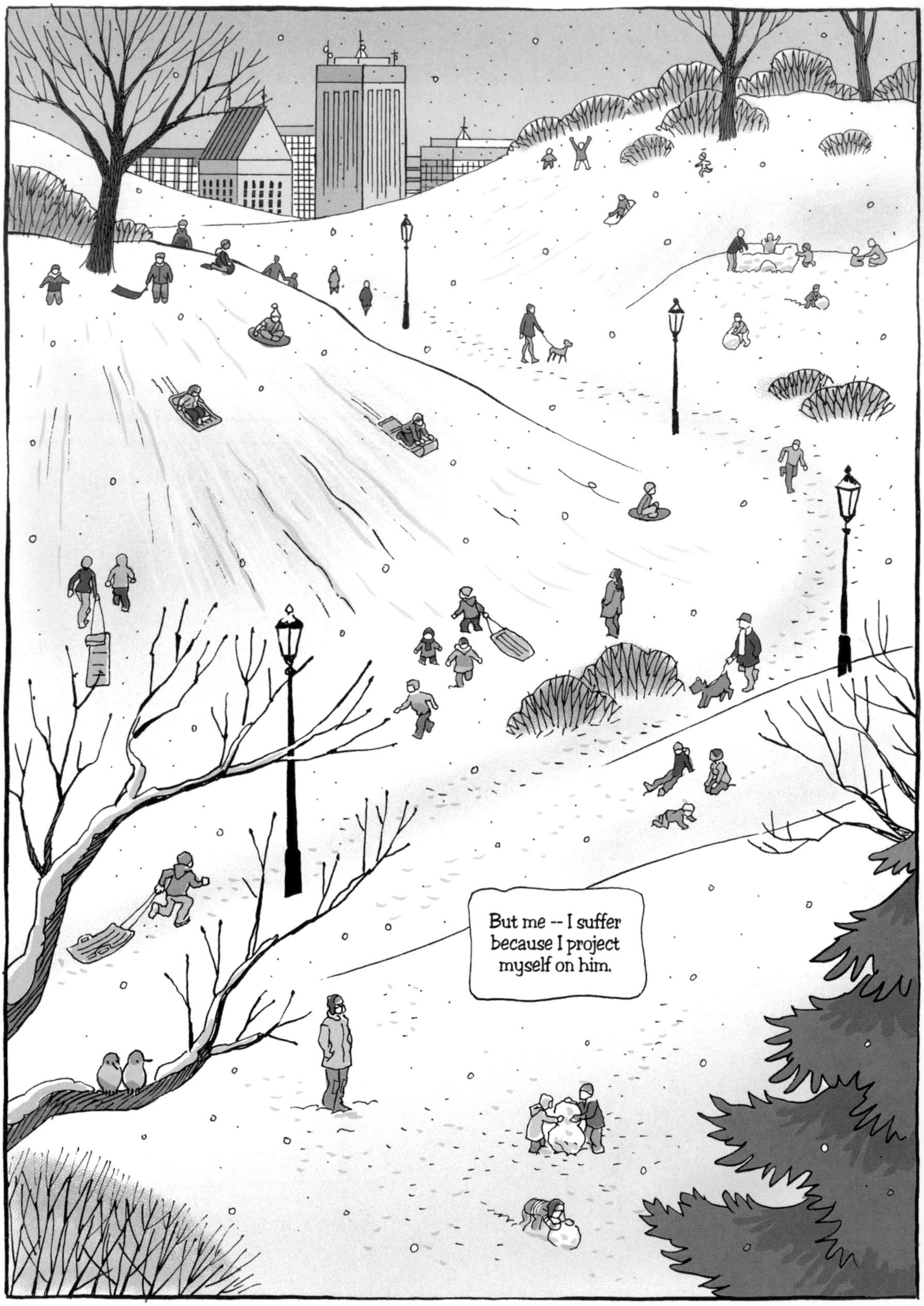
But me -- I suffer because I project myself on him.

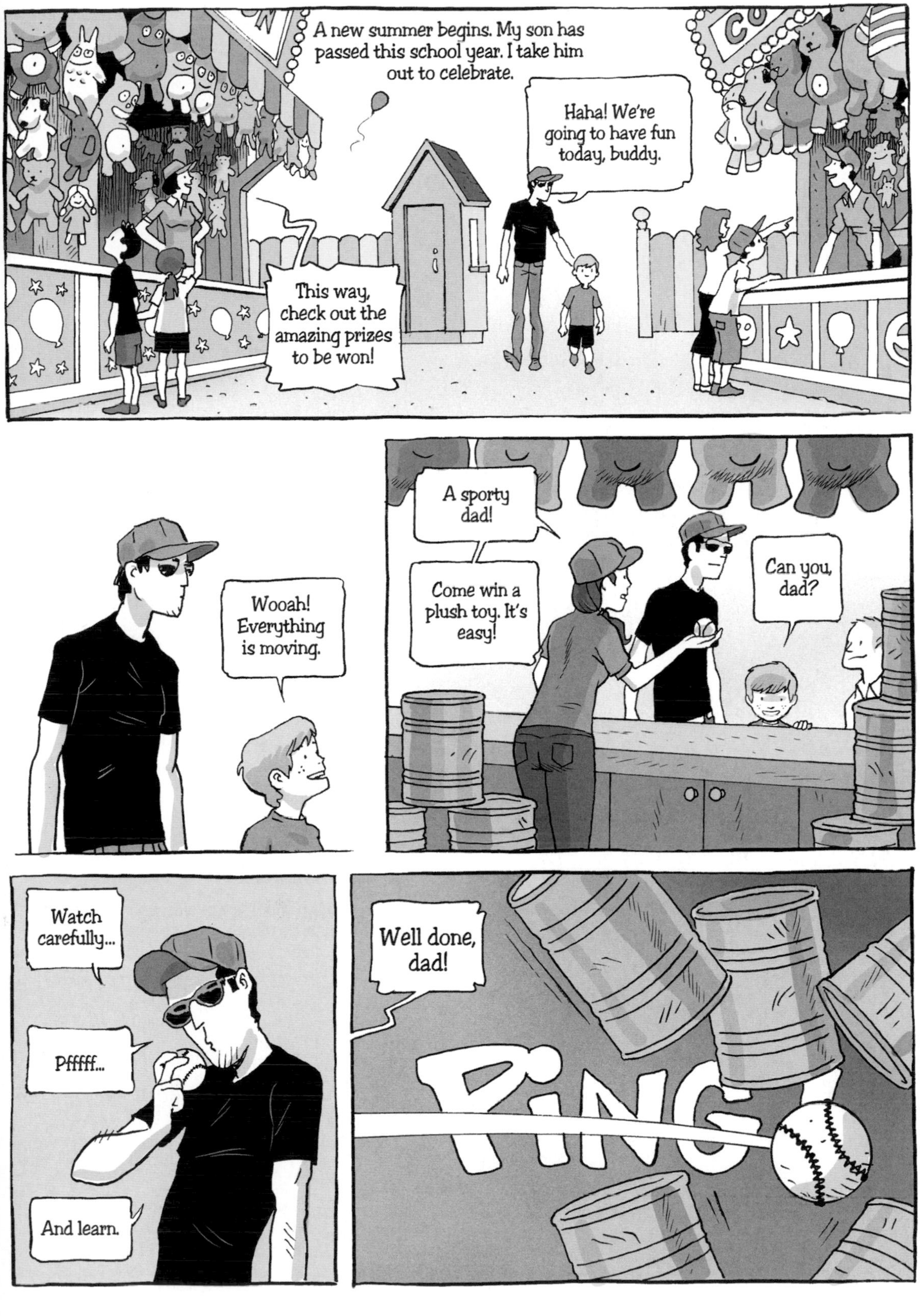
A new summer begins. My son has passed this school year. I take him out to celebrate.
Haha! We're going to have fun today, buddy.
This way, check out the amazing prizes to be won!
Wooah! Everything is moving.
A sporty dad!
Come win a plush toy. It's easy!
Can you, dad?
Watch carefully...
Pfffff...
And learn.
Well done, dad!
PING

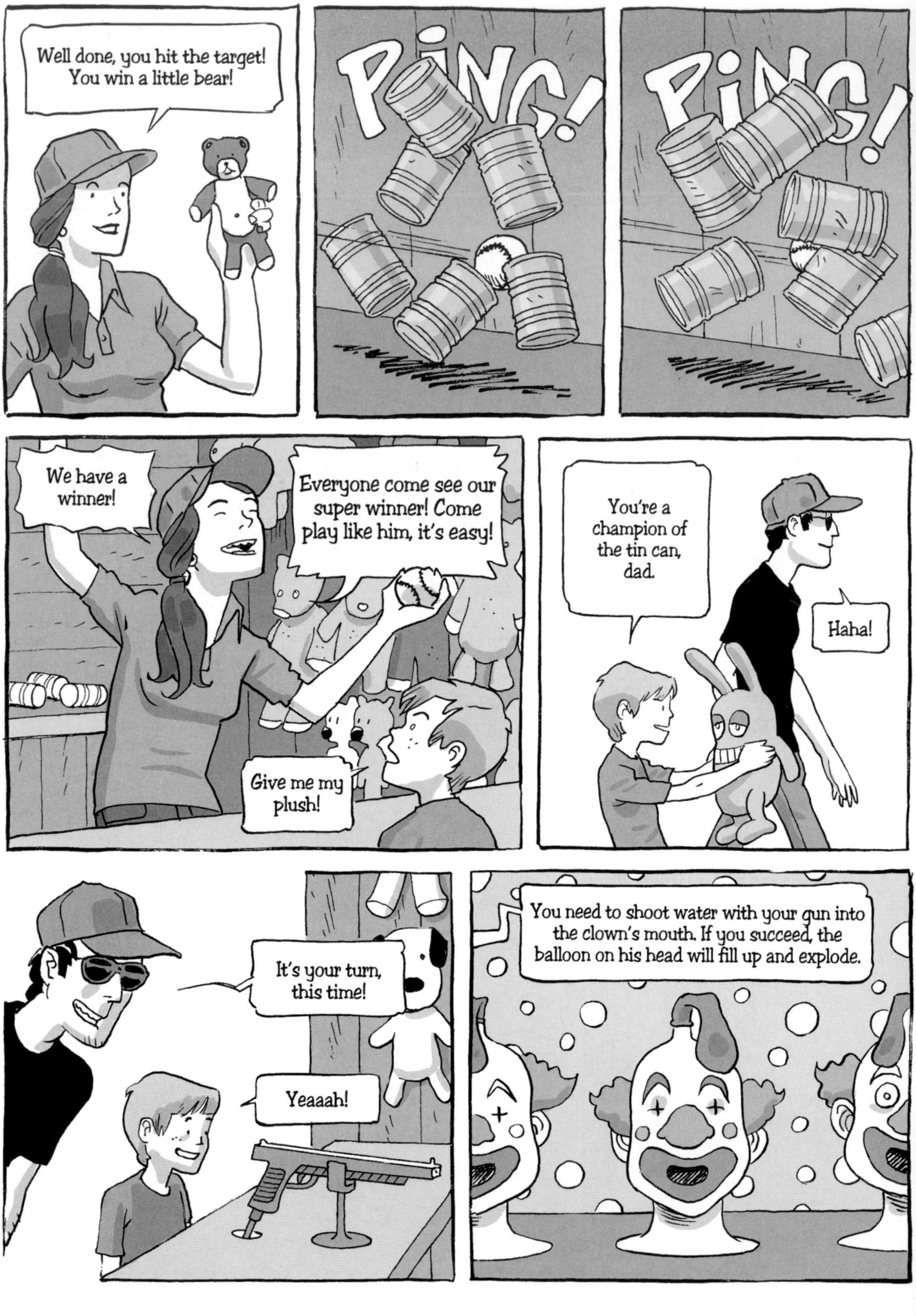
Well done, you hit the target! You win a little bear!
PING!
PING!
We have a winner!
Everyone come see our super winner! Come play like him, it's easy!
Give me my plush!
You're a champion of the tin can, dad.
Haha!
It's your turn, this time!
Yeaaah!
You need to shoot water with your gun into the clown's mouth. If you succeed, the balloon on his head will fill up and explode.

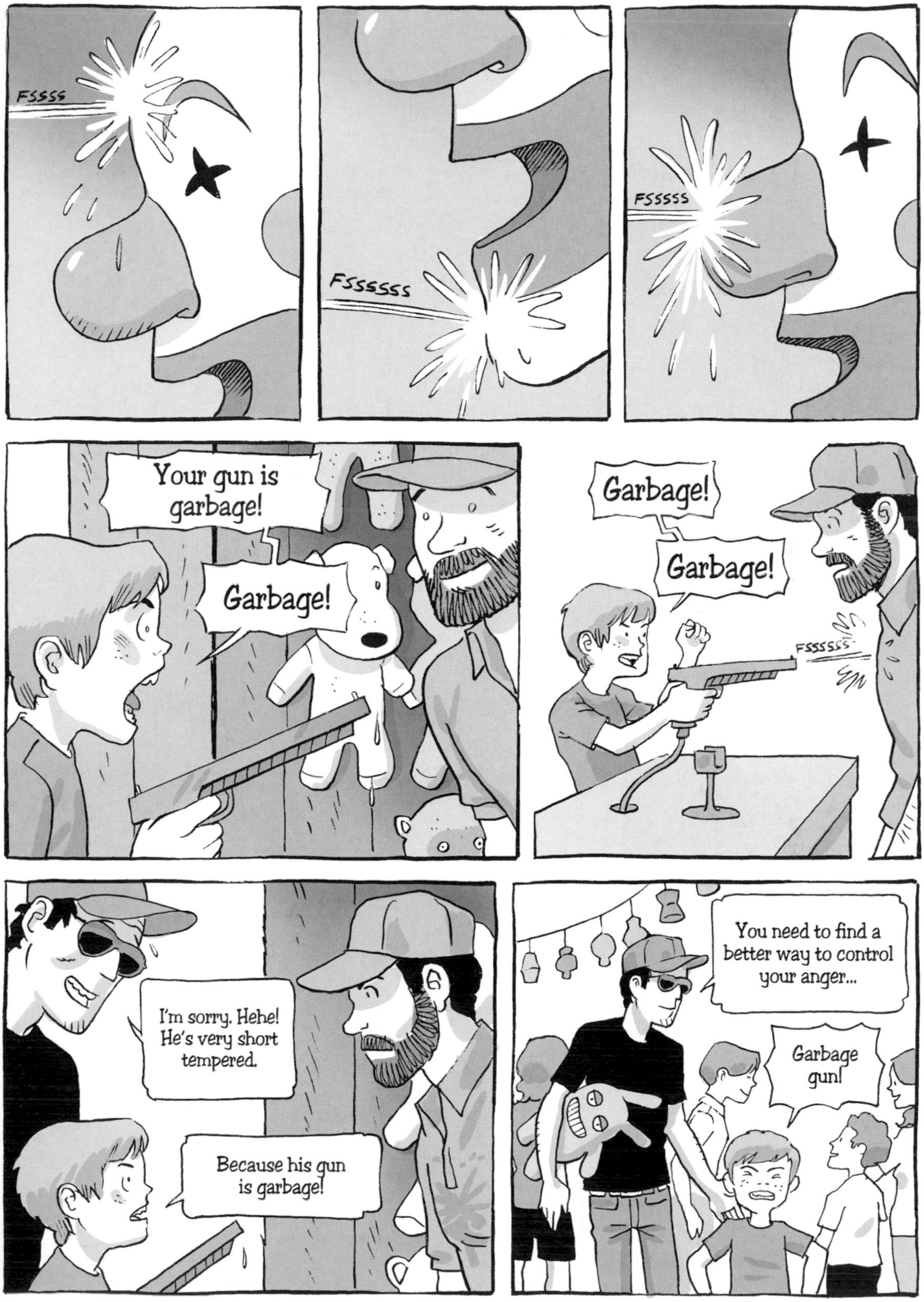
FSSSS
FSSSSSS
FSSSSS
Your gun is garbage!
Garbage!
Garbage!
Garbage!
FSSSSSS
I'm sorry. Hehe! He's very short tempered.
Because his gun is garbage!
You need to find a better way to control your anger...
Garbage gun!

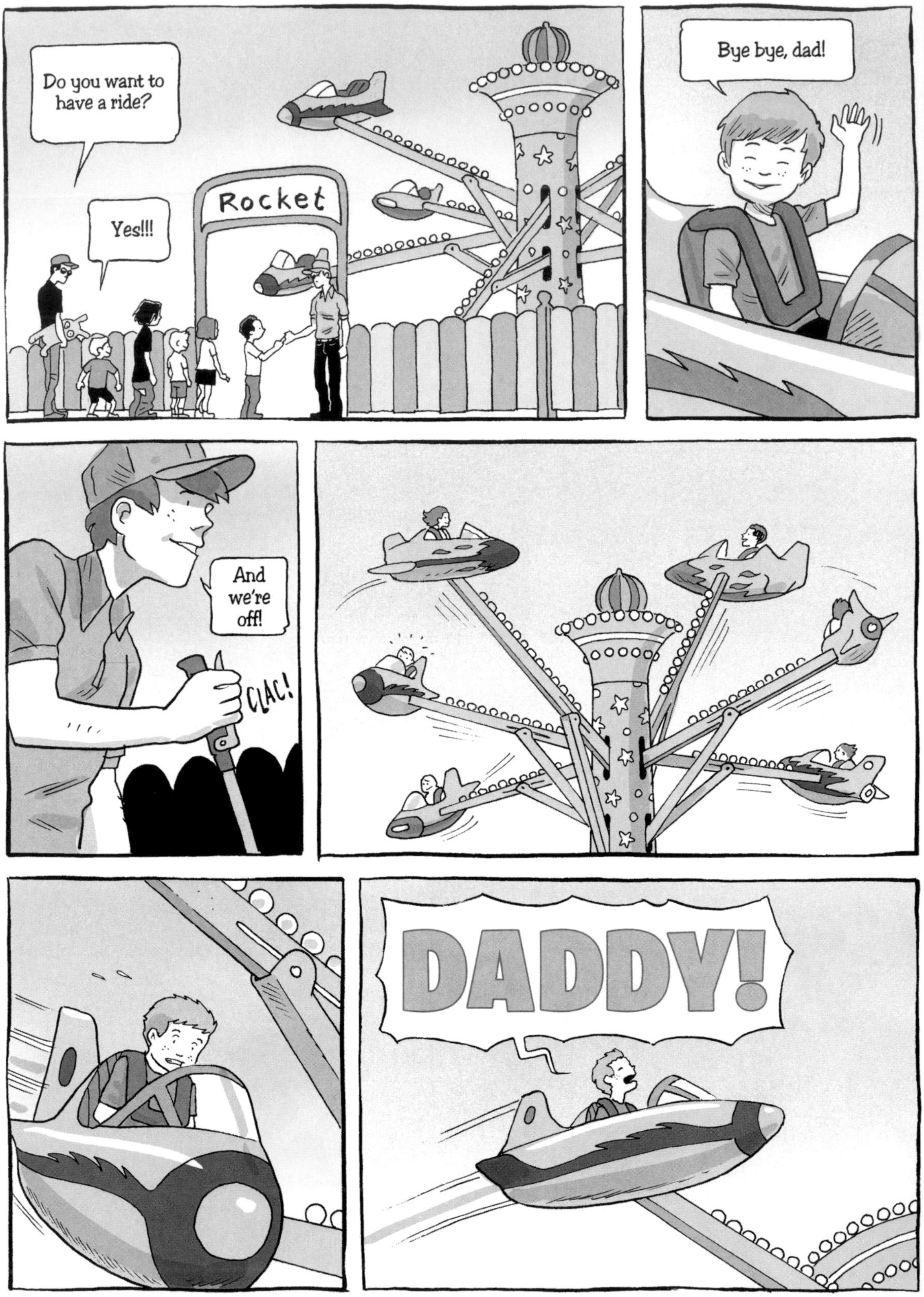
Do you want to have a ride?
Yes!!!
Rocket
Bye bye, dad!
And we're off!
CLAC!
DADDY!

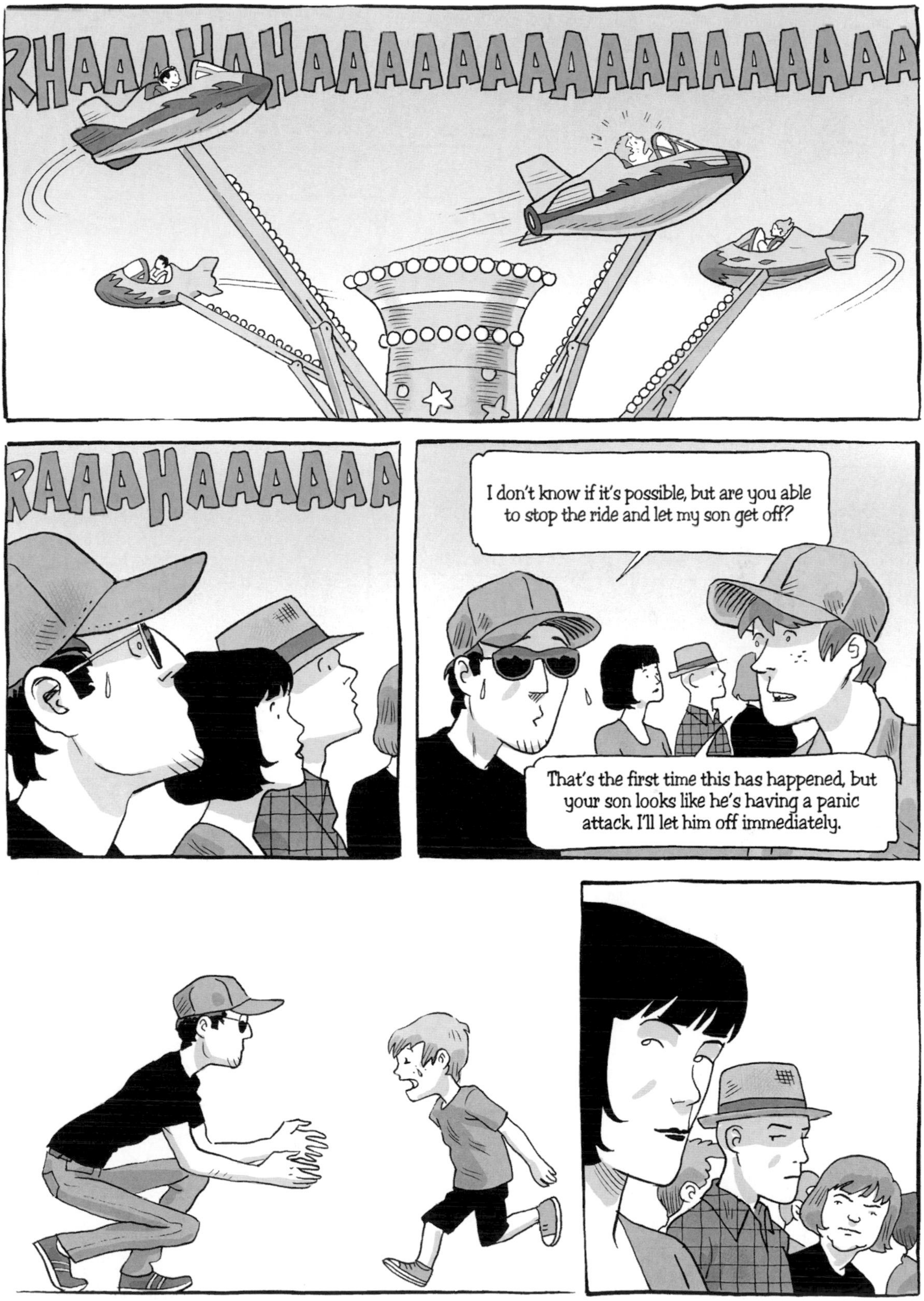
RHAAAHAHAAAAAAAAAAAAAAAAAA
RAAAHAAAAAA
I don't know if it's possible, but are you able to stop the ride and let my son get off?
That's the first time this has happened, but your son looks like he's having a panic attack. I'll let him off immediately.

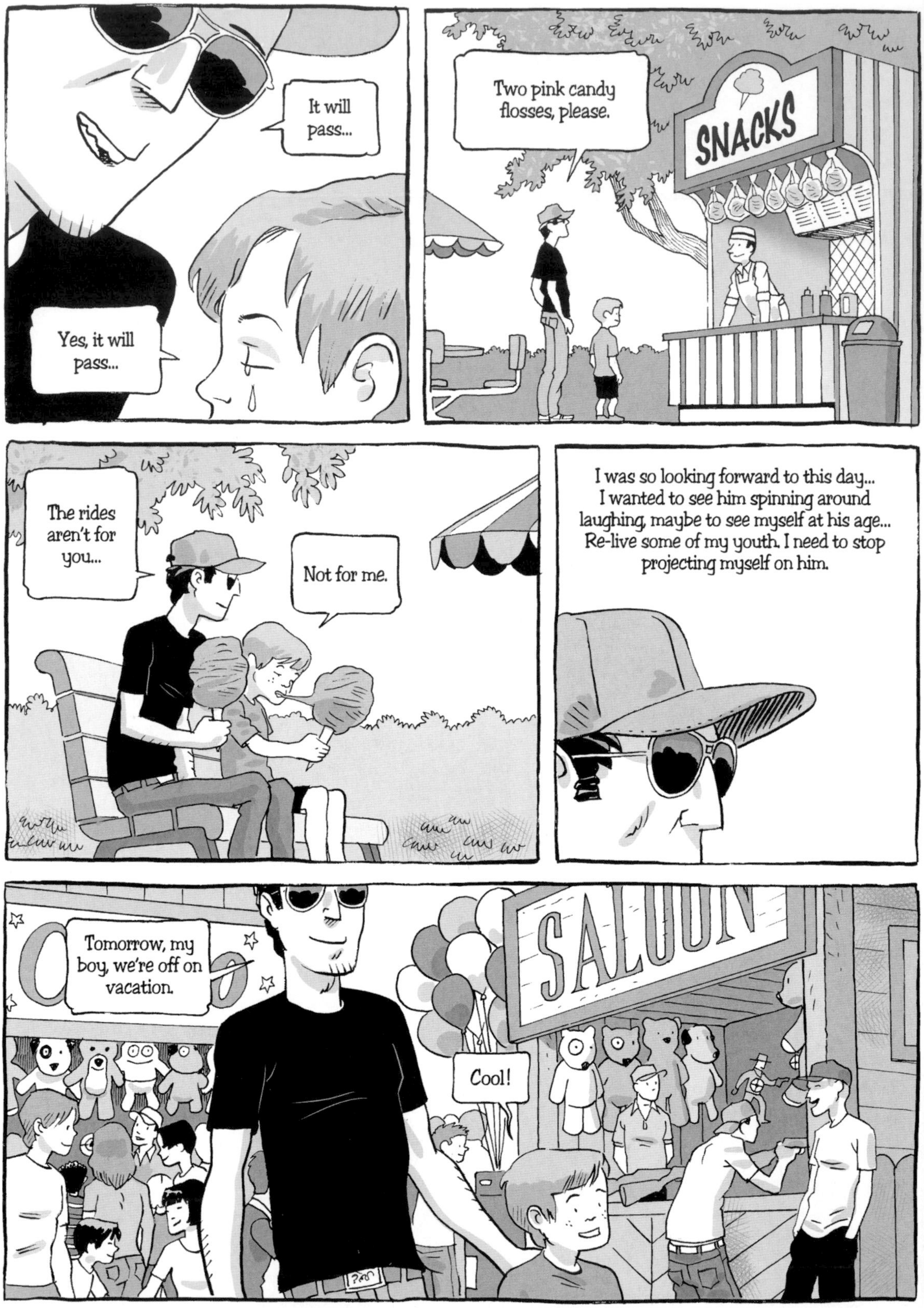
It will pass...
Yes, it will pass...
Two pink candy flosses, please.
SNACKS
The rides aren't for you...
Not for me.
I was so looking forward to this day... I wanted to see him spinning around laughing, maybe to see myself at his age... Re-live some of my youth. I need to stop projecting myself on him.
SALOON
Tomorrow, my boy, we're off on vacation.
Cool!

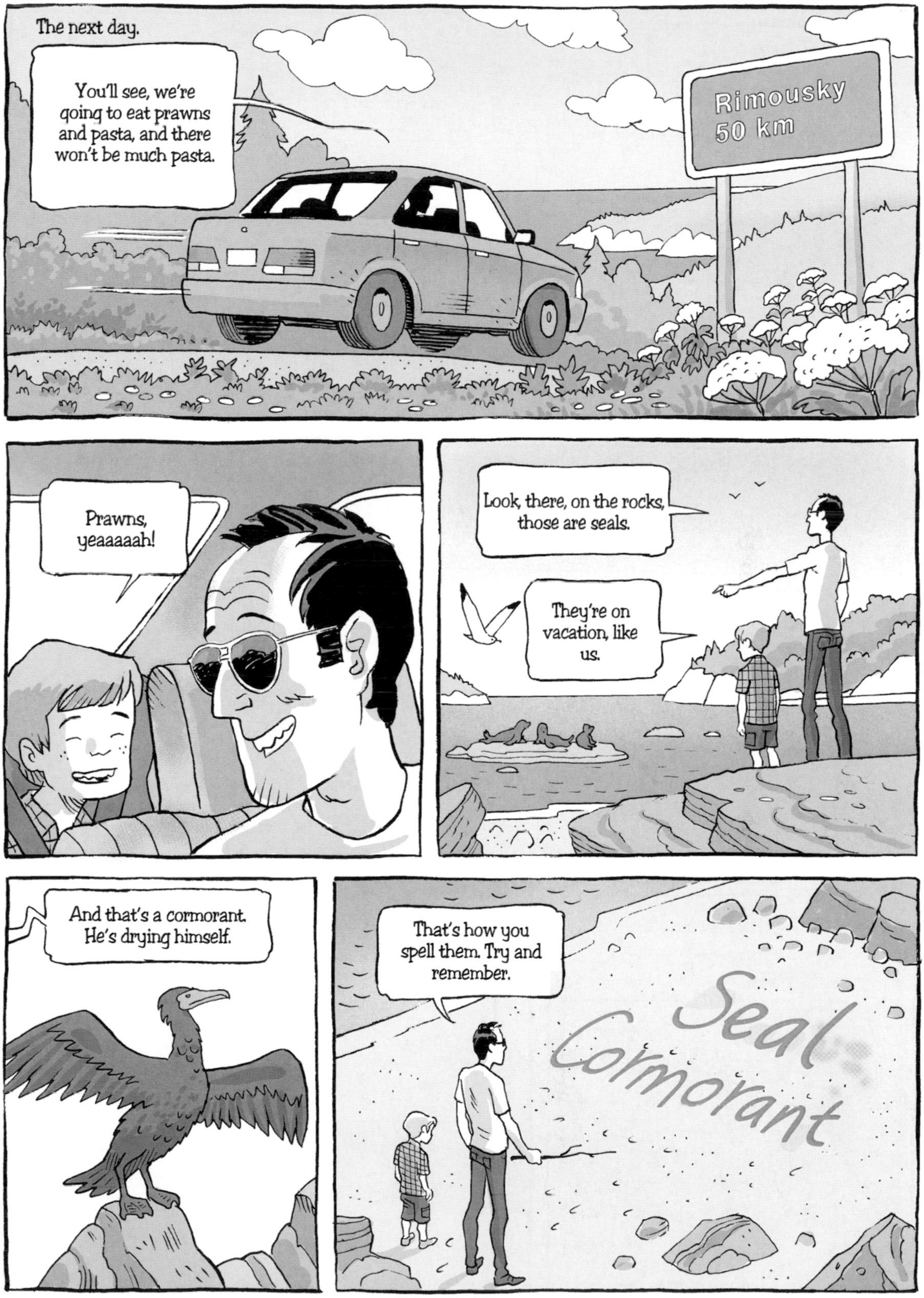
The next day.
You'll see, we're going to eat prawns and pasta, and there won't be much pasta.
Rimousky 50 km
Prawns, yeaaaaah!
Look, there, on the rocks, those are seals.
They're on vacation, like us.
And that's a cormorant. He's drying himself.
That's how you spell them. Try and remember.
Seal
Cormorant

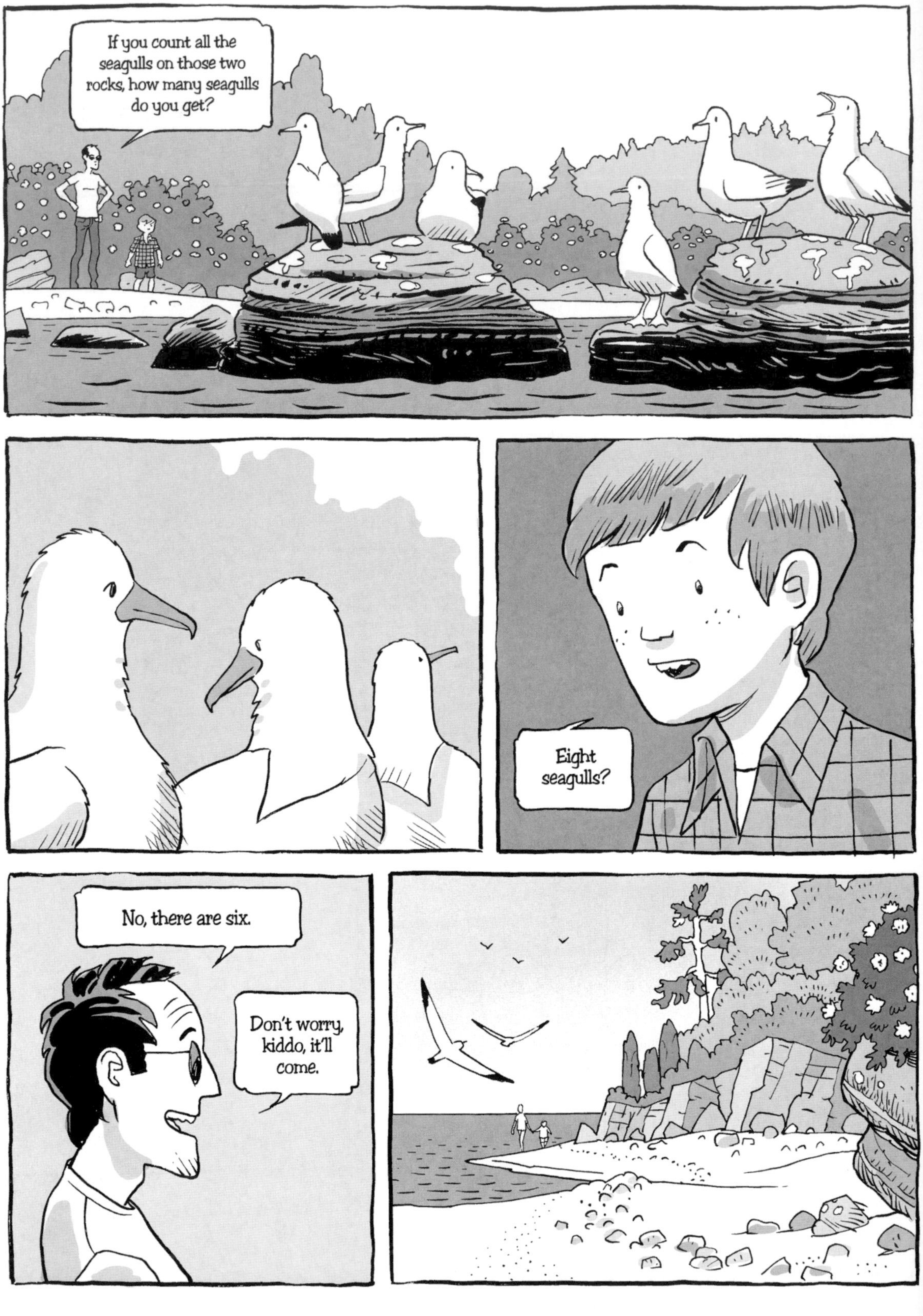
If you count all the seagulls on those two rocks, how many seagulls do you get?
Eight seagulls?
No, there are six.
Don't worry, kiddo, it'll come.

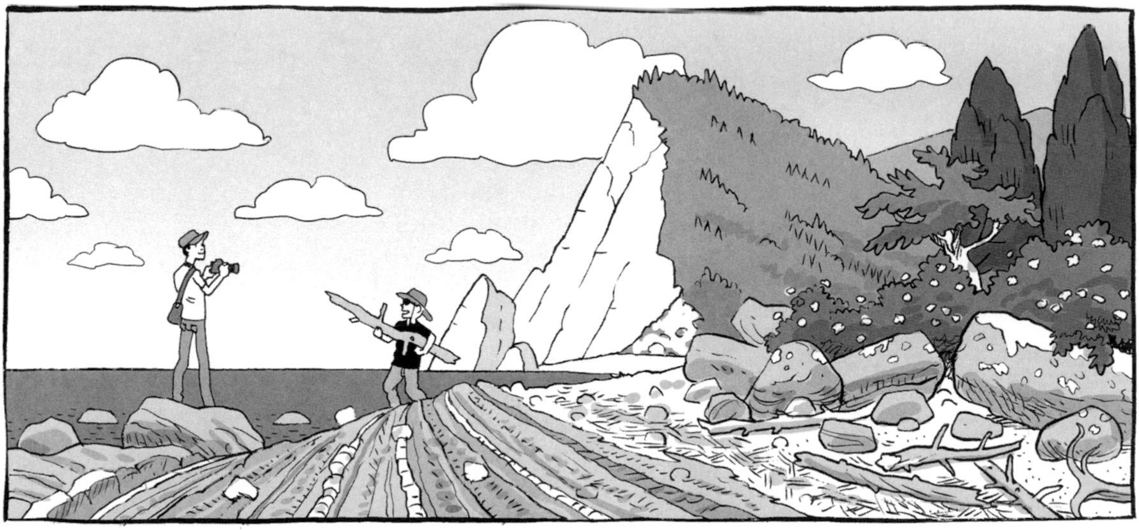

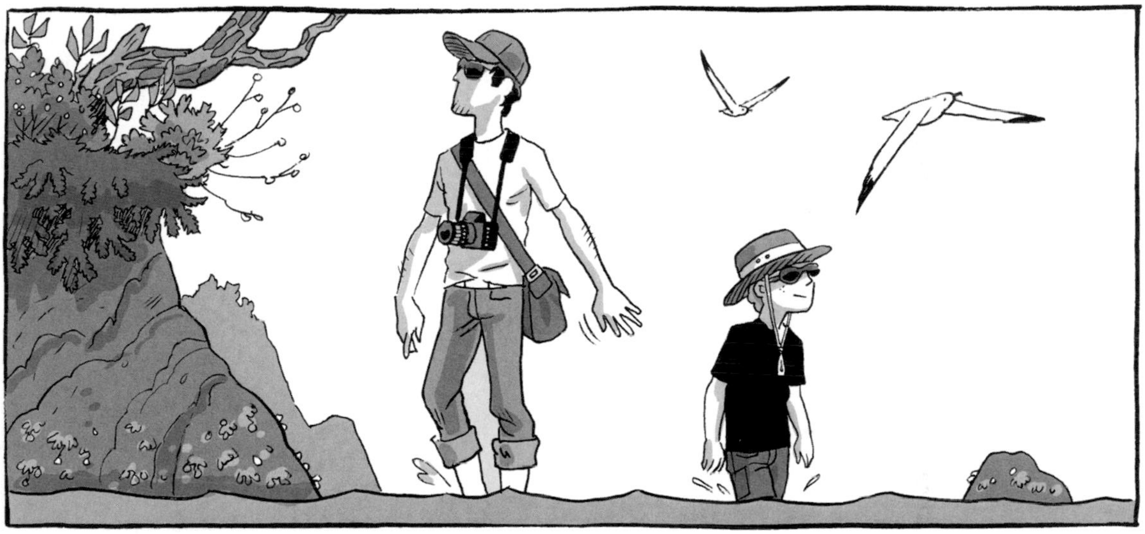

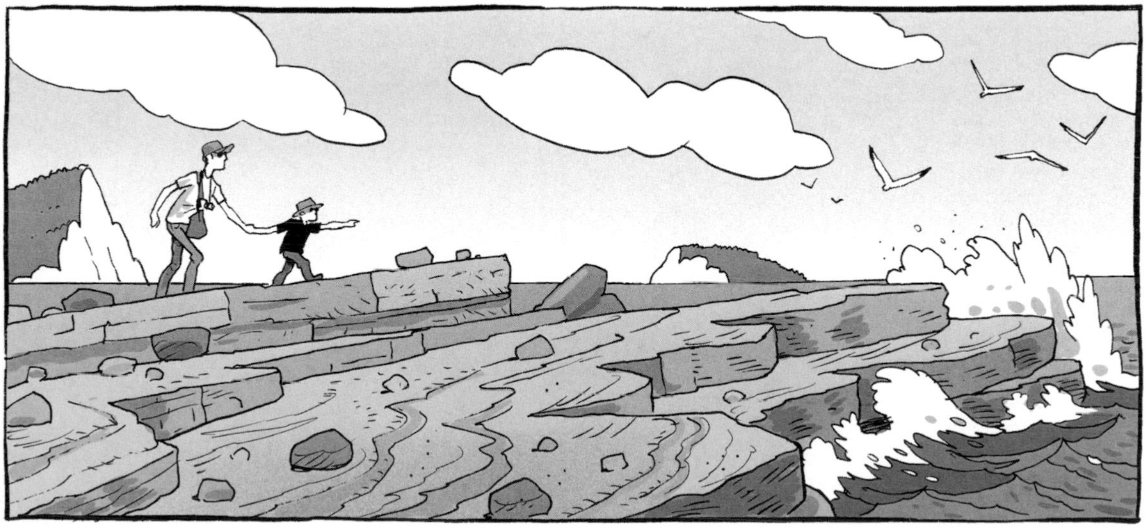

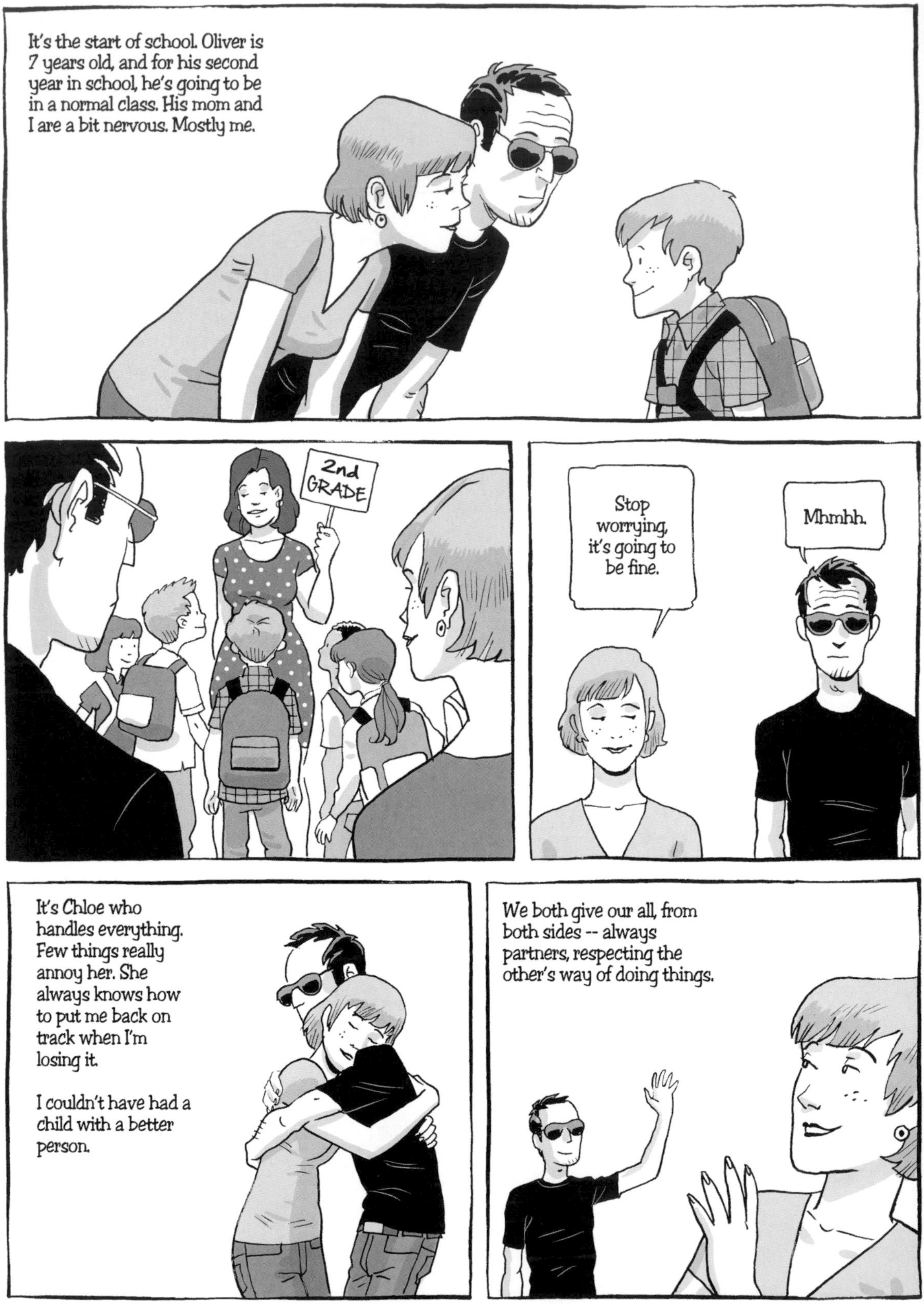
It's the start of school. Oliver is 7 years old, and for his second year in school, he's going to be in a normal class. His mom and I are a bit nervous. Mostly me.
2nd GRADE
Stop worrying, it's going to be fine.
Mhmhh.
It's Chloe who handles everything. Few things really annoy her. She always knows how to put me back on track when I'm losing it.
I couldn't have had a child with a better person.
We both give our all, from both sides -- always partners, respecting the other's way of doing things.

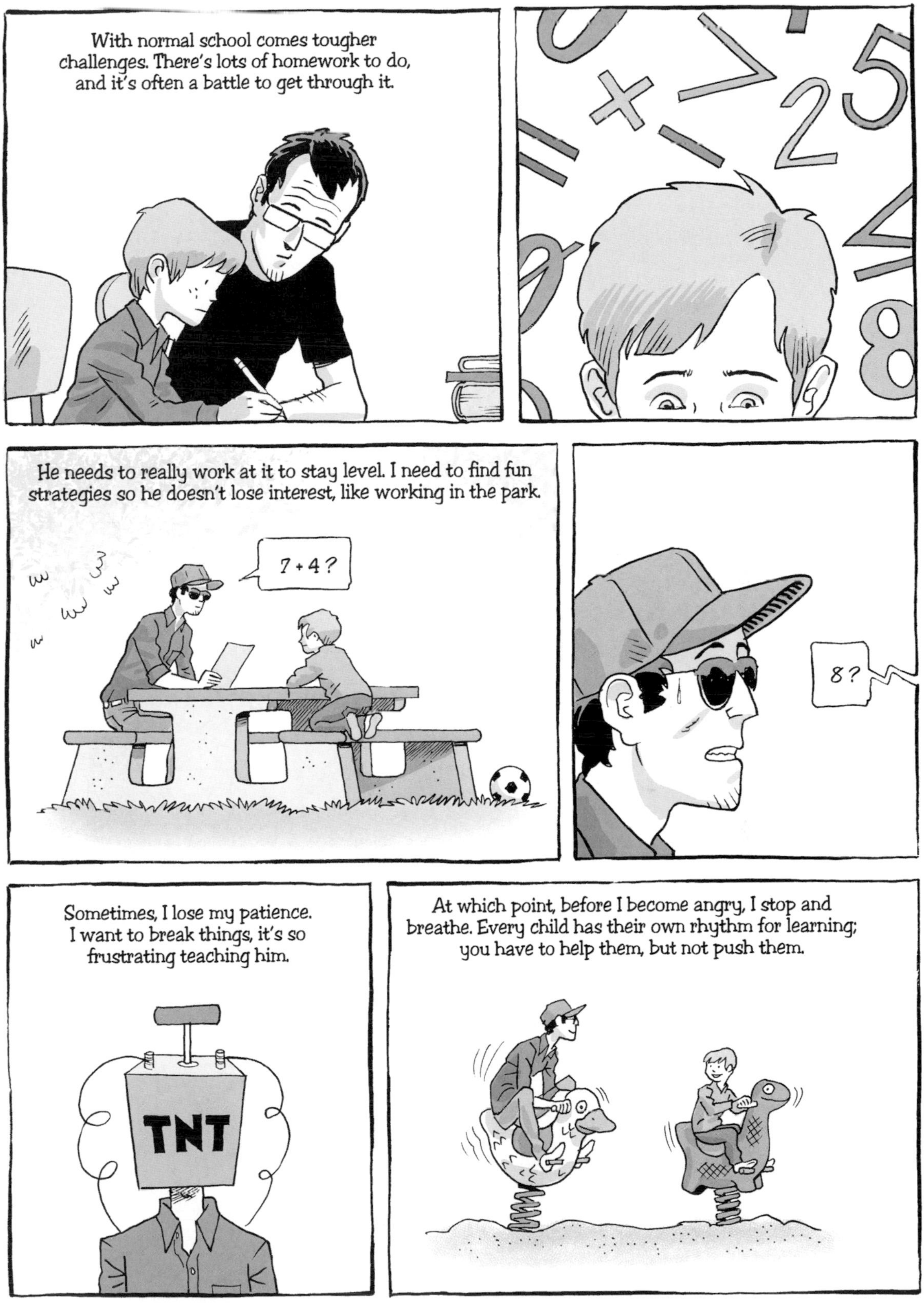
With normal school comes tougher challenges. There's lots of homework to do, and it's often a battle to get through it.
He needs to really work at it to stay level. I need to find fun strategies so he doesn't lose interest, like working in the park.
7 + 4?
8?
Sometimes, I lose my patience. I want to break things, it's so frustrating teaching him.
TNT
At which point, before I become angry, I stop and breathe. Every child has their own rhythm for learning; you have to help them, but not push them.

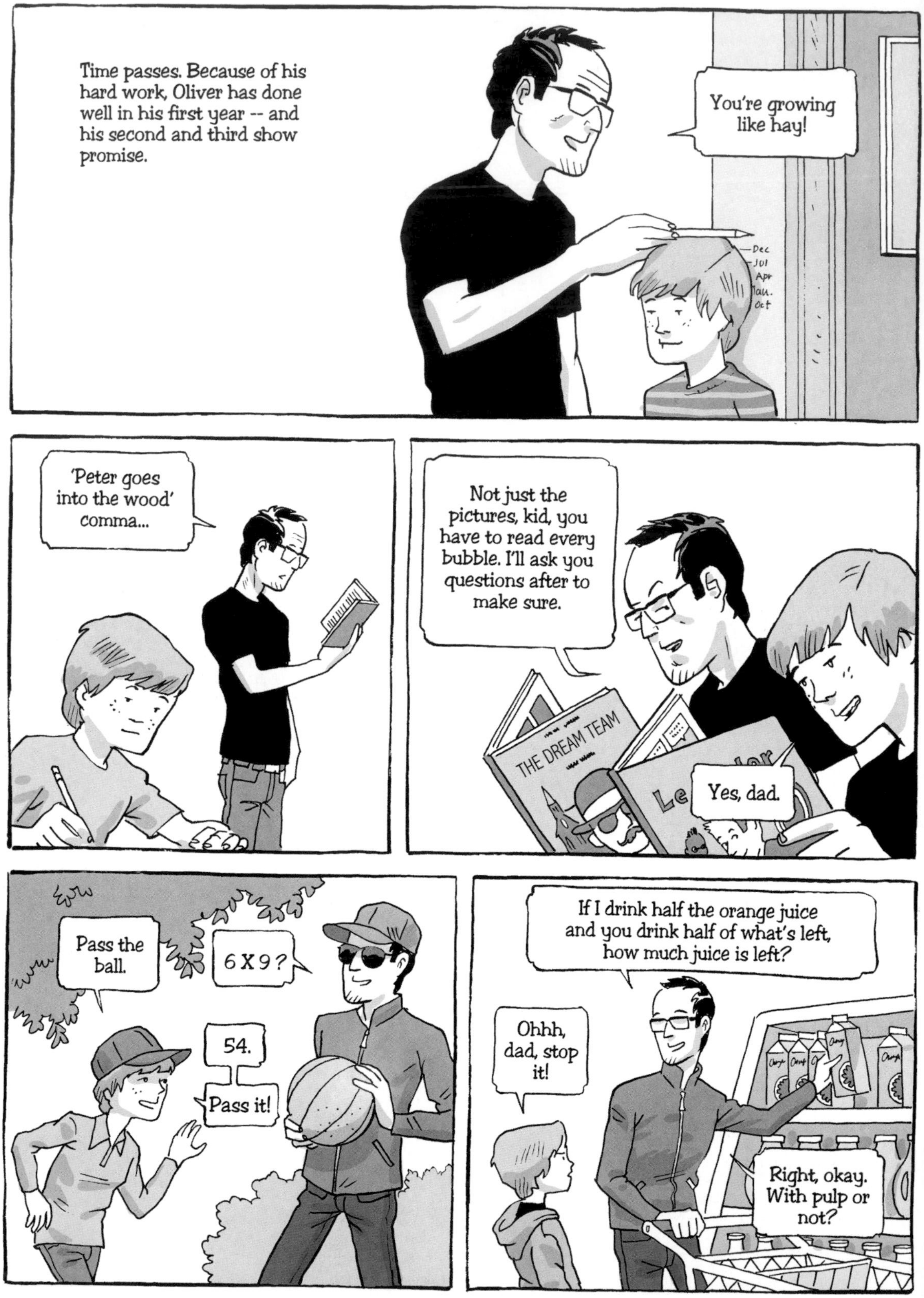
Time passes. Because of his hard work, Oliver has done well in his first year -- and his second and third show promise.
You're growing like hay!
Dec
Jul
Apr
Jan.
Oct
'Peter goes into the wood' comma...
Not just the pictures, kid, you have to read every bubble. I'll ask you questions after to make sure.
THE DREAM TEAM
Yes, dad.
Pass the ball.
6 X 9?
54.
Pass it!
If I drink half the orange juice and you drink half of what's left, how much juice is left?
Ohhh, dad, stop it!
Right, okay. With pulp or not?

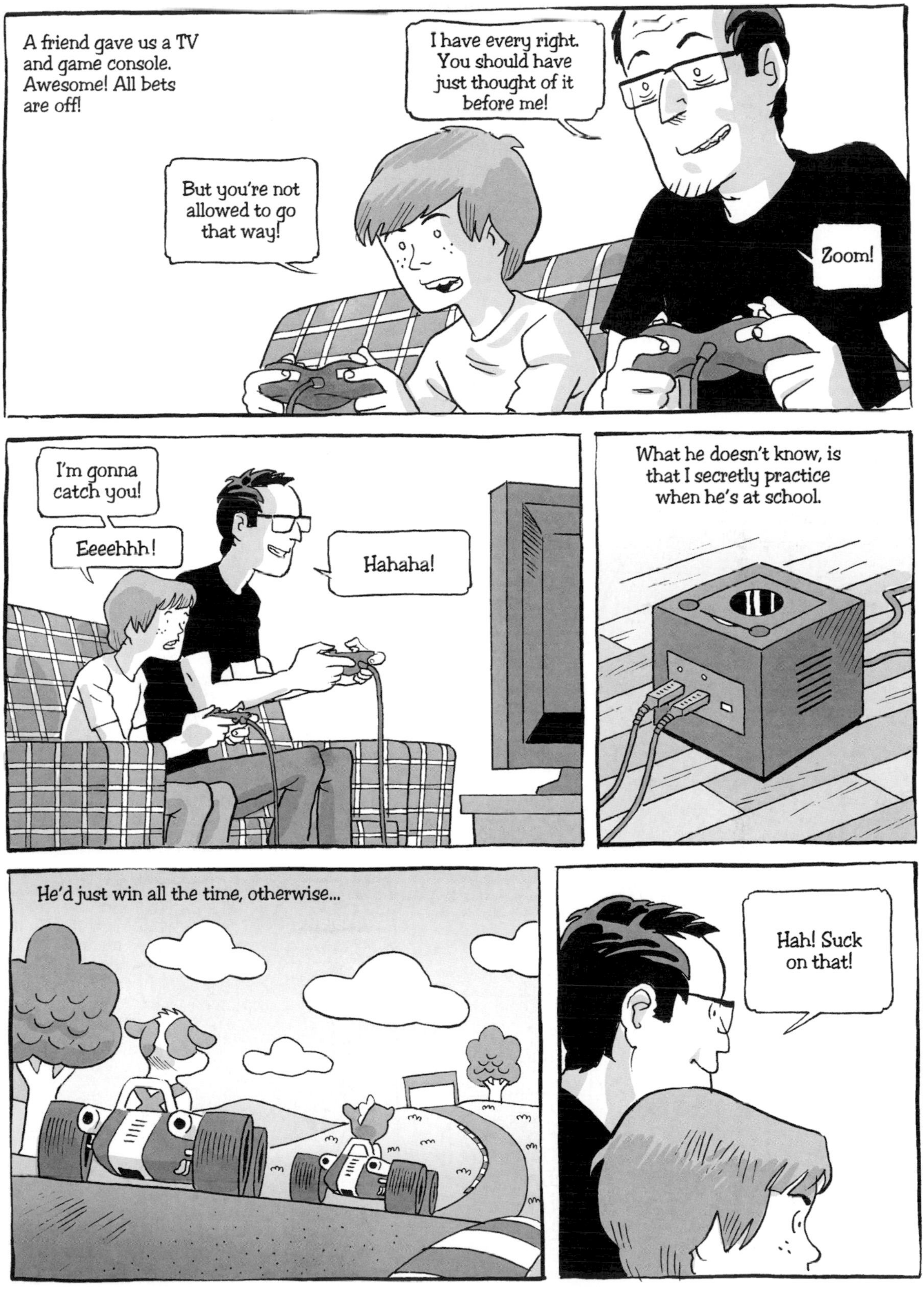
A friend gave us a TV and game console. Awesome! All bets are off!
I have every right. You should have just thought of it before me!
But you're not allowed to go that way!
Zoom!
I'm gonna catch you!
Eeeehhh!
Hahaha!
What he doesn't know, is that I secretly practice when he's at school.
He'd just win all the time, otherwise...
Hah! Suck on that!

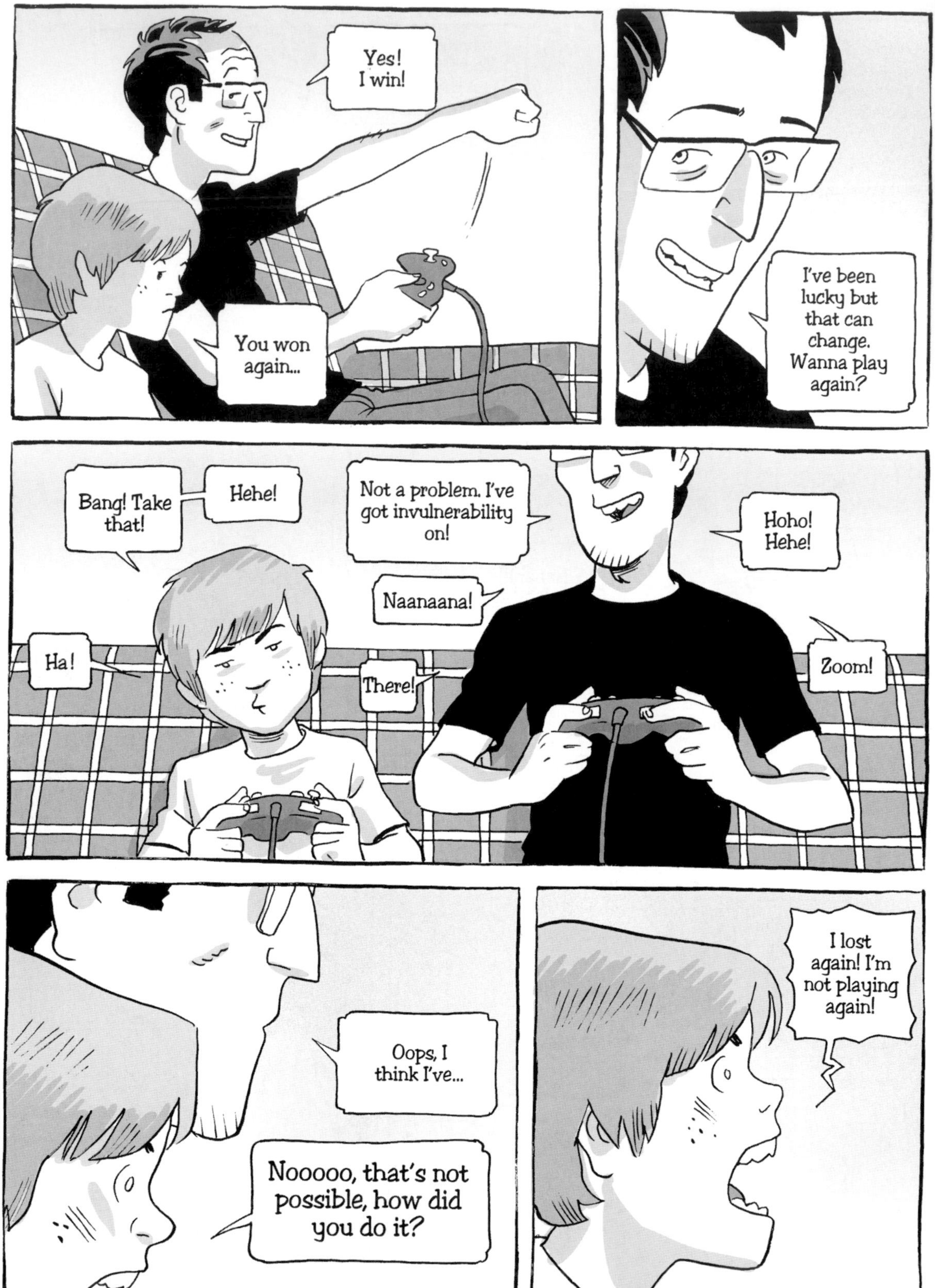
Yes! I win!
You won again...
I've been lucky but that can change. Wanna play again?
Bang! Take that!
Hehe!
Not a problem. I've got invulnerability on!
Hoho! Hehe!
Naanaana!
Ha!
There!
Zoom!
Oops, I think I've...
Nooooo, that's not possible, how did you do it?
I lost again! I'm not playing again!

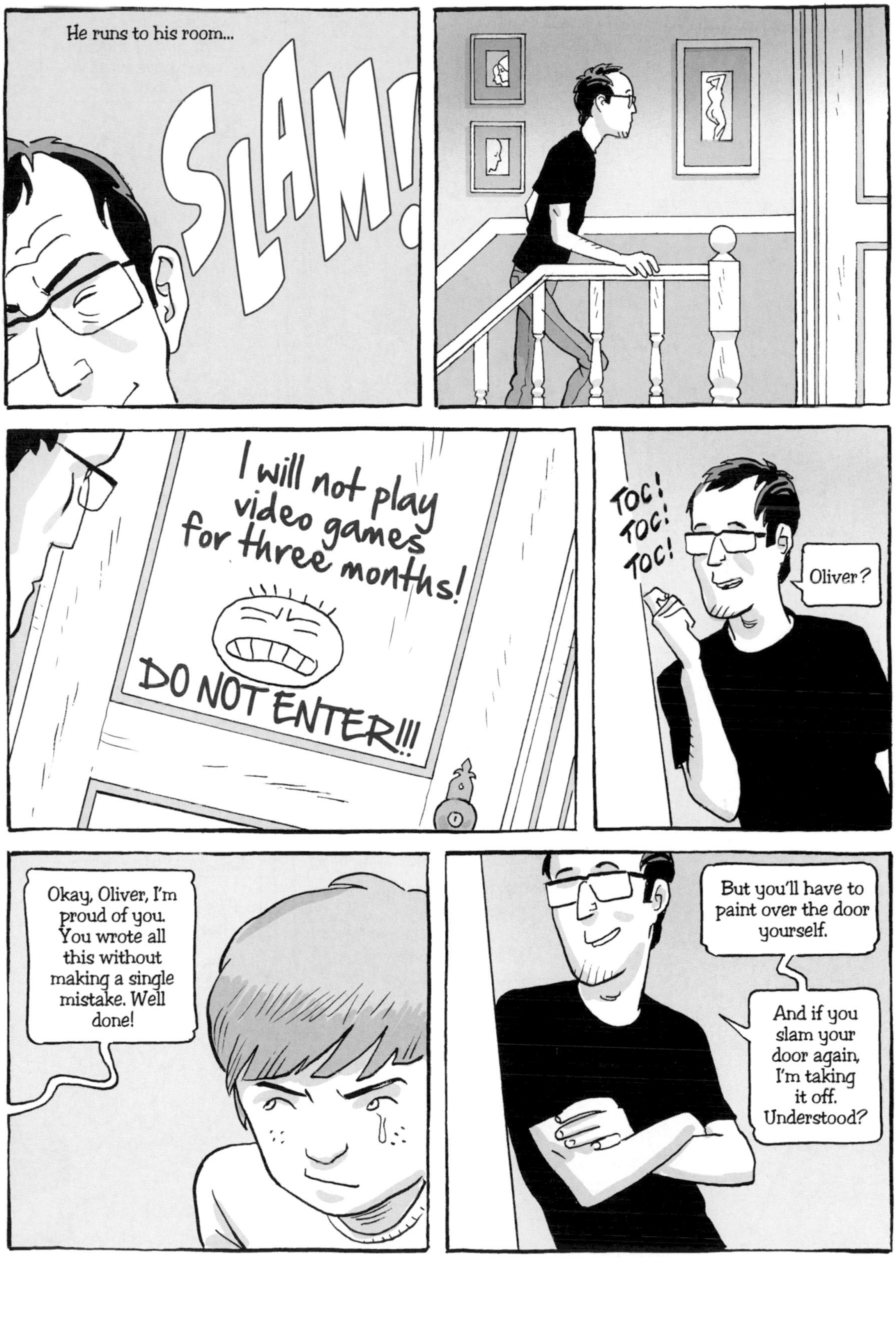
He runs to his room...
SLAM!
I will not play video games for three months!
DO NOT ENTER!!!
TOC! TOC! TOC!
Oliver?
Okay, Oliver, I'm proud of you. You wrote all this without making a single mistake. Well done!
But you'll have to paint over the door yourself.
And if you slam your door again, I'm taking it off. Understood?

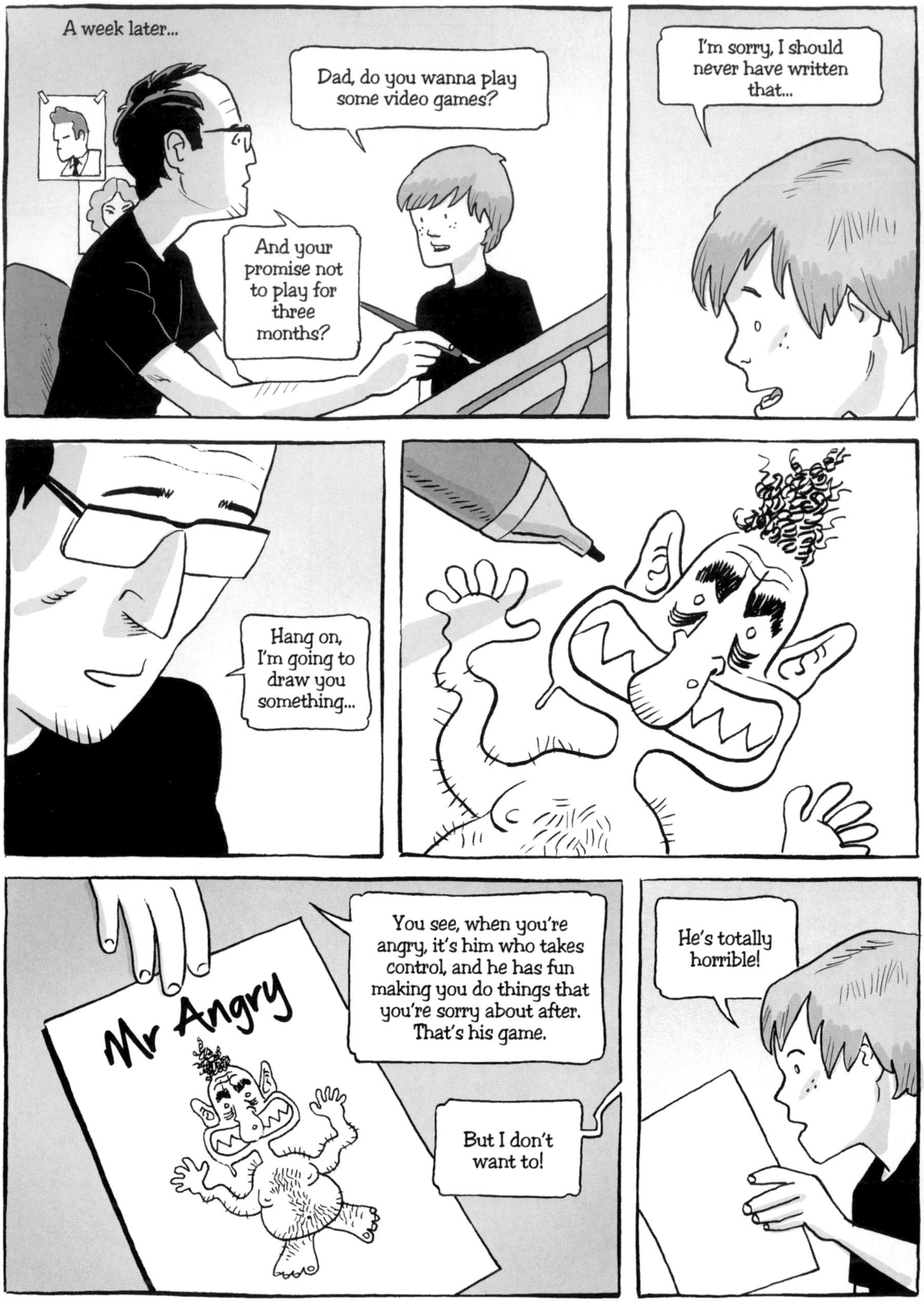
A week later...
Dad, do you wanna play some video games?
And your promise not to play for three months?
I'm sorry, I should never have written that...
Hang on, I'm going to draw you something...
Mr Angry
You see, when you're angry, it's him who takes control, and he has fun making you do things that you're sorry about after. That's his game.
But I don't want to!
He's totally horrible!

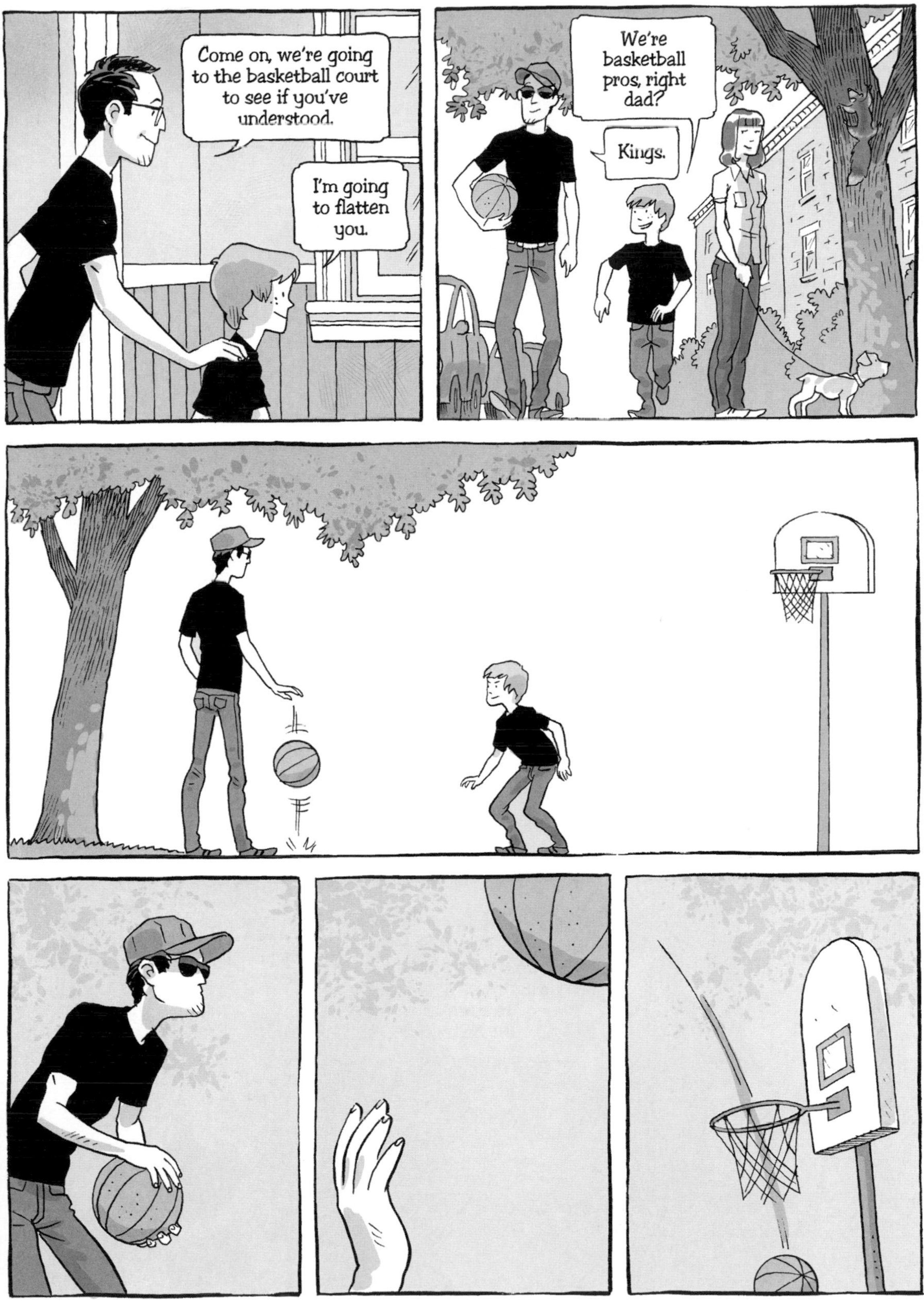
Come on, we're going to the basketball court to see if you've understood.
I'm going to flatten you.
We're basketball pros, right dad?
Kings.

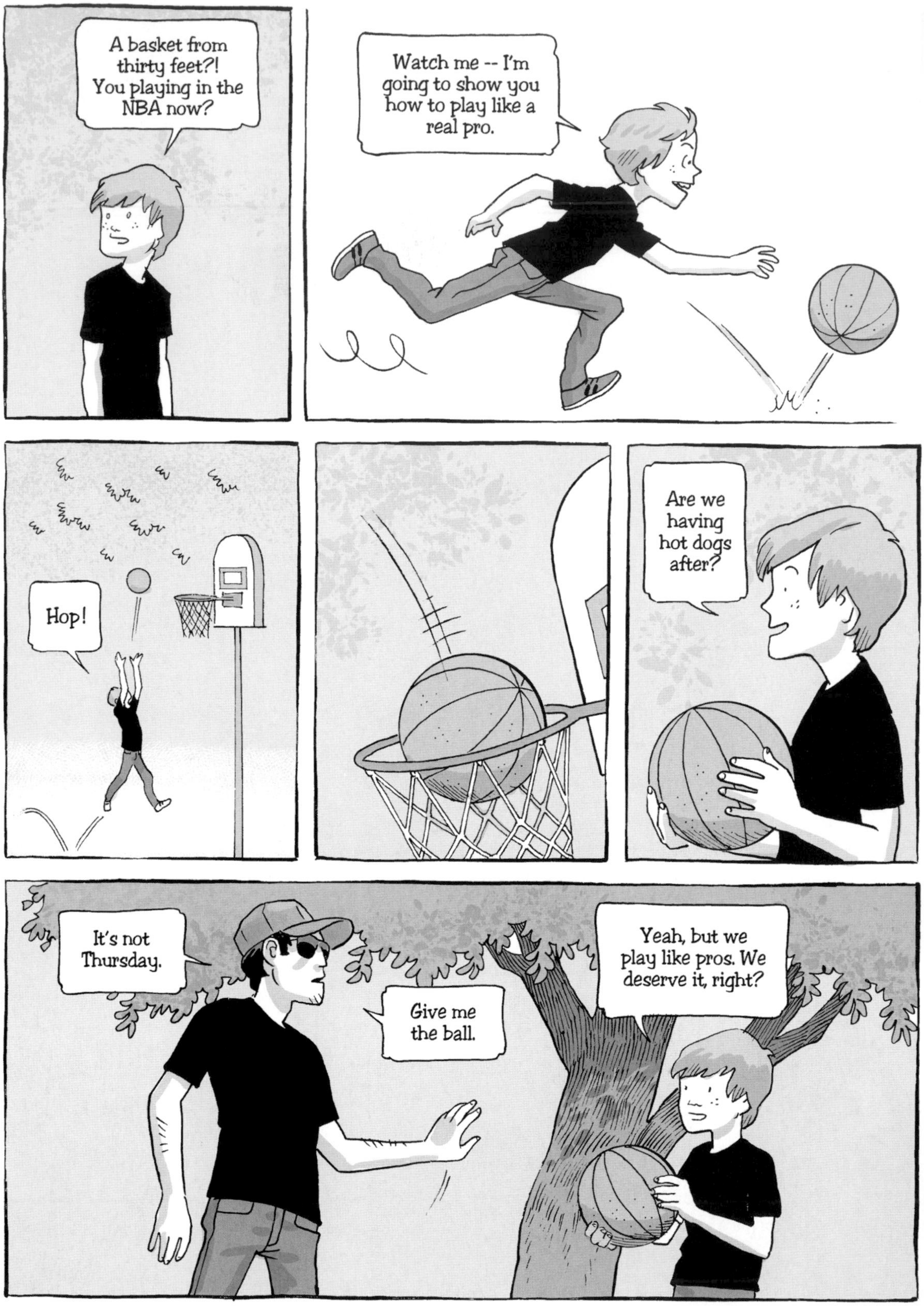
A basket from thirty feet?! You playing in the NBA now?
Watch me -- I'm going to show you how to play like a real pro.
Hop!
Are we having hot dogs after?
It's not Thursday.
Give me the ball.
Yeah, but we play like pros. We deserve it, right?

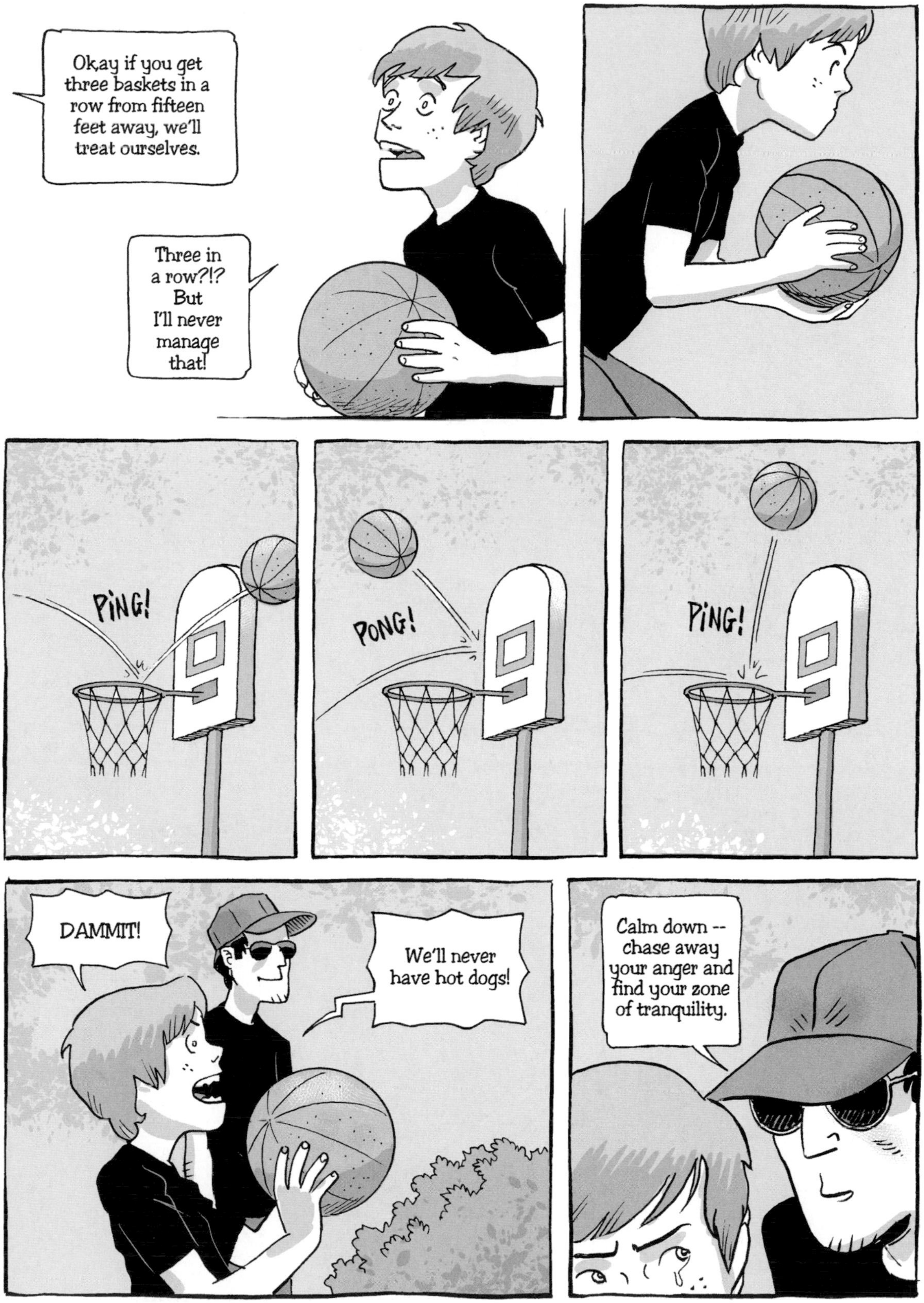
Okay if you get three baskets in a row from fifteen feet away, we'll treat ourselves.
Three in a row?!? But I'll never manage that!
PING!
PONG!
PING!
DAMMIT!
We'll never have hot dogs!
Calm down -- chase away your anger and find your zone of tranquility.

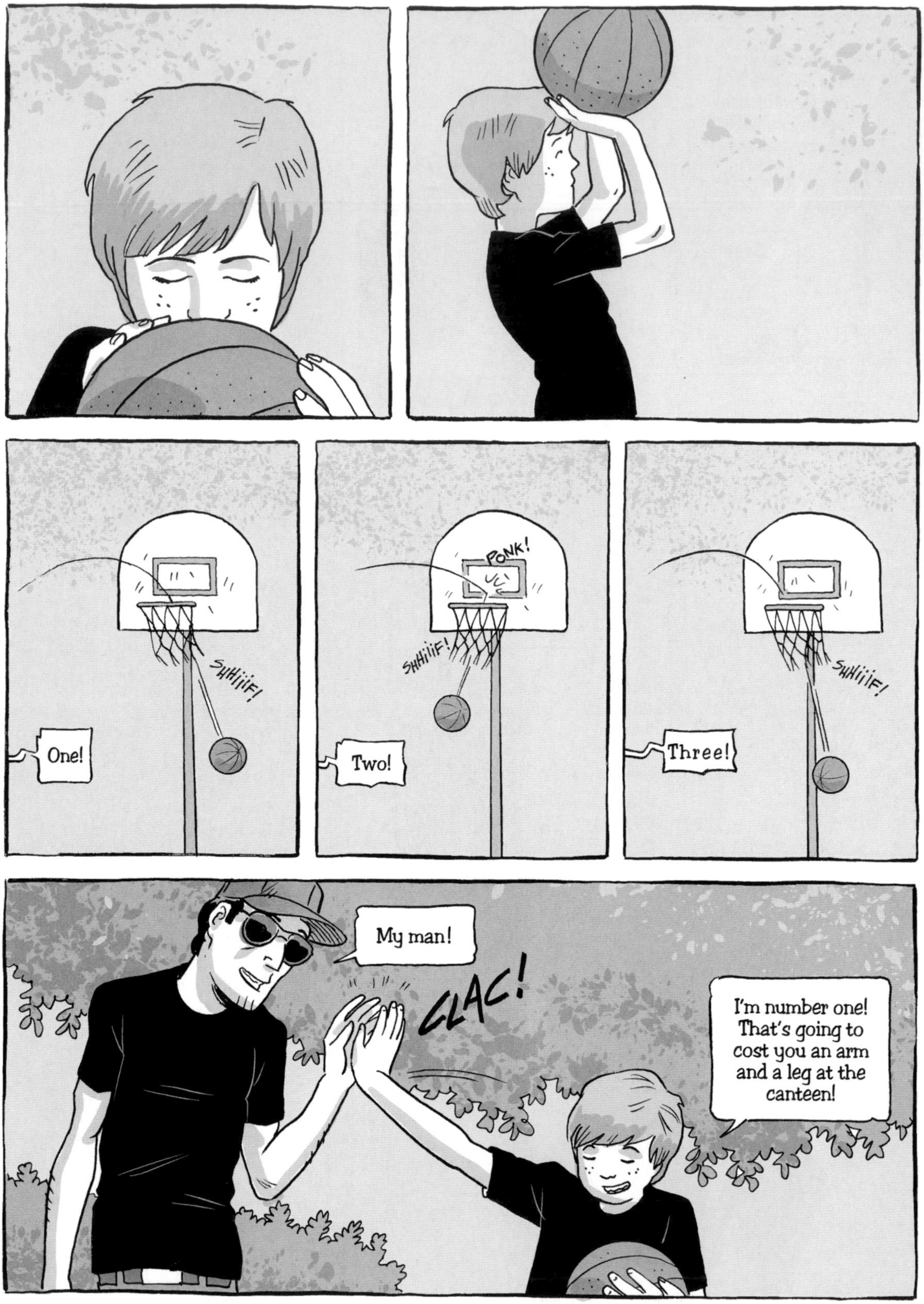
SHHIIIF!
One!
PONK!
SHHIIIF!
Two!
SHHIIIF!
Three!
My man!
CLAC!
I'm number one! That's going to cost you an arm and a leg at the canteen!

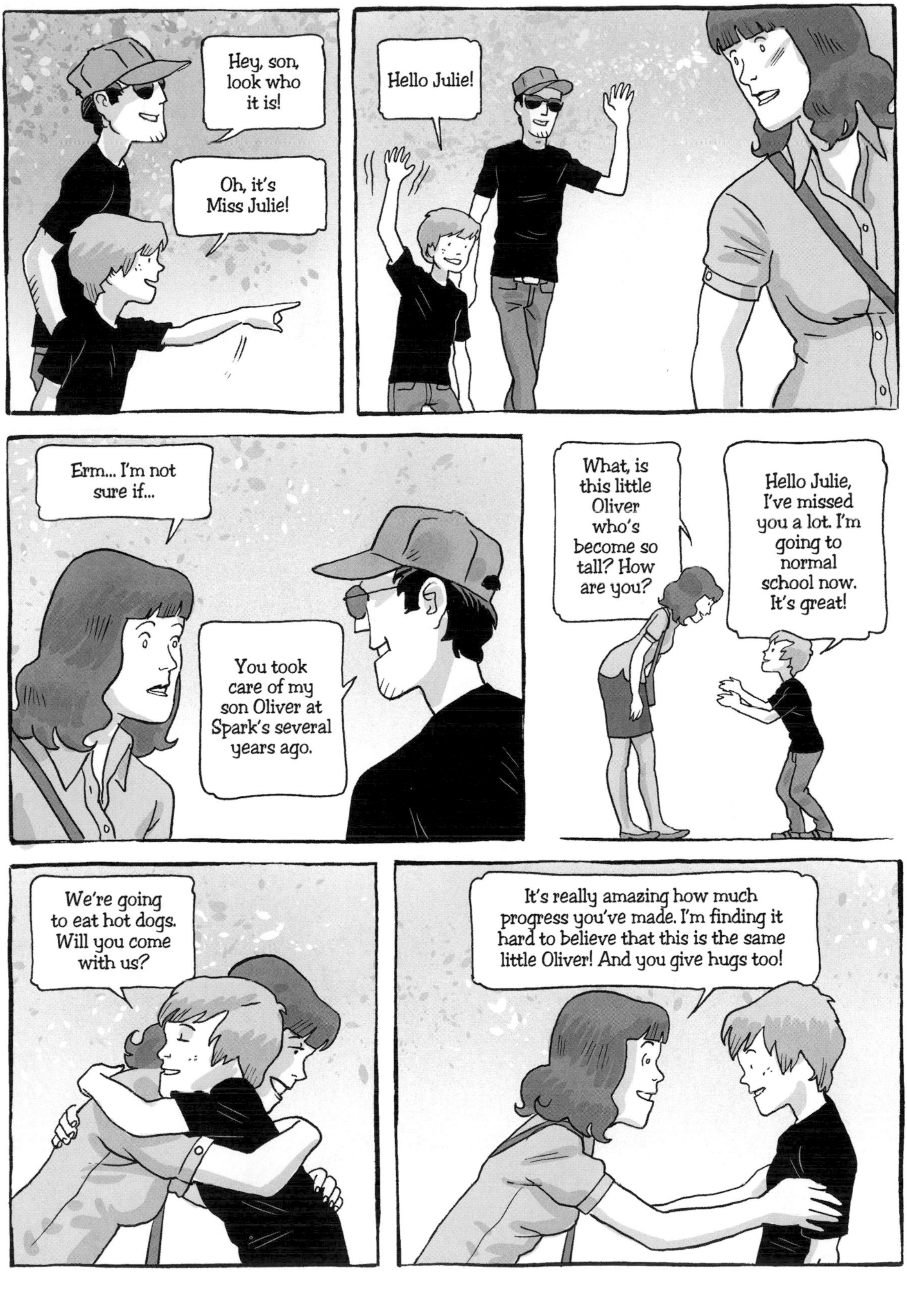
Hey, son, look who it is!
Oh, it's Miss Julie!
Hello Julie!
Erm... I'm not sure if...
You took care of my son Oliver at Spark's several years ago.
What, is this little Oliver who's become so tall? How are you?
Hello Julie, I've missed you a lot. I'm going to normal school now. It's great!
We're going to eat hot dogs. Will you come with us?
It's really amazing how much progress you've made. I'm finding it hard to believe that this is the same little Oliver! And you give hugs too!

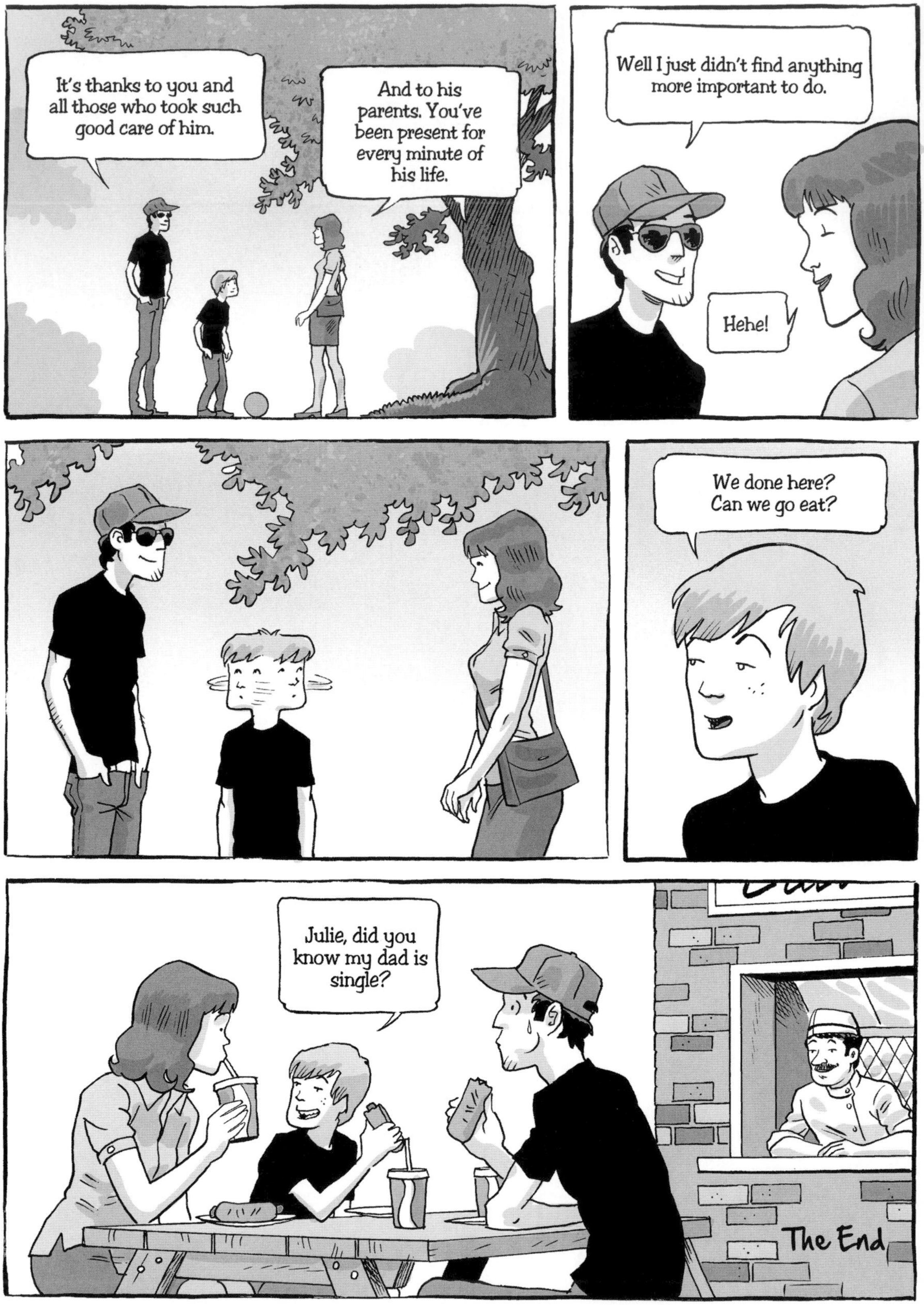
It's thanks to you and all those who took such good care of him.
And to his parents. You've been present for every minute of his life.
Well I just didn't find anything more important to do.
Hehe!
We done here? Can we go eat?
Julie, did you know my dad is single?
The End

*I dedicate this book to my son and his mother, who made me a man.*

*Thanks to :*
*Veronica for her unshakeable support*
*Bruno for his eagle eyes*
*Régis for his valuable advice*
*Tristan for his encouragement*
*Cindy for making rainy days sunny*
*Julie, Helsa and Marie-Josée for the wonderful work done together*

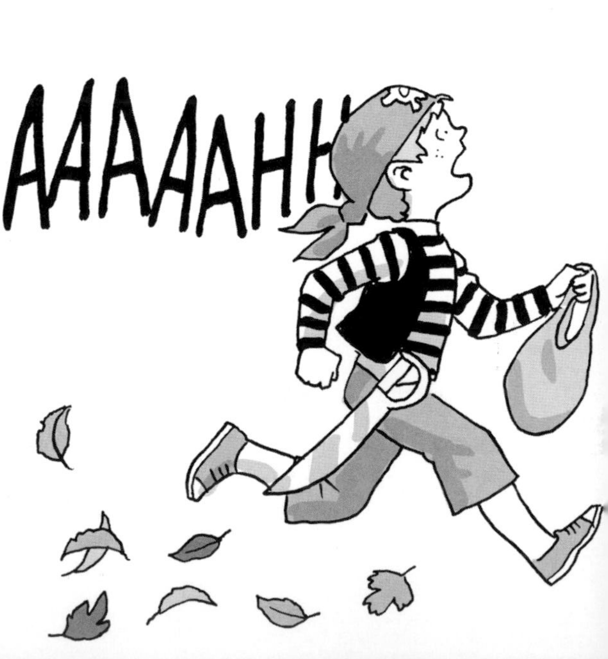
AAAAAHH

# YVON ROY BIO:

Yvon roy is a Canadian comic book writer and illustrator. Together with Jean-Blaise Dijan, he adapted the novel *Agaguk* by Yves Thérault, and several other children's stories.

In 2017, he produced his autobiographical work, *Little Victories,* detailing his experience raising his autistic son. The book received critical acclaim, garnering several awards, including Best Biography form the Disability Fund and Society. A film project is in the works.

Most recently he has completed another autobiographic graphic novel, *Graines de Bandits,* focussed on his troubled youth.

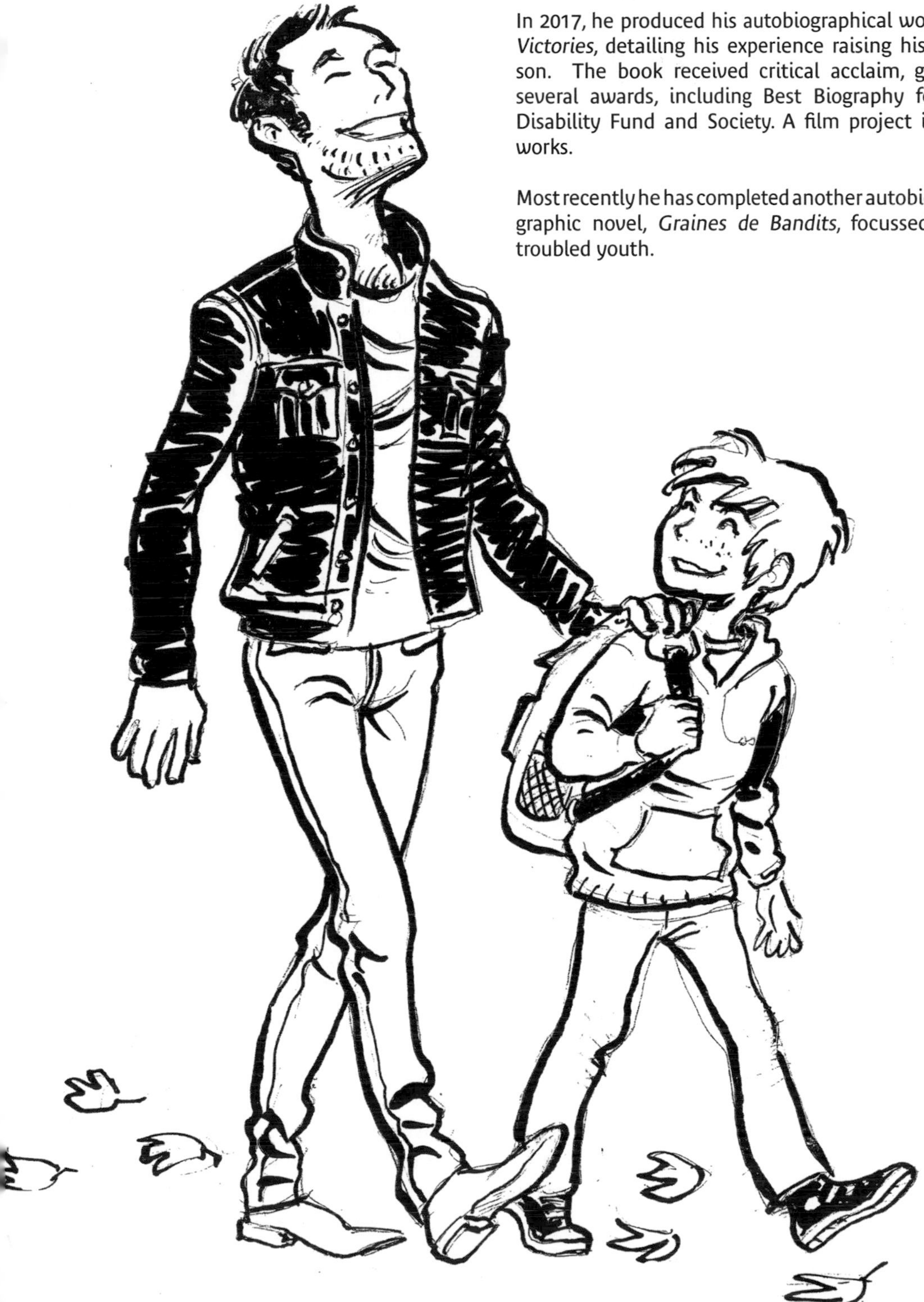

# ALSO FROM
## TITAN COMICS AND STATIX PRESS



**2021:** LOST CHILDREN
**ALISIK:** FALL
**ATAR GULL**
**ATLAS & AXIS**
**THE BEAUTIFUL DEATH**
**BILAL LIBRARY - CENTURY'S END**
**BILAL LIBRARY - THE NIKOPOL TRILOGY**
**BILAL LIBRARY - EXTERMINATOR 17**
**BILAL LIBRARY - MONSTER**
**CROMWELL STONE**
**THE CHIMERA BRIGADE -** BOOK 1
**THE CHIMERA BRIGADE -** BOOK 2
**THE CHIMERA BRIGADE -** BOOK 3
**THE CHRONICLES OF LEGION -** BOOK 1: RISE OF THE VAMPIRES
**THE CHRONICLES OF LEGION -** BOOK 2: THE THREE LIVES OF DRACULA
**THE DEATH OF STALIN**
**DEATH TO THE TSAR**
**DOCTOR RADAR**
**DRUILLET LIBRARY - THE 6 VOYAGES OF LONE SLOANE**
**DRUILLET LIBRARY - LONE SLOANE:** DELIRIUS
**DRUILLET LIBRARY - LONE SLOANE:** GAIL
**DRUILLET LIBRARY - YRAGAËL / URM THE MAD**
**DRUILLET LIBRARY - SALAMMBÔ**
**DRUILLET LIBRARY - THE NIGHT**
**EMMA G. WILDFORD**
**FACTORY**
**HERCULES:** WRATH OF THE HEAVENS
**KHAAL**
**KONUNGAR:** WAR OF CROWNS
**LITTLE VICTORIES**
**MANCHETTE'S FATALE**
**MASKED:** RISE OF THE ROCKET
**MCCAY**
**MONIKA -** BOOK 1: MASKED BALL
**MONIKA -** BOOK 2: VANILLA DOLLS
**NORMAN -** VOLUME 1
**NORMAN -** VOLUME 2: TEACHER'S PET
**NORMAN -** VOLUME 3: THE VENGEANCE OF GRACE
**NORMAN:** THE FIRST SLASH
**OSCAR MARTIN'S SOLO**
**PACIFIC**
**THE PRAGUE COUP**
**THE QUEST FOR THE TIME BIRD**
**THE RAGE -** BOOK 1: ZOMBIE GENERATION
**THE RAGE -** BOOK 2: KILL OR CURE
**RAVINA THE WITCH?**
**ROYAL BLOOD**
**SAMURAI:** THE ISLE WITH NO NAME
**SAMURAI:** BROTHERS IN ARMS
**THE SEASON OF THE SNAKE**
**SHOWMAN KILLER -** BOOK 1: HEARTLESS HERO
**SHOWMAN KILLER -** BOOK 2: THE GOLDEN CHILD
**SHOWMAN KILLER -** BOOK 3: THE INVISIBLE WOMAN
**SKY DOLL:** SPACESHIP
**SKY DOLL:** DECADE
**SKY DOLL:** SUDRA
**ULTIMATE SKY DOLL**
**SNOWPIERCER:** THE ESCAPE
**SNOWPIERCER:** THE EXPLORERS
**SNOWPIERCER:** TERMINUS
**SNOWPIERCER THE PREQUEL:** EXTINCTION
**THE THIRD TESTAMENT -** BOOK 1: THE LION AWAKES
**THE THIRD TESTAMENT -** BOOK 2: THE ANGEL'S FACE
**THE THIRD TESTAMENT -** BOOK 3: THE MIGHT OF THE OX
**THE THIRD TESTAMENT -** BOOK 4: THE DAY OF THE RAVEN
**TYLER CROSS:** BLACK ROCK
**TYLER CROSS:** ANGOLA
**UNDER:** SCOURGE OF THE SEWER
**UNIVERSAL WAR ONE**
**VOID**
**WORLD WAR X**
**THE WRATH OF FANTOMAS**